PETER

MW00355808

To my wife, Gail,
whose love, encouragement and
support have been a constant inspiration

PETER SELLERS
A Film History
Michael Seth Starr

McFarland & Company, Inc., Publishers
Jefferson, North Carolina, and London

The present work is a reprint of the library bound edition
of Peter Sellers: A Film History, first published in 1991
by McFarland.

LIBRARY OF CONGRESS CATALOGUING-IN-PUBLICATION DATA

Starr, Michael, 1961–
    Peter Sellers : a film history / Michael Seth Starr.
      p.   cm.
    Includes bibliographical references and index.

    ISBN 978-0-7864-7389-2
    softcover : acid free paper ∞

    1. Sellers, Peter, 1925– I. Title.
PN2598.S44S73 2012
791.43'028'092—dc20   89-43695

BRITISH LIBRARY CATALOGUING DATA ARE AVAILABLE

© 1991 Michael Seth Starr. All rights reserved

No part of this book may be reproduced or transmitted in any form
or by any means, electronic or mechanical, including photocopying
or recording, or by any information storage and retrieval system,
without permission in writing from the publisher.

On the cover: Peter Sellers as Chief Insp. Jacques Clouseau, *The
Pink Panther Strikes Again* (1976) (© United Artists/Photofest)

Manufactured in the United States of America

McFarland & Company, Inc., Publishers
  Box 611, Jefferson, North Carolina 28640
    www.mcfarlandpub.com

Contents

Part III: The Lost Decade (1965–1974)

Part IV: A Sellers Market (1975–1980)

Part V: Interview with Blake Edwards   225

Prologue

In myself, I have nothing to offer as a personality but as soon as I can get into some character I'm away. I use the characters to protect myself, as a shield—like getting into a hut and saying "nobody can see me."

        —Peter Sellers

He had a personality of his own. He felt better when he was living in someone else's skin for a while. What would happen was if it was stretched out too long there was no real substantial character there, it was "let's pretend." You can only pretend for a while and then you suddenly realize there's nothing really solid about the character.

        —Blake Edwards

In writing this first-ever comprehensive analysis of Peter Sellers's film career, I hoped to accomplish several objectives.

My first goal was to survey Sellers's more than fifty films, in so doing reminding readers of the inestimable impact Sellers had on the cinema in the early and later stages of his career.

Ten years after his death, Sellers is remembered chiefly as Jacques Clouseau, the bumbling, cartoonish inspector of the *Pink Panther* series now seen in fiberglass commercials chasing his still-elusive pink prey. That Sellers was so much more than Clouseau remains for many a moot point; who but the most ardent film buff remembers *Lolita*'s slyly sinister Clare Quilty or lascivious librarian John Lewis from *Only Two Can Play?* The casual observer may remember Sellers's Oscar-nominated triple-role stint in *Dr. Strangelove,* but he would be hard-pressed to recall Sellers's multi-character charades in *The Naked Truth* or *After the Fox.* Although the majority of Sellers's films are forgotten, they remain dusty relics of an immensely uneven, sometimes brilliant career.

I also probed aspects of Sellers's personality, theorizing that one could not appreciate an overview of his film career without trying to understand the motivations behind his progressively bizarre professional behavior. Toward this end, I consulted a variety of sources and conducted my own lengthy interview with writer-producer-director Blake Edwards, whose frank insights into Sellers's tortured psyche reveal a man far removed from his comedic on-screen creations.

Although this book isn't a biography, I felt it necessary to include specific biographical data to complete Sellers's overall portrait. For instance, it is necessary when tracing the development of his career to remember that Sellers didn't burst onto the film scene completely unnoticed; he had an established radio career as one-third of the BBC's legendary "Goon Show" (along with Spike Milligan and Harry Secombe), whose surrealistic antics paved the way for the Beyond the Fringe and Monty Python comedy troupes that would follow in its wake.

The "Goon Show" ran for roughly eight years (1951–1959), exposing Sellers's remarkable vocal talents to British audiences while providing an entrée into motion pictures with *Penny Points to Paradise* and *Down Among the Z Men*. Sellers also parlayed his "Goon Show" experience into film-dubbing jobs, providing Winston Churchill's voice for *The Man Who Never Was*, mimicking a parrot in *Our Girl Friday*, and looping some Humphrey Bogart dialogue for *Beat the Devil*, among other early film "roles."

References are also made to Sellers's half–Jewish, half–Protestant upbringing, an important factor in the shaping of his personality and career.

Raised in a theatrical atmosphere that he grew to despise, Sellers felt a strong emotional attachment to his great-great-grandfather, Jewish-Portuguese East End pugilist Daniel Mendoza, who used his fists and good looks to entertain Britain's high society in the late 1700s. Mendoza's theatrical flair was inherited by his granddaughter Welcome Mendoza (Sellers's maternal grandmother), who married at 44, birthed ten children, changed her name to Ma Ray, and founded England's first underwater revue called, appropriately enough, *Splash Me!*

Ma Ray's daughter Peg toured with the troupe and later married cathedral organist Bill Sellers. Peter Sellers was born on September 8, 1925, and was spoiled rotten by his doting mother, whom he referred to as "Peg." Bill Sellers faded into the background of his son's affections.

Sellers completed his mediocre academic career in several parochial schools; curiously, none of these were Jewish, no doubt contributing to Sellers's unwillingness later in life to claim any one religion as his own. During his teenage years, Sellers began playing the drums and toured with his father in a four-piece band before joining the RAF in 1943 as a lowly gunner's mate.

The war years helped shape Sellers's professional life. He joined Ralph Reader's "Gang Show" entertainment unit as a pianist-drummer and comedian, and honed his mimicking talents by impersonating high-ranking RAF officers (and never getting caught). It was also during this time that Sellers met Dennis Selinger, who would later become his first agent.

After the war, Sellers toured the country as a drummer, sired an illegitimate daughter (whom he never saw), and worked a variety of jobs (including strip-joint comedian) until getting his first big break.

In desperation, Sellers phoned BBC producer Roy Speer and impersonated Kenneth Horne and Dickie Murdoch, stars of the popular "Much Binding in the Marsh" series. "Ken" and "Dickie" gushed about a young comedian they'd seen—a fellow by the name of Sellers—who'd be perfect on the radio. When Sellers confessed his true identity to Speer, the producer was so taken aback, he booked Sellers on the "Show Time" variety series.

The rest is history.

Within a few years, after recurring roles on several BBC radio shows, Sellers helped launch the "Goon Show" and, ultimately, his film career.

"He had to inhabit, he's like a ghoul, he has to feast off somebody else," was Milligan's description of Sellers. "But he does it so well, it has become an art. He is not a genius, Sellers, he is a freak. There is nothing worthwhile that he could do on his own. He is a charming man, but I don't think that anybody would give him a job for that. So he requisitions these bodies, any body, any sound, any voice.... It is a freak gift and he is the only man in the world who can do it and consequently he is a very rare product."[1]

Part I:
The Road to Stardom
(1951–1959)

1

Down Among the Z Men

Cast:

Harry Jones	Harry Secombe
Major Bloodnok	Peter Sellers
Private Eccles	Spike Milligan
Professor Pureheart ...	Michael Bentine

STUDIO: E. J. Fancey Productions
RELEASE DATE: July 12, 1952
RUNNING TIME: 82 minutes (black and white)
DIRECTED BY: Maclean Rogers
PRODUCED BY: E. J. Fancey
WRITTEN BY: Jimmy Grafton and Francis Charles
PHOTOGRAPHY: Geoffrey Faithfull
MUSIC: Jack Jordan

Within a year of its BBC debut, the "Goon Show" made its first and last celluloid appearance in the low-budget comedy, *Down Among the Z Men.*

An amateurish, forgettable B-movie effort, *Down Among the Z Men* again paired Sellers with fellow Goons Harry Secombe and Spike Milligan, all three of whom had appeared in *Penny Points to Paradise* (1951), Sellers's first screen appearance. But *Down Among the Z Men* added Goonish teammate Michael Bentine to its mixture of hoary vaudeville comedy and B-movie antics. Sellers's close friend actor Graham Stark was also recruited for the project.

For Bentine, *Z Men* would be a last hurrah of sorts. An original "Crazy People" member (as the "Goon Show" was called in its inaugural year), Bentine first met Secombe in London at Vivian Van Damm's infamous Windmill Theater, a strip joint and comics's launching pad whose wartime motto, "We never closed," evolved into "We never clothed." Bentine was appearing as half of the forgettable "Sherwood and Forest" comedy musical duo.

(Sellers had also performed at the Windmill after the war; in fact, his name was inscribed after Secombe's on the theatre's plaque proclaiming *Stars of Today Who Started Their Careers in This Theatre.*[1])

2

Sellers played a lowly army private in *Orders Are Orders* (1954), his second big-screen effort and a remake of 1933's *Orders Is Orders*. (Courtesy National Film Archive, London.)

Bentine was an unlikely candidate for comedy; son of a Peruvian scientist, he was educated at Eton and the Sorbonne, and was an experienced Shakespearean actor. But introduced by Secombe to Milligan and Sellers, Bentine became an integral part of the Goons' Grafton Arms clique and developed his Professor Osrick Pureheart character, which became a popular "Crazy People" staple. Bentine left the fledgling radio show in its infancy to pursue a career in television and never looked back. "I was always a breakaway Goon with an urge to apply my logical nonsense as opposed to their nonsensical logic," he explained.[2]

Z Men's goonish roots stretched to cowriter Jimmy Grafton, in whose pub Milligan occupied an attic room under which the Goons hatched their outlandish surrealism. A war hero decorated with the Military Cross at the battle of Arnheim in 1944, Grafton also was a part-time BBC comedy writer. Having witnessed the Goons' birth—and the evolution of their zany characters—Grafton was able to construct a narrative framework around which Sellers, Secombe, Milligan, and Bentine could work their acts.

In fact, the team's *Down Among the Z Men* characters were "Goon Show" regulars, with the exception of Secombe's Harry Jones (whose thickheaded antics nonetheless bore a striking resemblance to the show's Neddy Seagoon). Sellers reprised his popular Major Bloodnok (here a colonel), turning the bluster down a notch but keeping a stiff upper lip; Bentine was the scatterbrained brilliant Professor Pureheart; and Milligan the half-witted Eccles, sounding like a human incarnation of Walt Disney's Pluto.

Sellers, Secombe, Milligan, and Bentine break out of character in the opening frame and introduce themselves to the audience, letting everyone know they aren't taking themselves too seriously.

Much of *Z Men*'s first half is devoted to the manic mugging of Secombe, playing butterfingered Crabb's shop clerk Harry Jones. An amateur thespian, Harry carries his only favorable press clipping in his wallet—for his turn as "Bats of the Yard" in a local production of *The Black Masquerader*—and fancies himself a novice detective.

Sent to retrieve £20 for his boss, Harry encounters a pair of crooks itching to steal the formula used by Professor Pureheart for his combination laughing–tear gas, known otherwise as the bicarbonate bomb. Pureheart already wrote the formula on the back of Harry's press notice while in Crabb's shop but forgot all about it. Meanwhile the crooks dupe Harry into thinking Pureheart is a foreign agent, and "Bats" springs into action. He finds Pureheart camped out in a nearby field and hides in his truck while Pureheart drives to Warwell Atomic Research Center to perfect his bomb.

A comely MI-5 agent (Carole Carr) is assigned to protect Pureheart while he conducts his research. She poses as the daughter of Warwell's commanding officer, Colonel Bloodnok, who assigns the idiotic Private Eccles to oversee the new Z-man recruits. When Pureheart arrives at the center, Harry is mistaken for a Z man and lumped with the recruits.

One of the thugs, disguised as an adjutant, also arrives at Warwell, still searching for Pureheart's formula. And he finds it, thanks to Harry's insistence on tacking his *Black Masquerader* press clipping to the wall of his barracks. But the formula is saved when a wild chase ensues, the crooks are caught red-handed, and everything ends happily ever after.

Down Among the Z Men plays more like an extended "Goon Show" sketch than a motion picture, with the Goons improvising frequently and furiously to plug the film's narrative holes. *Z Men* was clearly intended to expose the radio team to a wider audience and discarded any semblance of coherent plot structure in favor of showcasing the individual team members.

This is most apparent when the action shifts to Warwell and all four Goons are thrown into the *Z Men* mixture. Two extended sequences—completely unrelated to the film's flimsy central plot—illustrate this point. In the first scene, Harry and Eccles are assigned to "train" a group of shapely women recruits (played by Leslie Roberts's "Twelve Toppers"). With phonograph in tow, Harry and Eccles both clown for the camera—

Sellers had a cameo role as a dimwitted bobby in *John and Julie* (1955), the lighthearted tale of two children who journey to London to see the queen's coronation.

Harry "selecting" the appropriate exercise music (smashing a few records and setting the wrong phonograph speed) while Eccles leads the women through a series of loony exercises. The women, of course, are in excellent shape as they break into a syncopated orchestrated dance number reminiscent of a Ziegfeld musical (and ridiculously out of place here).

In the film's most interesting scene, the Warwell officers stage a variety revue, allowing both Sellers and Bentine to repeat — on film — bits of their real-life stage acts. Sellers launches into a sketch about a young American army officer complete with American accents, while Bentine cleverly demonstrates the many uses of a wooden chair.

Down Among the Z Men didn't enhance the Goons's film careers, but it wasn't for lack of trying. Given the thin material, Sellers and company were at least entertaining, and the film provides a unique historical perspective of the four original Goons and their stab at breaking into mainstream cinema.

(Unbeknownst to the Goons, they had a willing ally in the film industry.

John Redway, Sellers's future agent, was working as a casting director at the Associated British Picture Corporation. He recommended his company put the team under contract, but his suggestion was ignored.[3])

2
The Ladykillers

Cast:
Professor Marcus   .... Alec Guinness
Mrs. Wilberforce ..... Katie Johnson
Harry .... Peter Sellers
One-Round .... Danny Green
Louie .... Herbert Lom
The Major .... Cecil Parker

STUDIO: Ealing Studios
RELEASE DATE: February 24, 1956
RUNNING TIME: 90 minutes (Technicolor)
DIRECTED BY: Alexander Mackendrick
PRODUCED BY: Michael Balcon
WRITTEN BY: William Rose
PHOTOGRAPHY: Otto Heller
MUSIC: Tristram Cary

By the mid–1950s the names Alec Guinness and Ealing Studios were synonymous with classic British comedy. Ealing's social satires—*Kind Hearts and Coronets* (1949), *The Man in the White Suit* (1951), and *The Lavender Hill Mob* (1951)—had provided the multitalented Guinness some of his finest roles and a springboard to fame. Ealing and Guinness would also propel Peter Sellers across the cinematic transom, unlocking the door to his burgeoning film career.

After bit parts as a lowly army private in *Orders Are Orders* (1954) and a small-town bobby in *John and Julie* (1955), Sellers was sent by his agent, Dennis Selinger, to audition for the commanding role of an illiterate bully in Ealing's latest comedy, *The Ladykillers*. But the soft, overweight radio star didn't quite fit the bill; instead, he was cast as a greasy-haired henchman opposite his idol, Guinness.

Sellers had long admired Guinness for his comedic quick-change virtuosity (showcased in *Kind Hearts and Coronets*) and impressive range as a dramatic actor. In Guinness, Sellers found an artistic soulmate, the plain-looking everyman who virtually disappeared into his on-screen personae.

In hindsight, the opportunity to work with Guinness meant more to Sellers's career than personal gratification. Not only was the Ealing-Guinness combination a dynamic audience grabber, but *The Ladykillers* marked one of Ealing's last major successes before the studio was sold to BBC television toward the end of the 1950s. Fortunately, it remained in existence long enough to record for posterity the pairing of Guinness and Sellers—the professional old hand and his impressionable protégé soon to be labeled England's "next Guinness."

But for now there was only one Guinness, and he starred in *The Lady-killers* as "Professor" Marcus, a cadaverous bucktoothed criminal master-mind plotting his next job. Requiring a secret lair in which to assemble his thieving gang, Marcus rents a pair of upstairs rooms from Mrs. Wilberforce (Katie Johnson), a sweet old bitty who lives alone in her Victorian house with a bevy of exotic birds. The house is perfect for Marcus's needs; not only does it sit at a darkened street's end just above a London stockyard, but it's within striking distance of the gang's planned heist at King's Cross railway station.

Posing as a string quintet practicing in Marcus's rooms, the motley mob assembles at the house clumsily bearing musical instrument cases. There's Harry Robinson (Sellers), a dim-witted cockney teddy boy given to fits of despair; One-Round (Danny Green), a thickheaded ex-boxer; the harmless Major (Cecil Parker), complete with walrus mustache and genteel manners; and Louie (Herbert Lom), a nervous, sinister gunman dressed in mob-style pinstripes and white tie.

Louie carries a professed hatred for little old women, and after a few hours it's easy to see why. While the gang hashes over their plan in a back room—and a melodious phonograph record re-creates their "practice"—they're constantly interrupted by Mrs. Wilberforce bearing tea and crumpets (or asking the men to retrieve her errant parrot, General Gordon). Each knock on the door sends the gang dashing wildly for their instruments and striking an artistic (if not quite musically correct) pose when Mrs. Wilberforce enters the room.

But that's OK; after all, Mrs. Wilberforce is going to make the men rich by playing a key role in the robbery. For after they sabotage an armored truck and stuff £60,000 in a steamer trunk dumped at the railway station, Marcus asks "Mrs. W." if she will bring his trunk back to the house for him.

The plan works like clockwork, with one slight complication—Mrs. Wilberforce. Taking a cab to King's Cross, she retrieves the trunk as promised but stops on the way home to lambaste a grocer yelling at a horse eating his produce. The man tells Mrs. W. to mind her own business and vents his rage at the poor cabdriver coming to her aid. While the horrified

Marcus gang watches in dumbstruck agony, the crazed grocer slugs the cabdriver, damages his cab, and is hauled off to the police station along with Mrs. Wilberforce and the steamer trunk.

But the police fail to inspect the trunk, personally transporting it and Mrs. W. back to the house. Breathing a huge sigh of relief, the gang counts the money, each man stuffing his share into his instrument case. They're about to make their getaway when One-Round's cello case gets stuck in Mrs. W.'s front door and flies open, exposing the stolen loot to an astonished Mrs. W.

Fearing she'll go to the police, the gang returns to the house to lie about the money when a gaggle of Mrs. W.'s friends show up for afternoon tea. One of them has the afternoon newspaper with its blaring headlines about the robbery, and Mrs. W. puts 2 and 2 together. She punishes the men by making them stay for tea and entertain her friends, and when the women leave, Marcus and company try to explain their motives while helping Mrs. W. wash the dishes.

> *Marcus:* Let me try to explain, Mrs. Wilberforce. You see, in this case it would do no good to take the money back. As strange as it may seem to you, nobody wants the money back.
> *Mrs. W.:* Don't expect me to believe that.
> *Marcus:* But it's true Mrs. Wilberforce. You see this particular shipment was insured. So now the insurance company simply pays to the factory £60,000 and then in order to recover its money, it puts one farthing on all the premiums on all the policies for the next year. You see? So how much real harm have we done anybody? One farthing's worth, Mrs. Wilberforce, one farthing's worth. Now you hadn't thought of it like that, had you?
> *One-Round* (whispers to Harry): Hey, you know what, I never thought of it like that either.
> *Mrs. W.:* Surely it isn't as simple as all that.
> *Marcus:* I assure you, if we tried to take the money back now it would simply confuse the whole issue.
> *Harry:* They wouldn't even take it back.
> *Major:* That's perfectly true.

Mrs. W. remains skeptical of Marcus's explanation until the Major re-.counts the sad story leading to his life of crime. "Well, it's just that at this very moment, Mrs. Wilberforce, there is waiting an invalid; a dear, sweet little old lady not may heaven bless, unlike yourself, waiting with patient serenity, but with high hope that she has nothing more to fear—[pregnant pause] my mother."

But Mrs. W. still insists on going to the police, until Marcus informs her she's an accessory to the crime. Didn't she bring the "lolly" back to the house? The gang could swear she was innocent, but who'd believe them? It looks like she's likely to spend the rest of her days in prison, sewing mailbags.

Screenwriter William Rose shifts his narrative into high comedic gear when the gang reluctantly decides to kill Mrs. W., who still insists on going to the police. It's one thing knocking off a bank job, but killing an old lady? Although he would never admit it, each man has in some way grown attached to the pesky Mrs. W., a motherly substitute for their rotten upbringing. She's affectionately called "Mrs. Lopsided" by One-Round and "Mum" by Harry. Even trigger-happy Louie can't bring himself to murder his worst nightmare.

So after a process of elimination, the Major is picked to murder Mrs. W. But he has no intention of committing the dirty deed; instead, he sneaks out the bedroom window with the loot, only to be chased and killed by Louie. After One-Round dumps the Major's corpse into a passing freight train, it's Harry's turn to kill the old lady. Like the Major, he can't face the prospect of strangling poor Mum, so he also tries to sneak off with the lolly, before being caught and fatally clubbed by One-Round. As soon as Harry's body is dumped, it's One-Round's turn to meet his maker; he's killed by Louie, who in turn is killed by Marcus, who in turn is killed by a steel beam as his body falls into a freight car.

The Ladykillers's plot is ludicrous but good fun nonetheless and draws interesting parallels between the performing styles of Guinness and Sellers. Guinness liked to clothe his characters internally and work outward, and he limned Marcus as the epitome of evil-minded ruthlessness, complete with maniacal glint. But he added a further cartoonish dimension to the character by wearing his hair wildly, using false buck teeth, and adopting a stoop.

"Mr. Guinness, got up with monstrous buck teeth and eyes sunk darkly in his head, is perhaps the most farcically fiendish character he has ever played," wrote Bosley Crowther in the *New York Times*. "He has the unctuous and wicked personality of Captain Hook in 'Peter Pan,' the hollow and angular appearance of that other great British comic, Alastair Sim. In his long, flapping coat and wayward muffler, he would seem an invincible rogue. But the old lady defeats him. And that is the substance of the joke."[1]

Sellers, who needed to find his character's voice before working out the physical details, said later that he was "emerald with envy" at the voice Guinness chose for Marcus.[2] When he made *Ladykillers*, Sellers was still considered a topflight mimic and unproven screen talent relegated to supporting roles. He was hired by Mackendrick not for his slapstick genius—brought to fruition nearly a decade later in *The Pink Panther*—but for his ability to *sound* like a teddy boy. It was the sort of stock role Sellers could avoid in a few years. But for now it provided him with valuable on-the-job training next to some of the English cinema's finest character actors.

One-Round tries to explain his celloful of loot to Mrs. Wilberforce (Katie Johnson) as Harry and Professor Marcus panic. Sellers had originally auditioned for the role of One-Round but was judged unsuitable for the thick-eared muscleman.

Green, Parker, and Lom (with whom Sellers would reappear in *Mr. Topaze*, *A Shot in the Dark*, and subsequent *Panther* films) all turned in excellent performances, guided by Mackendrick's sure-handed direction and Rose's witty screenplay (for which he won a British Oscar). The 77-year-old Johnson, who died two years later in 1957, was voted 1955's best actress by the British Film Academy.

"Guinness tends to overact the sinister leader while Cecil Parker strikes just the right note as a con man posing as an army officer," wrote *Variety*. "Herbert Lom broods gloomily as the most ruthless of the plotters, with Peter Sellers contrasting well as the dumb muscleman."[3]

Still, even in such stellar company, Sellers had his moments of inspiration, which didn't go unnoticed by the critics. Whether chasing Mrs. Wilberforce's parrot or nonchalantly catching the Major's errant violin case from the roof, Sellers hinted at the mixture of broad comedy and subtle characterization of which he was capable if given the proper showcase.

3
The Smallest Show on Earth

Cast:

Matthew Spenser	Bill Travers
Jean Spenser	Virginia McKenna
Mrs. Fazackalee	Margaret Rutherford
Mr. Quill	Peter Sellers
Tom	Bernard Miles
Hardcastle	Francis De Wolff

STUDIO: British Lion
RELEASE DATE: April 11, 1957
RUNNING TIME: 81 minutes (black and white)
DIRECTED BY: Basil Dearden
PRODUCED BY: Michael Relph
WRITTEN BY: William Rose and John Eldridge
PHOTOGRAPHY: Douglas Slocombe
MUSIC: William Alwyn

As Sellers was learning the hard way, maintaining a steady career in the crowded British cinema of the 1950s wasn't an easy task. Although his work in *Ladykillers* caught the critics' attention, film producers weren't yet beating down his door with offers. But Sellers's sporadic film career was complemented by his work on the "Goon Show"—still going strong in 1957—and his frequent appearances on television.

William "Mate" Cobblers—a hoary old boy and one of Sellers's more popular "Goon Show" characters—made his television debut in a show called "Idiot Weekly" and consequently helped Sellers snare his next film role. The producers of *The Smallest Show on Earth*, searching for a decrepit, 68-year-old movie-house projectionist, chanced upon Sellers in his Cobblers makeup. Impressed with his physical transformation—and the way the 32-year-old comedian slipped into the guise of someone twice his age—they cast Sellers in *The Smallest Show on Earth*.[1]

As in *Ladykillers*, Sellers was teamed with a daunting ensemble company, this time featuring screen legends Margaret Rutherford and Bernard Miles. Although he would later complain that his best moments were swept away from the cutting-room floor, Sellers's performance in *Smallest Show on Earth* only solidified his growing reputation as an actor of remarkable range.

Bill Travers and Virginia McKenna, later to gain fame as the lion-rearing Adamsons of *Born Free* (1965), were cast in the lead roles as Matthew and Jean Spenser, a young married couple trying to make ends meet while Matthew completes his novel. Their luck takes a drastic turn when Matthew learns he's inherited a cinema from his great-uncle Simon, a champion beer drinker who died in a pub after winning a drinking contest. Thinking they've hit the jackpot, the couple take a train to the small town where they hope to claim their prize.

But there's a major problem. Uncle Simon's legacy lives only in the rat-infested broken-down Bijou Kinema, the town's laughingstock referred to locally as the Flea Pit. A former music hall and legitimate theater, the Bijou in its time was the elegant grand dame of cinemas, the first of its kind in this part of England. But mismanagement by hard-drinking Uncle Simon, adjacent railroad tracks that literally shake the Bijou's rafters, and the opening of the Grand—a resplendent domed cinema just yards away—have driven the Flea Pit out of business.

Although despondent over their inheritance, the Spensers hope they can sell the Bijou to Hardcastle (Francis De Wolff), the Grand's blustery owner who once offered Simon £2,000 for the Bijou property. Hardcastle needs the land to build a parking lot for his expanding empire, but the Spensers are insulted by his take-it-or-leave-it offer of £750.

Hoping to frighten Hardcastle into increasing his offer, the Spensers make mock preparations to reopen the Bijou. But they first have to convince their mothballed staff of three they mean business.

There's Mrs. Fazackalee (Rutherford), the venerable box-office matron who provided the piano soundtrack in the Bijou's silent-movie days and conducted a long affair with Uncle Simon; Tom (Miles), the Bijou's stooped ancient usher still bitter about the uniform he was promised but never received; and Percy Quill (Sellers), the cinema's alcoholic pensioner projectionist always complaining about his dilapidated equipment.

Having been together for decades, the Bijou staff are more than coworkers; they're a small, tightly-knit family, bickering constantly like bratty siblings, yet fused together by a bond of love for each other and for the only home they've ever known—the Bijou.

Screenwriters William Rose and John Eldridge poignantly illustrate these familial feelings in two sequential scenes where Matthew is confronted by Mrs. Fazackalee and Quill, complaining about each other's behavior. In the first scene, Matthew and Mrs. Fazackalee are sitting in the Bijou office when she suddenly spouts off about Quill.

> *Mrs. Fazackalee:* Unless something is done about Mr. Quill, I am not prepared to continue in my present position.
> *Matthew:* Oh?
> *Mrs. Fazackalee:* I can no longer tolerate his insulting and unseemly behavior.
> *Matthew:* Well then, what are you suggesting, Mrs. Fazackalee? That I should give him the sack?

Alcoholic projectionist Percy Quill reminisces about the old silent-movie days with Jean and Matthew Spenser (Virginia McKenna and Bill Travers). (Courtesy National Film Archive, London.)

Mrs. Fazackalee: Sack Mr. Quill? Sack Mr. Quill?! Oh, I'm afraid that would be quite out of the question, on account of the projection equipment, you know. Nobody else could possibly understand it. In fact, in 1937, when Mr. Quill had to go and have his appendix out and the late Mr. Spenser called in another projectionist to take over, it was only three days before *he* had to have *his* appendix out. Oh, no, I merely wondered if you would say something rude ... or unpleasant ... to him.

[Matthew tells Mrs. Fazackalee he'll see what he can do and leaves the room, only to be pulled aside by Quill.]

Quill: It's about that woman, sir, that Mrs. Fazackalee. She's a trouble-maker, sir. She does nothing else but make trouble; make trouble here, make trouble there....

Matthew: Oh, yes, well....

Quill: Well, now that the old scoundrel's dead ... oh, I beg your pardon, sir, no offense intended I assure you ... now that the old gentleman's gone to his dear rest, do we have to have that awful old hag hangin' 'round this place?!

Matthew: What do you suggest I do, sack her?

Quill: Sack Mrs. Fazackalee! I don't think you properly appreciate the position, Mr. Spenser. Mrs. Fazackalee's been here since the silent days.

She used to play the piano. She's the only one what knows how the place runs! Sack Mrs. Fazackalee! You'll be wanting to sack old Tom next!
Matthew: What you really mean is you just want me to say something rude and unpleasant to her.
Quill: Yes ... yes....

So with peace reigning among the troops, Matthew and crew clean, repair, and polish the Bijou to its former glory. Hardcastle, alarmed at what this could mean to the Grand's business, offers £2,000 pounds cash for the property. But Tom overhears Matthew's plan to sell the "dump" and tells the Grand's chief usher, who in turn relays the news to Hardcastle. Knowing now that Matthew had no intention of reopening the cinema, Hardcastle reverts to his original offer of £750.

But instead of cowering into a corner—and having nothing to lose—the Spensers decide to go for broke and actually reopen the Bijou, promising to provide for Quill, Tom, and Mrs. Fazackalee should they decide to sell the place. Quill vows to stop drinking—his ultimate sacrifice for the old Bijou—and in one of the film's most touching scenes, Matthew promises a skulking Tom his elusive uniform. The teary-eyed look of excitement and disbelief on Tom's timeworn face—like that of a small child unwrapping a toy—is priceless.

At the end of its first week, the Bijou surprisingly has made a £1.70 profit—not much but enough to spur a visit by Matthew and Jean to the Grand to see how a "real" cinema is run. The Grand itself puts on more of a show than the films it screens. A live orchestra serenades the audience while scantily clad girls parade up and down the aisles hawking ice cream and cigarettes. It's all spectacle, but it pulls in business. Before long, Jean is doubling as the Bijou's ice-cream girl, raising ticket sales and the libidos of the Bijou's male clientele.

But the crowds really start to pour in when Matthew hires a comely blond named Marlene to sell ice cream. In a flash of inspiration and business acumen, Matthew cranks up the Bijou's steam valves while the audience watches a desert picture. At a strategic point in the picture, with the audience gasping for air in the humid theater, out pops Marlene, who's almost trampled in the patrons' stampede for the ice cream.

For Tom, Quill, and Mrs. Fazackalee, the Bijou's rebirth harks back to the good old days, and after hours the three veterans touchingly relive their golden years. While Quill screens the silent movies he's kept all these years—a look of beatific contentment on his face as he peers through the projection-room peephole—Tom listens in rapture as Mrs. Fazackalee provides her grandiloquent piano accompaniment. Life, for these cinematic old-timers, just doesn't get any better.

Not to be outdone by his rival's sudden success, Hardcastle plots to destroy the Bijou by planting a bottle of whiskey in Quill's newsreel delivery box. Screening the desert picture and battling a powerful thirst, Quill gives in to his alcoholic urges and downs the bottle, leaving the Bijou in shame when he's unable to work the projection equipment.

It's all downhill for the Bijou following Quill's hasty departure. Matthew fights a losing battle with the equipment, a now-pregnant Marlene is forced to quit her job, and ticket sales are down. When the Spensers learn that Jean is pregnant, they decide to sell the Bijou to Hardcastle for his original £750 offer.

But Tom, eavesdropping once again, isn't going to let that happen. The Bijou means more to him than a share of money; it's his home. He decides to take matters into his own hands. Grabbing a can of gasoline, he sneaks into the Grand and starts a huge fire, completely destroying the cinema. Hardcastle, now forced to use the Bijou to recoup his losses, pays the Spensers £10,000 pounds for their property with the stipulation he be allowed to rename it the New Bijou.

Save for wooden performances from Travers and the sickeningly sweet McKenna, *The Smallest Show on Earth* was an actor's showcase, highlighted by the emotional interplay between Sellers, Rutherford, and Miles.

Working behind heavy makeup, bushy gray mustache, and granny glasses, Sellers was completely believable as the broken-down Quill, scurrying round his beloved projection booth and rejoicing in his new lease on life. Sellers imbued Quill with an affectionate Old-World demeanor not unlike the goonish William Cobblers, keeping pace with Rutherford and Miles and leaving little doubt he could tackle more substantive roles should they be offered.

Quill was more than just makeup and a funny voice, and one scene in particular illustrated Sellers's ability to capture an emotionally charged moment with a single gesture. Leaving the Bijou after opening night—"Only one breakdown tonight!" he happily reports to the Spensers—Quill walks down the street, a big smile on his face as he jauntily flaps his arms at his side and gives a little jump for joy.

The film received mixed notices upon its release. While *Variety* thought that "Peter Sellers, a noted impressionist, gives an old-time air to the boothman,"[2] *Newsweek* was confused by the proceedings:

> The projectionist briefly fights his alcoholic craving, and gives up; a girl who sells refreshments in the theater becomes pregnant; the novelist-hero, Travers, is accused of being the girl's seducer. That is the story—suddenly brought to an ending when the caretaker-arsonist sets fire to the competing movie house across the street, and the Flea Pit's new owner guarantees its employees continued employment. (The movie just drops the subject of the pregnant girl, which seems odd, but not nearly as odd as the movie.)[3]

The *New York Times*, labeling the film "a little package of nonsense," praised its cast. "Bill Travers and Virginia McKenna are fine as the new owners of the Bijou. Thanks to the script by William Rose and John Eldridge, from a story by Mr. Rose, Margaret Rutherford's cashier, Peter Sellers' projectionist and Bernard Miles' doorman are gems."[4]

The Smallest Show on Earth—his sixth film in six years—marked Sellers's last strictly supporting role. From this strategic jumping-off point, he would land firmer film offers in larger projects, beginning with his next picture, *The Naked Truth*.

4
The Naked Truth

Cast:
Sonny MacGregor   ... Peter Sellers
Lord Mayley   .... Terry-Thomas
Nigel Dennis   .... Dennis Price
Flora Ransom   ...... Peggy Mount
Melissa Right   .... Shirley Eaton
Lady Mayley   .... Georgina Cookson
Rev. Bastable   .... Miles Malleson

STUDIO: Rank
RELEASE DATE: January 2, 1958
RUNNING TIME: 92 minutes (black and white)
DIRECTED BY: Mario Zampi
PRODUCED BY: Mario Zampi
WRITTEN BY: Michael Pertwee
PHOTOGRAPHY: Stan Pavey
MUSIC: Stanley Black

As he struggled to gain momentum as a film actor in the mid-1950s, Sellers continued his vocal exploits on the "Goon Show," making occasional forays into television with only moderate success. Although his work in *Ladykillers* and *Smallest Show on Earth* showed Sellers's comedic potential, "the man of a thousand voices" had yet to convince the British public (and his critics) that he could transcend radio's confines and prove he was more than a mouthful of funny voices. It was Sellers's performance in *The Naked Truth* that would change that perception, enhancing his reputation as a screen chameleon on a par with Alec Guinness.

The Naked Truth marked several important milestones in Sellers's film career. Not only was he cast in his first multiple role—and given the chance to showcase his remarkable versatility in character as well as voice—but he was teamed with Terry-Thomas, a rising star on the British film scene whose career would intertwine with Sellers's over the next several years.

Thomas (born Thomas Terry Hoar Stevens) was an established radio and television personality when the cinema beckoned; hits like *Private's Progress*, *Blue Murder at St. Trinian's*, and *Too Many Crooks* followed shortly thereafter. As did Sellers during his wartime stint in Ralph Reader's "Gang Show," Thomas—a sergeant in the Royal Signals—had performed in the "Stars in Battledress" entertainment unit before segueing into a radio career after being demobbed. By the time he appeared in *The Naked Truth*, Thomas's gap-toothed smile and mustached visage were instantly recognizable trademarks, boding well for the film's box-office potential and Sellers's supporting role.

Expertly directed by Mario Zampi from Michael Pertwee's clever screenplay, *The Naked Truth* lampooned the yellow journalism of England's headline-screaming tabloids, in this case a fictional rag called *The Naked Truth*, written, edited, and about to be published by suavely decadent Nigel Dennis (Dennis Price).

Dennis is more than a hack journalist out to make a quick buck; he's a blackmail artist threatening to destroy the careers of England's finest by revealing scandalous information just this side of libel. The price for Dennis's silence is £10,000, paid in two weeks' time or his seedy publication goes to press.

That wouldn't be in the best interests of lecherous insurance executive Lord Mayley (Thomas), more interested in seducing young women than quoting premiums, nor beloved Scottish television host Wee Sonny Mac-Gregor (Sellers), the "jack of all faces" quick-change artist who unbeknownst to his adoring pensioner audience doubles as their slumlord, or Flora Ransom (Peggy Mount), the famous authoress who years before cheated on her husband and is now engaged to a reverend, or Melissa Wright (Shirley Eaton), an aspiring model with a checkered past and violently jealous boyfriend.

But Dennis's victims have no intention of being blackmailed, and each devises his own scheme to silence *The Naked Truth*'s blaring innuendoes.

Wee Sonny, whose specialty is impersonating his audience members, decides to test the waters of reality by disguising himself as a doddering old salt and casing Dennis's floating office barge in which resides the filing cabinet containing dossiers of *The Naked Truth*'s intended victims. While Sonny snoops around outside, Melissa is inside, pleading with Dennis not to publish her dirty deeds. ("I hope this isn't an appeal to my better nature," Dennis tells her. "I haven't one.")

Slumlord–television star Wee Sonny MacGregor and skirt-chasing Lord Mayley (Terry-Thomas) are exposed to *The Naked Truth*. (Courtesy National Film Archive, London.)

Meanwhile Flora, known for her popular detective thrillers, decides to murder Dennis by luring him to her home, plying him with a Mickey Finn, then stuffing his body in a trunk and disposing of the remains in a swamp. She recruits her fluttery daughter Ethel (Joan Sims) for the dirty deed, but the plan goes awry when Mayley pays a visit to discuss Dennis's blackmail scheme. Ethel mistakes Mayley for Dennis, and he wakes up a short time later floating helplessly in the swamp.

Sonny's murder attempts also fall short of their intended mark when he tries to procure a bomb to destroy Dennis's barge and all the evidence contained therein. Sellers was at his best in these scenes, imbuing his free-form comedic riffs with a surrealistic twist recalling his Goonish roots.

Posing as an Irish safecracker complete with thick brogue, ridiculous wig, and shamrock in his lapel, Sonny visits a Dublin bar, orders a drink, and parks himself at a table peopled by two Irish thugs, one of whom has a cauliflower ear and broken nose. "Me name's Lalichan, and I'm from across the water. You'll be O'Toole and a straight lad I am to meet ya," Sonny says to the broken-nosed tough, getting only an angry stare in response.

Somewhat taken aback, Sonny leans toward the other tough and launches into his conspiratorial pitch for the bomb. "I'm descended from the kings, you know, and the halls of Tara. It's like this, we're doin' a job in London, 'tis the Albert Hall at all, and we've run right out of the jelly. So if you could be letting me have a little of the gel ignite, b'gad, I could do the job."

Answered again only by a blank stare and sensing he's in trouble, Sonny pulls out all the stops. "But why are we talking in the cursed tongue when we have the Gaelic?" he says, rubbing his hands together and launching into Gaelic-flavored gibberish before being punched in the nose by the broken-nose tough.

"It's an Englishman, all right," says the other thug, as Sonny hits the deck and is dragged out of the bar.

Forced to make his bomb from a do-it-yourself kit, Sonny then disguises himself as an English country gentleman and visits a gun shop in search of the final ingredient—gunpowder—armed with a plummy aristocratic accent and walking stick.

Shop Manager: Good afternoon, sir.
Sonny: Good afternoon. Look here, I'm having a day's rough shooting. I want some bullets, please.
Manager (pointedly): Cartridges. Certainly, sir. Any particular make?
Sonny: Oh no, I shouldn't think so, as long as they've got gunpowder in them, what.
Manager: What bore?
Sonny: Boor? Oh boar ... no, no ... I shoot rabbits, pheasants, small fry, you know....
Manager: No, no, no, sir—bore, B-O-R-E.
Sonny: Oh, bore! Hmmm....
Manager: Twelve, twenty, or four-ten?
Sonny: Uh, definitely, yes....
Manager: Well, which sir?
Sonny: The largest you have, surely.
Manager: Twelve bore. And how many sir, 50?
Sonny: No, no.... I think you'd better make it a thousand.
Manager: A thousand?!
Sonny: Yes.
Manager: But didn't you say a day's rough shooting?
Sonny: (stuttering): Yes I did, and it may be pretty rough. On second thought, I think you'd better make it fifteen hundred perhaps?

Sonny, once again disguised as the old salt, plants his homemade bomb in Dennis's filing cabinet, which is subsequently stolen by Flora and Ethel. When Dennis shows up at Flora's flat, demanding £5,000 up front for witnessing the Mayley swamp incident, Flora realizes Ethel drugged the wrong man. She takes her daughter aside and tells her to sneak out with the filing cabinet and return it to the barge so Dennis won't suspect anything amiss.

Meanwhile, Sonny, waiting outside after following Dennis to the Ransom residence, removes the bomb from the cabinet and plants it on the street, hoping to kill Dennis when he leaves the flat. Mayley arrives and recognizes Sonny just as the bomb explodes and destroys Mayley's car.

The plot thickens later when Mayley and Melissa return to Flora's flat and are soon joined by Sonny, disguised this time as a bobby. Flora isn't home, but the guests are greeted by Cedrick (Miles Malleson), Flora's pious fiancé who is totally unaware of Dennis's blackmail scheme. Cedrick offers his guests a drink from the drugged alcohol, and Flora and Ethel return home to a roomful of unconscious people.

But now that they're all in the same place at the same time, the would-be blackmail victims plot a scheme of their own to wipe Dennis off the face of the earth. Mayley and Sonny record some insurance dialogue ("Here are the figures, MacGregor, have a look at them." "You mean to say I get all that with such a small premium?") in Mayley's home. While Mayley plays the tape over and over again to fool his wife, MacGregor, disguised as the old salt, returns to Dennis's barge to finish him off. But Dennis is arrested for his blackmail attempts, telling the cops he'll "blow them all sky high" if he's put on trial.

Fearing Dennis will expose them at his trial, Mayley, Sonny, and Flora, backed by three hundred high-powered Brits entangled in Dennis's scheme, "rescue" Dennis on his way to prison, knock him out, and transport him by helicopter, boat, and zeppelin out of the country. Every time Dennis wakes up, he's knocked out with a rubber truncheon; when he's finally allowed to regain his senses, Dennis tells the group (assembled in the zeppelin) he wasn't going to talk at his trial, since they had already destroyed all the evidence. Not realizing he's in a zeppelin over the Atlantic, Dennis steps out for some "fresh air" and plunges to his death, much to the glee of his captors. Their joy, however, is short-lived when Sonny fires off his gun in celebration, puncturing the zeppelin and sending it spiraling toward the ocean.

Although Pertwee's busy zigzagging plot at times threatens to throw *The Naked Truth* off its comedic course, Zampi managed to keep the film's narrative flowing in a jolly vein, mining humor from almost every farcical situation.

Sellers turned in the film's finest performance, slipping in and out of Sonny's phony Bonnie accent to suit the particular occasion and maintaining his momentum among his more seasoned costars. The role was attuned to Sellers's reputation at the time as the owlish, somewhat rebellious "Goon Show" member, and he obviously relished the chance to lampoon Wilfrid Pickles, the popular radio quiz-show host upon whom Sonny was based. (*The Naked Truth* also led to Sellers's chance meeting with director Joe McGrath, who would later direct him in *Casino Royale*, *The Magic Christian*, and *The Great McGonagall*. McGrath, coming out of a showing of *The Naked Truth* after it opened in London, spied Sellers waiting in the theater's foyer, eavesdropping on the audience's remarks. McGrath strode over to Sellers and announced, "You are the real Peter Sellers, and I claim the ten-pound prize!" Sellers appreciated McGrath's sense of humor, and the two men struck up an instant friendship.[1])

Although it did quite well at the box office, *The Naked Truth* (*Your Past Is Showing* in the United States) opened to mixed reviews, with most critics complaining about the film's narrative overindulgence but enthusiastically praising Sellers. "Mario Zampi's well-made farce sets out to get the patrons' yocks and achieves its purpose.... Though relying more on the sledge hammer than the rapier for its effects, it has few dull moments," wrote *Variety*. "Major acting honors must go to Peter Sellers, top UK TV and radio comedian, as the tele star. He shapes as a fine character comedian in a wide range of impersonations."[2]

The *New York Times*'s Bosley Crowther panned the film, noting that "we're bound to report the only murder that is positively done in this film is performed by the couple of fellows who wrote and directed it.... But don't hold the actors responsible. They try to whip life into the thing with the violent determination of gypsies flailing away at a dead mule.... Occasionally one or the other wrenches free of the death grip of the script and does something fairly funny that is worth a halfway guffaw. But, for the most part, it is labored, witless going...."[3]

But regardless of *The Naked Truth*'s critical reception, Sellers was now in a position to launch a full-time film career. Having earned his cinematic stripes with some of Britain's finest actors, his drive and ambition now carried him further along the road to stardom.

5

tom thumb

Cast:

Tom	Russ Tamblyn
Jonathan	Bernard Miles
Woody	Alan Young
Ivan	Terry-Thomas
Tony	Peter Sellers
Anna	Jessie Matthews
Queeny	June Thornburn

STUDIO: MGM
RELEASE DATE: December 24, 1958
RUNNING TIME: 98 minutes (Eastmancolor)
DIRECTED BY: George Pal
PRODUCED BY: George Pal
WRITTEN BY: Ladislas Fodor
PHOTOGRAPHY: Georges Perinal
MUSIC: Douglas Gamley and Kenneth Jones

Teamed once again with Terry-Thomas, Sellers continued his burgeoning film career with a supporting role as an overweight bumbling thief
in the George Pal–directed children's film tom thumb.

Tom thumb represented a major stepping-stone for Sellers. Not only
was he teamed again with Thomas—a fruitful partnership that would blos-
som in future screen endeavors—but this was his first, albeit transatlantic,
brush with Hollywood's studio system. Tom thumb, produced under the
MGM banner, was filmed mostly in England but fared well in America,
where Sellers hoped to establish a solid audience base.

Pal's film, written by Ladislas Fodor, also represented an early international packaging concept, with Sellers and Thomas playing opposite American stars Russ Tamblyn (who reportedly won the role much to the chagrin
of Donald O'Connor), Alan Young, and the voice of advertising whiz/
satirist Stan Freberg. (Like Sellers's earlier dubbing jobs on Malaga (1954)
and 1953's Beat the Devil—in which he dubbed some of Humphrey Bogart's
lines—Freberg remained faceless while supplying a puppet's voice. Unlike
Sellers, however, he received a screen credit for his vocal duties.)

Even in today's age of high-tech sophistication, tom thumb remains a
virtuoso study in cinematic special effects. Before embarking on the project, Pal had already won four Oscars—a special Oscar for his 1944 Puppe-
toon pictures and special effects Oscars for Destination Moon (1950), When
Worlds Collide (1953), and War of the Worlds (1953).

Long on special effects but short on plot, tom thumb remained true to
its two-inch hero, sent to the humble childless home of Honest Jonathan
(Bernard Miles) the woodcutter, and his loyal wife, Anna (Jessie Mat-
thews, who was coaxed by Pal out of a fifteen-year retirement).

Jonathan, chopping down an oak tree in the Great Forest, is approached
by Queeny (Thornburn), a magical wood nymph who grants him three
wishes if he saves the tree for the animals. Acceding to Queeny's request,
Jonathan returns home and tells Anna about their good luck. But the couple proceed to waste their wishes on a sausage during a silly argument and
before long are pining for just one more wish—a son. "I'd love him with
all my heart, even if he were no bigger than my thumb," Anna says, perhaps
thinking of the bedroom she's already filled with toys. Queeny responds to

her plea, sending a whistling Tom (Tamblyn) to the couple's log cabin in the dead of night.

Overjoyed at their new arrival, Jonathan and Anna welcome Tom with open arms despite his minuscule size. After celebrating with a "birthday cake"—in his case, a doughnut ten times his size—Tom is put to bed, only to discover that the "toys" in his room come alive in his presence. Tom proceeds to dance with and talk to the toys in the film's most technically impressive sequence mixing animation with live-action footage. (Pal took painstaking efforts to achieve the illusion of Tom's tiny size. A hat appearing with Tom was, in actuality, sixteen feet high, while Tom's crib was fifty-five feet long and a cobbler's bench eighty feet.)

"We had two camera crews in England so one always could be working ahead of us, preparing the next set in a different stage," Pal said. "We revolved between stages continuously. As soon as we would finish with one set, another invariably also filling the entire stage would be put into construction in its place. For one set, our nursery where Tom dances with the dolls, we had to open two stages and utilize them both simultaneously. For another, we made a hole in the room of one stage so our camera could draw far enough away for a long shot of the entire set."[1]

The next day, on their way to the forest, Tom and Jonathan encounter Woody (Young), the friendly local musician in love with Queeny. Woody doesn't bat an eye at Tom's size or the fact that Jonathan suddenly has a son. But then Woody's not planning a robbery, as are the black-clad Ivan (Thomas) and his corpulent Italian partner, Tony (Sellers). Spotting Tom upon their emergence from the Black Swamp, Ivan and Tony see not only a very small boy but an instrument to help them execute their heist of the town treasury. Ivan's offer to buy Tom from Jonathan, however, is abruptly rejected by the honorable woodcutter.

But the crooks are unwittingly helped by Woody, who takes Tom to town fair over the weekend. Searching for a gift for Queeny, Woody's attention is captured by a man selling magical "dancing shoes," which bop on their own, provided there's musical accompaniment. Woody has Tom try on a pair, with disastrous results; Tom can't control the shoes, and before long he's dancing wildly through the fairgrounds, grabbing a balloon that carries him within view of Ivan and Tony, preparing to break into the treasury.

Using a peashooter, Ivan torpedos the balloon and catches Tom in his hat, telling him the treasury money really belongs to the town's "poor orphans." The innocent Tom believes Ivan's story, agrees to be lowered down a rope into the treasury vault, and helps steal a sack of gold coins.

Sworn to secrecy for his "good deed" and given a stolen coin for his trouble, Tom returns home later that night to an angry Jonathan. Trying to sneak in through a kitchen window, Tom slips, and the coin drops into

Clumsy crooks Tony (Sellers) and Ivan (Terry-Thomas) plan to use Tom (Russ Tamblyn) to rob the local treasury.

a bowl of biscuit batter, the same batter used to feed some policemen questioning the couple about the robbery. When one of the cops bites into the coin, Anna and Jonathan are accused of the heist, arrested, and hauled into town for a public lashing.

Unable to open his bedroom door and help his parents, Tom finally escapes with the help of his toy friends. He finds Woody singing a lonely love song, and the pair set out to apprehend Ivan and Tony and bring them to justice. They find the crooks in their lair, gleefully counting the booty yet carefully watching each other.

But Woody's attempt to arrest the men falls flat when he's knocked unconscious by Tony, who begins to suspect he's being cheated by Ivan as Tom carefully manipulates the piles of gold coins. Tom's strategy pays off; Ivan and Tony's bickering eventually escalates into slapstick physical violence. They patch up their differences long enough to flee (with the loot) on horseback, but Tom is hiding in the horse's ear and directs his hooved friend to ride the crooks straight into the town center where Jonathan and

Anna are saved from the lash, Woody gets the girl, and everyone rejoices at their good luck.

"The only thing lower case about this production is the Metro spelling of *tom thumb*. Otherwise the film is top-drawer, a comic fairy tale with music that stacks up alongside some of the Disney classics of similar nature," *Variety* wrote in its review. "Terry-Thomas and Peter Sellers make a classic pair of comic villains, a hilarious combination of Rudolph Rassendale and Joe Weber complete with funny hat and Dutch low comedy accent."[2]

"Hollywood never fully succeeds in capturing the precise quality of fairy-tale fantasy," *Newsweek* opined. "George Pal's *tom thumb* is no exception; much of the magic of the original is missing. On the other hand, it is the best attempt to date at committing the spirit of the fairy tale to film."[3]

6
Up the Creek

Cast:

Humphrey Fairweather	David Tomlinson
Bosun Dockerty	Peter Sellers
Susanne	Liliane Sottane
Barker	Lionel Jeffries
Admiral Foley	Wilfrid Hyde-White

STUDIO: Byron Film Productions
RELEASE DATE: November 11, 1958
RUNNING TIME: 83 minutes (black and white)
DIRECTED BY: Val Guest
PRODUCED BY: Henry Halsted
WRITTEN BY: Val Guest
PHOTOGRAPHY: Arthur Grant
MUSIC: Tony Lowry

Sellers wasn't a recognized film star yet, but he was now working full-time on his career, making three pictures during the course of 1958. His second project, a simple naval farce entitled *Up the Creek*, was a remake of the 1937 hit *Oh Mr. Porter*, which starred Will Hay and was cowritten by Val Guest, *Up the Creek*'s writer-director.

Sellers was cast as Dockerty, Irish bosun of the HMS *Berkeley*, part of the Royal Navy's "mothball fleet" now docked near the countryside village of Meadows End. The *Berkeley* hasn't had a commanding officer in quite some time; in fact, the ship has been forgotten by headquarters and operates according to its own rules and regulations. But don't expect the *Berkeley*'s crew to be concentrating on nautical matters; they're too busy manning the ship's dry-cleaning service, bakery ("Auntie Berkeley's Goodies"), produce, and dry-goods business, which services the Meadows End populace and the Pig and Whistle Inn. The *Berkeley* is more of a petting zoo than a seaworthy vessel; pigs and chickens roam the decks freely, while the ship's boiler room is used as a clothes press.

The fledgling Berkeley Enterprises is supervised by Dockerty, who also keeps the books and organizes weekly "board meetings" to discuss profits, losses, and future quarterly projections.

But the *Berkeley*'s business days are jeopardized by the arrival of Lieutenant Humphrey Fairweather (David Tomlinson), appointed as the *Berkeley*'s new commanding officer. A quite decent chap, Fairweather hasn't ever really served near the sea, having spent almost his entire naval career behind a desk fiddling with his experimental "Fairweather Falcon" rockets. The rockets constantly cause trouble—blowing up naval property and the like—and Fairweather would have been discharged long ago if not for an uncle in high places. But when the Fairweather Falcon Mark III accidentally destroys the loo of a naval superior, Fairweather is banished to the Navy's furthermost outpost, Meadows End, as punishment.

The fresh-faced Fairweather arrives at the *Berkeley* full of hope and renewed vigor. After all, the Fairweather Falcon Mark IV will soon be here, and then there's Susanne (Liliane Sottane), the Italian beauty Fairweather met while stopping at the Pig and Whistle on his way to the ship.

The *Berkeley* crew, of course, knows they'll have to run the business at night when Fairweather is asleep. The plan is to rouse the CO early in the morning so he'll go to bed earlier at night, giving the men time to make their Meadows End deliveries.

But Fairweather senses something amiss almost immediately. For starters, there's that chicken he spots walking about the deck, and the ship's sow mascot, Esmeralda, who makes her home in the boiler room. And what about those roosters waking him up each morning? That must be a dream. And after all, Dockerty did say there weren't any regulations against having mascots, didn't he?

Fairweather's suspicions grow deeper when he decides to visit Dockerty's cabin and scan the ship's pay ledger. The bosun's room is elegantly furnished with the finest wood cabinets, a completely stocked bar, and a fancy phonograph, not to mention eiderdown bed linens. But it's Dockerty's reluctance to cough up the ledger that annoys Fairweather, and an examination of the book reveals some extremely odd entries somehow explained by Dockerty.

Bosun Dockerty itemizes Berkeley Enterprises's inventory while Cooky (John Warren) lends a hand. (Courtesy National Film Archive, London.)

What Dockerty can't explain, however, are the ship's egg deliveries, which Fairweather learns about from the townsfolk. It's up to Seaman Steady Barker (Lionel Jeffries), keeper of his beloved poultry, to absorb the blame for the eggs in order to cover up the rest of the ship's business operation. Barker, acting from a script written by Dockerty, tells Fairweather he has thirteen mouths to feed at home; Fairweather swallows the story hook, line, and sinker, and the *Berkeley* is safe for the time being.

At least Fairweather's attention is turned to other matters when the Fairweather Falcon Mark IV arrives at the post office. But after installing the rocket in the *Berkeley*—its nose cone peeking through the ship's deck—Fairweather learns from Susanne about the whole *Berkeley* business operation. He threatens to court-martial the entire crew until Dockerty blackmails him into reconsidering. After all, what's Fairweather's word against the eleven crew members'? And hadn't he abetted Berkeley Enterprises by his contribution to the general fund?

And there's more trouble on the way. While Fairweather drives into Meadows End to retrieve some paint, Admiral Foley (Wilfrid Hyde-White) decides to visit the *Berkeley* for a routine inspection. Seaman Perkins (Lionel Murton) assumes the role of Fairweather and nearly pulls it off until he's recognized by Foley as a troublemaker who once served under his command. But the admiral, after being warned by Fairweather several times, gets himself into trouble when he pounds the Mark IV's ignition button, discharging the rocket, which lands directly on the *Berkeley* and sinks the ship.

Fairweather and Dockerty band together to persuade Foley into explaining the *Berkeley*'s demise as a natural occurrence (after all, Foley *was* warned about hitting the Mark IV's triggering mechanism). *Up the Creek* ends in an appropriately jolly vein as Fairweather is sent off to an Australian command while the rest of the *Berkeley* crew set sail on the HMS *Incompatible,* presumably to begin their operations anew.

"*Up the Creek* is an amiable navy farce, which rates a fair measure of guffaws, but often has its slim joke stretched to the breaking point," wrote *Variety.* "The cast play this tiny anecdote for laughs and get them effortlessly. Tomlinson, Sellers and Wilfrid Hyde-White head a cast which is experienced in making a jest look like a full-powered joke.... Mostly, however, *Up the Creek* depends on a ripe and fruity performance by tv [sic] and radio comedian Peter Sellers and it is somewhat disconcerting to find that a sequel, *Further Up the Creek,* has been started without Sellers, who has another engagement...."[1]

Sellers handled himself with ease in his role as Dockerty, assuming an Irish accent and breezing through the part with little difficulty. Although *Up the Creek* didn't stretch Sellers's talents, it kept his name in the fickle public eye and lent his film career some valuable exposure.

7

Carlton-Browne of the F.O.

Cast:

Cadogan de Vere Carlton-Browne	Terry-Thomas
Amphibulos	Peter Sellers
Colonel Bellingham	Thorley Walters
The King	Ian Bannen
Davidson	Miles Malleson
F.O. Minister	Raymond Huntley
Princess Ilyena	Luciana Paoluzzi
Grand Duke Alexis	John Le Mesurier

STUDIO: Charter Films/British Lion
RELEASE DATE: March 13, 1959
RUNNING TIME: 87 minutes (black and white)
DIRECTED BY: Roy Boulting and Jeffrey Dell
PRODUCED BY: John Boulting
WRITTEN BY: Roy Boulting and Jeffrey Dell
PHOTOGRAPHY: Max Greene
MUSIC: John Addison

Sellers and Terry-Thomas reprised their comedic rapport in *Carlton-Browne of the F.O.*, the latest satire from Britain's cinematic bad boys, the Boulting brothers.

The twin Boultings, John and Roy, had already carved their niche in British film history with a string of dramas and comedies reflecting the country's changing social mores. *The Guinea Pig, Fame Is the Spur, Brothers in Law, Private's Progress,* and *Lucky Jim* were just a few of the brother's postwar hits, many of which featured an ensemble cast headed by Ian Carmichael and Thomas. (The Boultings often took turns in the director's chair while the other handled producing duties. *Carlton-Browne of the F.O.* marked a departure of sorts in that writer-director Roy Boulting shared directing credit with Jeffrey Dell, who also cowrote the film's screenplay.)

At this point in his film career, Sellers was still relegated to second-banana status and (the "Goon Show" and other radio roles notwithstanding) was supplementing his income and broadening his exposure by appearing frequently on television. (The "Goon Show" format eventually would be transplanted, with only moderate success, to television, where Sellers and crew indulged in shows like "Yes, It's the Cathode Ray Tube Show" and "A Show Called Fred.") It was from the small screen that Sellers would be introduced to the Boultings and stake his cinematic territory. His agent, John Redway, telephoned John Boulting and asked him to watch Sellers perform a television sketch that night in which he played a sarcastic schoolmaster complete with mortarboard and gown but sans makeup. While Roy Boulting kept a dinner date, John intently watched Sellers, who was unaware of Redway's telephone call.

"We could see what we were getting, and he looked ordinary enough," Boulting said. "But the way he played—acid-tongued, very incisive. Brilliant. No need of a funny voice, either. As I recall, his voice sounded rather like Alec Guinness's."[1]

The Boultings immediately signed Sellers to a £100,000, five-year nonexclusive contract—he could appear in other films, adding that time to his contract—and cast him in *Carlton-Browne of the F.O.*, a satiric look at British foreign diplomacy.[2]

Although the film starred Terry-Thomas—deservedly so—Sellers received second billing in a key role that required his on-screen presence in a number of important scenes. Rounding out the impressive cast were Ian Bannen, Thorley Walters, John Le Mesurier, Raymond Huntley, and Luciana Paoluzzi.

Carlton-Browne opens in 1959 when a mysterious letter arrives at the foreign office from the Mediterranean island of Gaillardia, a long-forgotten British colony operating under local rule since 1916. It seems no one ever told doddering British envoy Davidson (Miles Malleson) that he was supposed to leave the island forty-three years before; he's still conducting business as usual, and fighting a bad case of gout, when a Soviet dance troupe unexpectedly arrives.

Smelling a rat, Davidson hastily posts his letter to the home office where a visit to the FO's dank archives reveals the island to be under the jurisdiction of Cadogan de Vere Carlton-Browne (Thomas), a blundering low-level bureaucrat who inherited his position as head of the FO's undistinguished Department of Miscellaneous Territories from his equally inadequate father. True to Britain's traditionally elitist white-collar labor force, Carlton-Browne spends his time playing squash at the club while his seldom-used office gathers dust.

But there's an apparent crisis at hand, and reluctantly pressed into service, Carlton-Browne is forced to reach a decision concerning Gaillardia. His first plan—sending the British Council disguised as dancers into the island to spy on the Russians—fails miserably when Gaillardia's King Lawrence and his son are assassinated. With much reservation and through a process of elimination, the FO decides to send Carlton-Browne to Gaillardia on a diplomatic mission to foster good relations and meet with its new king (Ian Bannen), an Oxford-educated medical student thrust on the throne.

Accompanied by military attaché General Bellingham (Walters), an airsick Carlton-Browne is greeted at the Gaillardia airstrip by Amphibulos (Sellers), the country's double-dealing oily prime minister, who immediately curries favor with the Brits by arranging an exotic dinner complete with dancing girls. Meanwhile, the king's uncle—Lawrence's nasty brother Grand Duke Alexis (Le Mesurier)—implores the king to abdicate in favor of Ilyena (Paoluzzi), the "rightful" heir to the throne.

The plot thickens when Davidson tells Carlton-Browne of the holes being dug around the island. It's actually the work of the British, searching for cobalt deposits to help build a hydrogen bomb. Soon the Russians and Americans have secretly joined the cobalt hunt and Carlton-Browne, trying to avert an international crisis, proposes dividing the country into two sectors, north and south. The plan, surprisingly, is accepted by the United Nations, which sends a task force to paint (literally) a white partition across Gaillardia's middle.

The king (Ian Bannen), backed by the oily Amphibulos (Sellers), explains Gaillardia's balance of power to Carlton-Browne (Terry-Thomas) and decrepit foreign service officer Davidson (Miles Malleson).

But the king isn't happy with his newly divided country and flies to London with Amphibulos to meet with Carlton-Browne and his FO superiors. Unbeknownst to the king, the British have discovered cobalt in the Russian (southern) sector of Gaillardia and are secretly negotiating a purchase agreement with Alexis. Amphibulos slithers behind the king's back and telephones Alexis, trying to arrange some kind of deal by helping to remove the king from his throne. But the king discovers his treachery, just in time to fly back to Gaillardia where a civil war has erupted. Carlton-Browne and Bellingham, sent back to the island in a peacekeeping effort, somehow manage to be captured by the king's men before restoring peace to the island. The film ends on an ironic note as Carlton-Browne is knighted for his diplomatic efforts while Amphibulos and Alexis are banished to Portugal.

Terry-Thomas, as usual, was excellent as the idiotic Carlton-Browne and managed to sustain his funny performance even while *Carlton-Browne of the F.O.* veered off into confusing tangents and eventually ran out of comedic steam.

Sellers, foreshadowing what would become a dilemma on each successive film for him, found it difficult to "get" Amphibulos's character once shooting got under way. But Roy Boulting, knowing that screenwriter Jeffrey Dell had fashioned Amphibulos after Italian film entrepreneur Filippo del Guidice, did his best del Guidice impression for Sellers. "As well as I could, I gave Peter my impression of Del and, within two minutes, on the sidewalk, he proceeded to improvise dialogue and put on an act as a man he'd never seen which was more 'Del' than Del himself," Boulting said later.[3]

Carlton-Browne of the F.O., released in the United States as *Man in a Cocked Hat*, opened to generally favorable reviews. Sellers, performing admirably in his supporting role, received mixed notices from critics not yet familiar with his evolving comic style. "Peter Sellers, whose screen star has risen phenomenally since he made this film, may not have as fat a role in it as Terry-Thomas, but, as the conniving prime minister of Gaillardia, he is an unctuous scoundrel who tosses off exotic-accented dialogue as if to the manner born," A.H. Weiler wrote in the *New York Times*.[4]

The Boultings, noted *Variety*, "put their faith in two comedians who are far too associated with their own tele personalities to fit snugly into the general scheme of things. Terry-Thomas and Peter Sellers are often wildly funny but they cannot be accepted in the roles they are playing.... Sellers plays the Gaillardian blackguard of a Prime Minister with relish. But here again, the Sellers personality tends to throw the part off-balance."[5]

8
The Mouse That Roared

Cast:
Count Mountjoy/
  Duchess Gloriana/
    Tully Bascombe ... Peter Sellers
Helen .... Jean Seberg
Dr. Kokintz .... David Kossoff
Benter .... Leo McKern
Will .... William Hartnell

STUDIO: Columbia
RELEASE DATE: July 17, 1959
RUNNING TIME: 85 minutes (Technicolor)
DIRECTED BY: Jack Arnold
PRODUCED BY: Carl Foreman

WRITTEN BY: Roger MacDougall and Stanley
Mann (from a novel by Leonard Wibberley)
PHOTOGRAPHY: John Wilcox
MUSIC: Edwin Astley

In early 1958, fresh from his successful costarring role in *Carlton-Browne,* Sellers was approached by theatrical producer Peter Hall, impressed by Sellers's performance in *The Naked Truth,* to star in a legitimate stage comedy entitled *Brouhaha* about a scheming Arab potentate who invents an oil crisis to help pay off his gambling debts. Although he hated the theater, associating its smells and atmosphere with his unhappy, rootless childhood, Sellers jumped at the opportunity to flex his improvisatory muscles and work a live audience, elements he had missed during the rigors of filmmaking.

Sellers approached his *Brouhaha* role with typical enthusiasm and gusto—a sure sign boredom was just around the corner. Having to repeat the performance night after night began to take its toll, and soon after the play opened to mixed reviews, Sellers began improvising his own dialogue, costumes, and entrances—much to the chagrin of his costars.

"He was such a quick, instinctive performer that, unlike most actors, he didn't want to master, standardize, and refine his performance—he wanted to change it, give himself problems to solve," Hall said. "The result was a daily nightmare for the rest of the cast. No one knew for sure what any particular night would bring."[1]

Sellers's short-lived stage career ended soon after he showed up drunk for a performance after attending a party in honor of Alec Guinness, who had just been knighted. Halfway through his performance, he broke traditional theatrical decorum by announcing to the audience that he was "sloshed" and offering to let his understudy complete the play. But his public had paid good money to see Sellers and enthusiastically urged him to stagger through the remainder of his performance. "I can't remember too much about it after my confession—which was all too superfluous—but I'm told it was a memorable evening," Sellers said later.

The pressures of his nightly stage performances were compounded by Sellers's daily routine at Columbia's British studios, where he was filming his newest comedy, *The Mouse That Roared,* for sci-fi director Jack Arnold. By a remarkable coincidence, *Mouse* was strikingly similar to *Brouhaha* in content and theme, targeting the folly of international diplomacy and America's benevolent Marshall Plan for lightly satiric treatment. Sellers burned the candle at both ends, day and night, incorporating aspects of each vehicle into his diverse performances.

Mouse called for Sellers to undertake his second multiple-role assignment in the guise of monocled Count "Bobo" Mountjoy, wimpy Tully

Bascombe, and senile Duchess Gloriana, residents of the tiny Duchy of Grand Fenwick, Europe's only English-speaking country. Lying somewhere in the French Pyrenees and taking its name from founder Sir Roger Fenwick, Grand Fenwick is a simple, peaceful country, relying on the export of its native wine — Pinot Grand Fenwick — to stimulate its local economy.

But 1959 is a bad year for Pinot Grand Fenwick, driven out of the market when a California winery introduces its own copycat brand called (naturally) Pinot Grand Enwick. In his infinite wisdom, Prime Minister Mountjoy formulates a "can't miss" plan to help Grand Fenwick recoup its losses. Why not declare war on the United States? There's no doubt the country will lose, thereby insuring its "rehabilitation" by the United States in the form of millions of dollars to be used for schools, homes, and other public works projects.

Mountjoy mails a formal declaration of war to Washington, D.C., and instructs the bumbling Tully Bascombe — a plump, pleasant lad who also doubles as Grand Fenwick's hereditary field marshal — to assemble a twenty-man army and mount a U.S. invasion. It should be, in Mountjoy's words, "the best investment this country ever made." Mountjoy's plan is met with cautionary approval from Duchess Gloriana, Fenwick's aged royal figurehead who's given to bouts of melancholia over her dear departed husband, Leopold.

So, armed with crossbows and attired in medieval military chain mail, Tully and his men prepare for their American defeat. Unable to afford an attack vessel of their own, they take a bus to the port of Marseilles, board a merchant ship, and set sail for New York City. Tully, ever the old salt, spends the entire overseas trip crippled by seasickness.

But unknown to Grand Fenwick's army, the American government had declared a citywide air-raid alert while brilliant physicist Dr. Alfred Kokintz (David Kossoff) perfects a working prototype of his football-shaped Q-bomb, hundreds of times more powerful than the H-bomb and able to decimate an area of two million square miles.

Tully and company, arriving at a desolate and completely empty city, take a cautious stroll through the streets of lower Manhattan, using *Cook's Guide to New York* as their "invasion map" but finding no one who'll take them prisoner. Stumbling upon Dr. Kokintz and his attractive daughter Helen (Jean Seberg), Tully mistakenly decides to take them — and the Q-bomb — back to Grand Fenwick for a stronger bargaining chip once his country surrenders. Rounding out his quota of "prisoners" are a Pentagon general and three New York City cops the army captures in Central Park.

But instead of surrendering, Grand Fenwick is suddenly courted by the world's superpowers, frightened of the Q-bomb's destructive potential.

Tully Bascombe leads Grand Fenwick's army on the streets of New York.

Tully quickly falls in love with Helen and is chosen by Gloriana to replace Mountjoy. Meanwhile, the United States is forced to surrender and accept Grand Fenwick's terms for peace—taking Pinot Grand Enwick off the market, providing $1 million in aid, and helping establish the League of Little Nations to look after the Q-bomb and engender eternal worldwide harmony.

Clocking in at a short eighty-five minutes, *Mouse* had many flaws, among them the totally unbelievable and plastic romance between Tully and Helen, few genuine laughs, and some cheesy-looking studio scenery (surprising in light of Director Jack Arnold's reputation as the craftsman behind *The Incredible Shrinking Man*).

Yet somehow, despite its syrupy plotline and forced jocularity, *Mouse* caught the world's fancy. One must keep in mind that Sellers, by now a British institution, was still relatively unknown everywhere else. This would change significantly when *Mouse* premiered in 1959 shortly before *I'm All Right, Jack,* the breakthrough role that established Sellers as a major star.

Mouse also provided an impatient Sellers his transatlantic entree into the United States, where it hit a populist nerve in a receptive American audience. Sellers himself was amazed at the film's American impact. "In the first four weeks of its American run it took over a million dollars, which is more money than any other British picture ever to play there has taken in the same length of time," he said. "In New York they were queuing four deep, if you please, from the Guild Cinema right around the block."[2]

What film fans were flocking to see was Sellers's comic dexterity and the ease with which he embodied two of his three *Mouse* characters. Mountjoy, sounding a bit like the "Goon Show's" Hercules Grytpype-Thynne and Duchess Gloriana, a lovable parody of British aristocracy, were enjoyably light in tone and saved *Mouse* from plunging into total mediocrity. Sellers, at the time still a bit overweight, even seemed to grow physically thinner while playing the dashing Mountjoy.

It was in the guise of Bascombe—played in his own voice and without any makeup—that Sellers ran into a stone wall: He was boring playing himself. It was around this time that Sellers began claiming he had no personality of his own—that he needed a role to inhabit—and Bascombe certainly helped Sellers prove his point. He limned Tully in a flat and colorless fashion, making Bascombe's love for Helen (the identically wooden Seberg) even harder to swallow.

But audiences loved the film and loved Sellers. By November of 1959, *Life* magazine had dubbed him the "funniest actor England has sent to America since Alec Guinness,"[3] and his *Mouse* performance generally garnered good to excellent notices. "Mr. Sellers is the dominant performer and is most persistent in the role of the horn-rimmed-spectacled Field Marshal who is carried away by zeal," wrote Bosley Crowther in the *New York Times*. "But his prissy primness as the duchess and his elegant swash as the Prime Minister make for a great deal of amusement in the British comedy vein."[4]

"With versatility in voice and subtle characterization Sellers scores cheerfully in all three roles, with the Prime Minister probably being the best," wrote *Variety*. "While not necessary for one man to play all three roles, it is a standout gimmick which adds greatly to the fun."[5]

Several critics, however, chastised the film for its smugness. "Emulating Alec Guinness, who played so many assorted roles in *Kind Hearts and Coronets*, Peter Sellers, in the English film *The Mouse That Roared*, portrays a grand duchess, a Prime Minister, and a field marshal.... Mr. Sellers is competent in each of these assignments, but the picture, after a fairly amusing start, runs down badly," John McCarten wrote in the *New Yorker*. "...The film meanders aimlessly into a discussion of what might happen if the United States had to sue for peace with a modest little principality like Grand Fenwick, and finally all the humor of the situation is dissipated."[6]

"Parts of *The Mouse That Roared* will undoubtedly seem a bit too coy to suit some tastes. Considerable footage is devoted to fooling around with animation, mock-documentary narration, captions, subtitles and rather parochial sight gags, some of them not very funny," wrote the *Reporter*'s Jay Jacobs. "But there are any number of genuinely comic passages along the way, ranging from brief touches of extreme subtlety to elaborate bouts of out-and-out slapstick...."[7]

So, with his first outright screen triumph in hand, Sellers embarked on the role that would alter the course of his career and point him toward the road to international stardom.

9

I'm All Right, Jack

Cast:

Fred Kite	Peter Sellers
Stanley Windrush	Ian Carmichael
Major Hitchcock	Terry-Thomas
"Uncle Bertie" Tracepurcel	Dennis Price
Sidney De Vere Cox	Richard Attenborough
Cynthia Kite	Liz Fraser
Mrs. Kite	Irene Handl
Aunt Dolly	Margaret Rutherford
Waters	John Le Mesurier

RELEASE DATE: August 13, 1959
RUNNING TIME: 104 minutes (black and white)
DIRECTED BY: John Boulting
PRODUCED BY: Roy Boulting
WRITTEN BY: Frank Harvey, John Boulting
and Alan Hackney (from Alan Hackney's
novel, "Private Life")
PHOTOGRAPHY: Max Greene
MUSIC: Ken Hare

Sellers's studied portrayal of Amphibulos in *Carlton-Browne* was in the Boultings' minds as they prepared to tackle their next project, a lampooning of Britain's postwar labor movement. *I'm All Right, Jack* was adapted from Alan Hackney's satiric novel *Private Life,* with a script by John Boulting, Frank Harvey, and Hackney. The Boultings (Roy would produce the film) thought Sellers perfect for the film's pivotal character, Shop Steward Fred Kite.

I'm All Right, Jack was intended as a sequel to the Boultings' 1956 smash *Private's Progress,* in which young, innocent Stanley Windrush (Ian Carmichael) joins the army and becomes the unwitting dupe of jewel thieves. *I'm All Right, Jack* continued Stanley's adventures and found him on equally precarious footing. Now a bumbling civilian, Stanley embarks on a career in industry. He's helped in this pursuit by his devious uncle Bertie (Dennis Price), owner of Missiles, Ltd., a missile factory that employs Stanley as a forklift operator. Unbeknownst to Stanley, Uncle Bertie is in cahoots with "Coxie" (Richard Attenborough), Stanley's former army chum who's now a rival missile manufacturer. The two men, well aware of his predilection for starting trouble, hope Stanley's brush with the factory's union mentality, spearheaded by Marxist Shop Steward Fred Kite—will cause a strike, diverting a substantial Middle Eastern contract to Coxie's missile company while both men share the profits.

Sellers enjoyed working with the Boultings on *Carlton-Browne* and was excited at the prospect of being written into *Jack*'s storyline. In late 1958 he was sent the film's script, which he read and flatly rejected: Kite's part wasn't funny enough.

Sellers's comic training had come by dint of radio where laughs were wrought from cartoonish characters delivering silly lines in front of a live audience. The instant gratification Sellers derived from these laughs—evidenced in his lifelong affection for his "Goon Show" days—was not there in the controlled environment of the movie studio. Here, human contact signaling success or failure was minimal.

This was a major roadblock Sellers needed to conquer, especially if he was to understand Kite's inherent comic subtleties. But he failed to see the humor in Kite, unable to align the shop steward's human foibles with his surrealistic notion of comedy. "He wanted the jokes, the obvious belly-laughs, and they just weren't there," Boulting said of Sellers's initial reluctance to play Kite.[1]

Boulting invited Sellers to his home, confident that an intense discussion of Kite would sway Sellers toward accepting the role. The two men talked long into the night, but Sellers still refused to commit to the project, insisting Kite wasn't a big enough character for an actor of his growing stature. A second meeting the next night followed the same script until Boulting used a little psychology on his unsuspecting guest. Boulting knew that Sellers didn't feel comfortable in a role until he went through the often agonizing process of "finding" the character's voice. This was the solid foundation upon which Sellers needed to build his character's personality.

Boulting suggested Sellers make a screen test, hoping the actor would feel more comfortable as Kite if outfitted in the character's on-screen attire. Though he reluctantly agreed, Sellers threw himself into the test preparation with characteristic relish. He went to Berman's, a fashionable London haberdashery, and left with an ill-fitting suit. His next stop was the barber shop where Sellers had his hair cropped in Kite's distinctly Teutonic style. Sellers's final embellishment was a suspiciously Hitlerlike mustache adding to Kite's porcine appearance.

Perfecting Kite's voice was, as usual, an agonizing process for Sellers. For about a week he screened footage of labor leaders and shop stewards, studying their every movement, nuance, and vocal inflection. When the time arrived for Sellers's screen test, Boulting was amazed at the metamorphosis the comedian had undergone. "It was an incredible transformation, yet apart from that hideous haircut and the mustache, he wore hardly a piece of makeup," Boulting said. "he looked at himself and he couldn't recognize himself. He was totally different, he wasn't Peter Sellers at all. It wasn't merely the physical appearance, it was the attitude. He was a man called Kite."[2]

Boulting knew the battle was partially won; all that remained was the crucial screen test. The two-minute test scene called for Kite to interrogate Stanley Windrush, played by an assistant director standing in for Ian Carmichael. The Boultings had based Kite on a shop steward they knew from one of the studios, a stock character with whom the workingman could identify. When Sellers completed his speech, spontaneous applause erupted from the crew.

"As he finished, he stood there lamely, looking anxiously at the camera," John Boulting said. "Suddenly there was a gale of laughter, a round of applause from the workers who had been listening this time round and were savoring something they'd never dreamed of hearing—their own shop stewards turned into recognizable figures of outrageous fun. Peter got his confidence back in a flash."[3]

Filming on *I'm All Right, Jack* could now begin, and Sellers, comfortably enveloped in the body and soul of Fred Kite, delivered one of the finest screen performances of his career. He joyously spouted Kite's muddled union ideology to anyone within earshot, waxed sentimental about Russia ("all them cornfields and ballet in the evening"), and wreaked unintentional havoc on the factory floor.

Kite was scripted as a cartoonish laughingstock, management's worst nightmare, yet Sellers dug deeper into the character, infusing Kite with an underlying sensitivity that added another dimension to the shop steward's buffoonish bluster. The film's narrative also allowed Sellers to take Kite off the factory floor and into the home, where the by-the-rules shop steward, so mindful of management, was a henpecked husband and ineffectual father. The inclusion of Kite's home life in the film's story line added a clever twist to the film's thematic framework of labor versus management.

In his own home, the bargaining tables are turned on Fred Kite. Instead of holding factory management at bay with strike threats and daily work stoppages, Kite is restricted by the home rule, operating under the demands of his doting yet sharp-tongued wife (Irene Handl) and free-spirited daughter (Liz Fraser). It's obvious, even to Kite, who wears the pants in the household. It's within this domestic environment that Sellers gleaned Kite's sensitivity and turned the well-meaning shop steward into a warm, sympathetic human being.

The stage is set when Stanley, now boarding with the Kites (to be closer to their busty daughter Cynthia), falls into Uncle Bertie's trap and unwittingly unearths Waters (John Le Mesurier), the "time and motion" agent hired by management for the sole purpose of secretly analyzing the workers' snaillike rate of production.

As expected, the news of Waters's study spreads like wildfire among the factory workers, and Kite immediately calls a strike, much to the delight of Uncle Bertie and Cox. But the conscientious Stanley—suspected by Kite and his yes-men of working with Waters—decides to defy the union and go back to work. When he's shut out of the factory, workers around the country walk off their jobs in sympathy, bringing England's industrial econ-. omy to a complete standstill.

Stanley becomes an overnight national hero, not only ruining his uncle's scheme but angering Kite, who throws Stanley out of the house. Mrs. Kite and her daughter, out for a day of shopping, return home to find Stanley gone. Kite, well aware of the women's fondness for Stanley, sheepishly admits to throwing the "blackleg" out, rationalizing the decision with some mumbled union gibberish. Mrs. Kite, reversing roles, declares a household work stoppage in sympathy with Stanley's abrupt departure. She and her daughter tearfully leave home, forcing Kite into the uncharacteristic role of menial laborer.

Kite and Hitchcock (Terry-Thomas) sew up their differences.

Meanwhile, back at Missiles, Uncle Bertie and Cox frantically order Major Hitchcock (Terry-Thomas), Tracepurcel's lazy, cynical personnel director, to visit Kite and propose a solution to the strike.

Cut to Kite, wearing an apron and gloomily tramping around the empty house, muttering to himself while Ken Hare's droopy musical score emphasizes his loneliness (and Kite's defeat as he surveys the mess he's created and resignedly steps on a piece of toast with his bare foot).

The ensuing scene between Sellers and Thomas remains one of the film's highlights, as Hitchcock arrives and Kite invites him in to "imbibe" while the pair discuss possible strike settlements and the maudlin Kite pines for his wife. While Hitchcock darns Kite's sock—symbolically "sewing up" the differences between labor and management—a now drunk Kite comes up with a plan: Why not declare Stanley mentally exhausted and unfit for work? That way, Stanley can be released from the factory, and Kite's men will come back to work.

Upon its British release in August 1959, *I'm All Right, Jack* ingrained itself into the national consciousness. Legend has it *Jack* helped the Conservative Party win a landslide victory the same year.

"I think it probably helped a bit," Sellers said. "I heard the Tories liked it. It probably did more good to them than it did to Labor."[4]

However strong its implications, *I'm All Right, Jack* remains to this day one of the country's best-loved films. Such was its influence that twenty years later, in 1979, BBC television canceled the film's election-eve broadcast, fearing it would cast a partisan shadow on the BBC.

Sellers had succeeded in turning Fred Kite into a lovable character and a household name. His subtle performance was singled out by the critics for its originality and deadly accuracy. "In the Boulting Brothers' hilarious satire on trade unions, *I'm All Right, Jack,* Peter Sellers is brilliant," wrote *Esquire.* "As the somewhat pompous, inflexible shop steward, Sellers never caricatures the role; he lives it, spouting clichés and dogma to a neophyte, quaking before his wife and daughter who have had enough of his labor nonsense, boldly leading the docile workers into strike. Sellers is exposing not only a pig-headed labor leader but also any man and every man who puts up a bold front to cover the fact that he is somewhat beyond his depth."[5]

"Many gifted mimics imagine that what they can imitate they have understood, but Sellers goes farther than that," *Time* opined. "His shop steward is the little man with the big dream, and he sees that if there is humor, there is also 'enormous sadness' in the grubby little doctrine monger's vision of a workers' paradise somewhere beyond the Vistula...."[6]

Sellers went on to win the British Academy Award for his portrayal of Kite, beating out Laurence Olivier, Richard Burton, and Peter Finch for the valued prize.

10
The Battle of the Sexes

Cast:

Mr. Martin	Peter Sellers
Angela Barrows	Constance Cummings
Robert Macpherson	Robert Morley
Andrew Darling	Jameson Clark
Macpherson	Ernest Thesiger

STUDIO: Prometheus
RELEASE DATE: February 25, 1960

RUNNING TIME: 83 minutes (black and white)
DIRECTED BY: Charles Crichton
PRODUCED BY: Monja Danischewsky
WRITTEN BY: Monja Danischewsky (based on
  "The Catbird Seat" by James Thurber)
PHOTOGRAPHY: Freddie Francis
MUSIC: Stanley Black

The year 1960 was the busiest of Sellers's film career. Not only did the Variety Club of Great Britain vote him the film actor of the year (for *The Millionairess, The Mouse That Roared, Two-Way Stretch,* and *Never Let Go*), but he was reunited with the Goons for an eleven-minute short, *The Running, Jumping and Standing Still Film,* directed on a £700 budget by Richard Lester (later to direct the Beatles in *A Hard Day's Night* and *Help!*). Shot in two days with Sellers's new camera, *The Running, Jumping and Standing Still Film* featured the Goons—and Graham Stark—cavorting in a London field. Produced on a lark, the film garnered an Oscar nomination and was awarded a "best fiction short subject" prize at the San Francisco International Film Festival.

At the same time, Sellers made a promotional trip to America where *I'm All Right, Jack* was making its Broadway premiere along with *The Battle of the Sexes,* Sellers's latest effort.

Adapted from James Thurber's short story "The Catbird Seat," *The Battle of the Sexes* (the title change accommodated English ignorance of the American baseball term) was another of Sellers's "little British comedies," given an Ealinglike twist by director Charles Crichton (*The Lavender Hill Mob*) and writer-producer Monja Danischewsky, an ex–Ealing studio aide.

When he inked his £9,000 *Sexes* contract,[1] Sellers was being inundated with scripts, many from Hollywood, and had already agreed to star with Sophia Loren in *The Millionairess,* which began filming shortly after he returned from America in May 1960. That he chose the unpretentious *Battle of the Sexes,* which premiered in Britain only two weeks after *Two-Way Stretch,* highlighted the shaky confidence he placed in his own burgeoning talent.

Unlike the broad brushstrokes with which he painted Fred Kite, Sellers's turn in *The Battle of the Sexes* was a more subtle sketch. He played Mr. Martin, the quiet, unassuming middle-aged chief accountant for the House of Macpherson, an Edinburgh tweed manufacturer operating under its own successful system of order within a paperwork chaos. A loyal 35-year Macpherson employee without any vices—he neither drinks nor smokes—Martin is summoned to the deathbed of old Mr. Macpherson (Ernest Thesiger) where he promises to look after Macpherson's doddering London-educated son Robert (Robert Morley), the firm's new president.

On his train into Edinburgh, Robert encounters Angela Barrows

Venerable accountant Mr. Martin steels himself for *The Battle of the Sexes* with American efficiency expert Angela Barrows (Constance Cummings). (Courtesy Academy of Motion Picture Arts and Sciences.)

(Constance Cummings), a pushy American "efficiency expert" banished to Scotland by her firm, ostensibly to oversee its foreign accounts. Robert and Angela take a liking to each other, and she agrees to observe the House of Macpherson's infrastructure upon their arrival in Edinburgh.

That's when the trouble starts. Robert, smitten with the comely American, soon hires Angela as the firm's industrial consultant, and within a matter of days she's making changes that upset Macpherson's loyal old workers, or "gremlins" as she insensitively labels them.

For starters, Angela decides not only to increase tweed production 1,000 percent—quite a problem since Macpherson's "factory workers" are represented by three hundred weavers spread throughout the Hebrides Islands using manual machines—but to revamp completely Martin's moldy accounting department, accustomed to a quirky filing system (based on *never* opening the windows lest the wind blow anything out of order); meticulous hand-written account ledgers; and cuff guards. Before long, Martin's men are using noisy adding machines and typewriters, while Angela's irritating squawk-box intercom system resonates throughout the building.

But Angela's plans to build a new factory, sack Martin and his "gremlin" cohorts, and manufacture (gasp!) *synthetic* tweed represent the final act of heresy. Something must be done to stop this demonic woman before she completely destroys the House of Macpherson, and the meek Martin—furious at Angela and ever loyal to the old company—decides to take matters into his own crafty hands.

His first act of defiance is purposely to break one of Angela's antique sculptures, proudly placed in old Mr. Macpherson's office, redecorated, of course, by Angela and now occupied by Robert. Going a step further, Martin sneaks around the office at night and sabotages the adding machines, intercom system, and filing system, forcing a red-faced Angela to apologize to Robert. And when she broaches the idea of time clocks to increase factory-worker efficiency (and talks about the dreaded "time and motion" study feared by Kite and crew in *I'm All Right, Jack*), Martin orders three hundred *individual* time clocks for each Hebrides weaver, much to Robert's horror.

But while Angela uses her feminine wiles in persuading Robert to keep the intercom system and adding machines, Martin is planning his next move—murder. Visiting a cinema one afternoon to watch a "perfect crime" flick, Martin decides that killing Angela is the only solution to Macpherson's problem. Following the on-screen murderer's modus operandi, Martin clumsily purchases a pack of cigarettes and flask of whiskey. When he overhears Angela invite Robert over to her apartment, telling him to ring three times so she'll answer the door, Martin decides to implement his homicidal scheme.

Of course, everything goes wrong from the get-go. Using the excuse that he's delivering a message from Robert, Martin rings Angela's bell three times and gets himself invited into her apartment where he plants the cigarettes and whiskey on her living-room table. When Martin tells her he can't remember Robert's message, Angela thinks he's visiting because he's lonely, and she invites him to stay for a drink.

But try as he might, Martin can't seem to do anything right. He tries to whack her over the head with a whiskey bottle but misses; tries to stab her with a kitchen knife but loses his nerve; goes to plunge a knife into her back, only to discover he's brandishing—lo and behold—an egg whisk; and, finally mustering the nerve *really* to stab Angela, is a victim of bad timing when in his deadly lunge the knife gets stuck in the swinging kitchen door as Angela sashays from the room.

Refusing to miss his golden opportunity, a desperate Martin proceeds to put his cinema-inspired "perfect murder" plan into action. Not only does he smoke his first cigarette and swill his first shot of whiskey, but he lures Angela to the window and is about to push her out when he hears a chorus of "All Things Bright and Beautiful" emanating from her television set.

Martin realizes he's a born Milquetoast, unable to commit murder, regardless of his intended victim. So, using his brains instead of his questionable brawn, he quickly shifts gears. If Robert thought Angela was crazy, he'd have to fire her. And what would be crazier than Angela's far-fetched story about a drug-crazed Martin smoking cigarettes, drinking, and attempting a seduction ("Come here, you naughty darling!") while babbling insanely about killing Robert? Which is exactly what Martin does, cleaning up the evidence and sneaking out of the apartment just as Robert shows up to "rescue" Angela from the clutches of wild-eyed Martin.

Robert, attributing Angela's unbelievable story to overwork and stress, fires the American efficiency expert when, out of frustration, she physically attacks him in his office. Martin has saved the House of Macpherson, and all is well.

But is it? Danischewsky and Crichton end their fable on an ambiguous note as Martin, spying a weeping Angela on the street corner, buys her a flower she readily accepts, thereby propagating the battle of the sexes and perhaps adding another chapter to the House of Macpherson's quirky little story.

Newsweek, calling Sellers's Martin "the very prototype of the worm that turned," labeled the film "a generally amusing and occasionally uproarious movie."[2] A. H. Weiler, in the *New York Times,* wrote: "As viewers will recall from his performance in the current *The Mouse That Roared,* Mr. Sellers' humor is both vocal and physical but rarely muscular. And, again in *The Battle of the Sexes,* he is a Casper Milquetoast to the manner born. A quiet man, who can toss a line away as well as project it . . . and whose voice is never raised above a respectful whisper."[3]

"Mr. Sellers plays with what is known as delicious roguery, and six months from now I shall be prepared to swear that I saw Alec Guinness in the part," *The Nation*'s Robert Hatch said of Sellers's performance. "*The Battle of the Sexes* is good formula fun."[4]

Sellers, armed with a thick Scottish burr, gray hair, too-big glasses, and droopy mustache, dished out doleful dollops of pathos as Martin, aided by Crichton's understated direction and Danischewsky's finely tuned narrative. Strong performances by Cummings and Morley and a fine supporting cast featuring Jameson Clark, Moultrie Kelsall, and Ernest Thesiger rounded out this fine effort, which further strengthened Sellers's hold on his newfound American audience.

Part II:
The Best Sellers List
(1960–1964)

11
Two-Way Stretch

Cast:

Dodger Lane	....	Peter Sellers
Jelly Knight	....	David Lodge
Lennie Price	....	Bernard Cribbins
Sidney Crout	....	Lionel Jeffries
Soapy Stevens	....	Wilfrid Hyde-White
Mrs. Price	....	Irene Handl
Ethel	....	Liz Fraser

STUDIO: British Lion/Shepperton
RELEASE DATE: February 11, 1960
RUNNING TIME: 87 minutes (black and white)
DIRECTED BY: Robert Day
PRODUCED BY: M. Smedley Aston
WRITTEN BY: John Warren and Len Heath
PHOTOGRAPHY: Geoffrey Faithfull
MUSIC: Ken Jones

Notwithstanding his growing reputation as a prima donna—fueled by the pressure of instant stardom—Sellers never forgot the mates who were there for him through good times and bad. One of his best friends was David Lodge, whom Sellers first met while entertaining the troops as a clownish drummer in Ralph Reader's "Gang Show" during World War II. Lodge had been transferred into the show and was immediately entranced by Sellers.

"We generally had a pianist, trumpet, tenor sax, a jazz accordionist, and drums," Lodge remembered. "Peter on the drums was one of the best performers ever. 'Drumming Man' was how he was billed. He closed the show. To see him do his jazz numbers was a show in itself, throwing up the sticks, catching them. Nothing could have followed him! He doubled as a comedian, sometimes in drag...."[1]

Sellers and Lodge remained lifelong friends, and Lodge appeared in quite a few Sellers films; along with Spike Milligan and Graham Stark, Lodge was a Sellers confidant, an eyewitness to the comedian's mercurial

48

psyche fueled in part by his strange relationship with Peg. "I thought Peter's relationship with Peg was too close for comfort; yet she didn't cow him," he said. "That boy did what he wanted. He was already showing the traits of a spoiled only child."[2]

Throughout the 1950s Lodge was something of a fourth Goon, working with the team in their variety stage incarnations (he often warmed up their act) and sharing in their off-stage lives. Sellers rewarded Lodge's loyalty with a small part in *I'm All Right, Jack*. In *Two-Way Stretch*, the first of his two prison comedies, Sellers's influence helped Lodge snag a leading role as Jelly Knight, a less-than-perfect safecracker.

Two-Way Stretch epitomizes Sellers's insecurity regarding his talents. As 1960 drew near, he impatiently awaited international recognition, especially after the transatlantic box office achievements of *I'm All Right, Jack* and *The Mouse That Roared*. It wasn't for lack of interest; Hollywood beckoned, but Sellers seemed reluctant to answer its call. Instead he chose "safe" vehicles, produced and directed in England, with familiar plots that didn't tax his range. Such was Sellers's popularity at the time that he was almost ensured of a hit regardless of the film's quality.

Two years after the release of *Two-Way Stretch*, Sellers would complain to the press about the "little man" roles he was offered by unimaginative producers. That he didn't comprehend the artfulness with which he laced these characterizations—just as Fred Kite wasn't "funny enough"—reveals Sellers's flawed judgment regarding his limitations as an actor. For now, though, the workaholic comedian reeled off a string of "little man" roles that represent some of his finest work.

Two-Way Stretch, sandwiched between *I'm All Right, Jack* and *The Battle of the Sexes*, was a good-natured prison comedy laced with smutty British humor. Sellers didn't strain himself in his role as prison ringleader Dodger Lane, wearing no makeup and embellishing Lane only with a Cockney accent. Although he received top billing as the film's major drawing card, Sellers was outshone by supporting players Lionel Jeffries—his *Brouhaha* costar—and Bernard Cribbins, a situation of which he was acutely aware as filming progressed. Not happy with his own performance, Sellers went so far as to call the Boultings, for whom he had just completed *I'm All Right, Jack*, to complain that Jeffries was "going over the top." The Boultings, all too familiar with Sellers's insecurities, interpreted this as Sellers's fear that Jeffries was delivering a better performance.[3]

Two-Way Stretch centers around Dodger and cellmates Jelly Knight and Lennie Price (Cribbins), leisurely serving the tail end of a three-year sentence in Huntleigh Prison.

Huntleigh is the picture of prison reform and every Conservative's nightmare. The prisoners carry keys to the front gate, "hard labor" consists of cultivating the warden's flower garden, and basket weaving has replaced

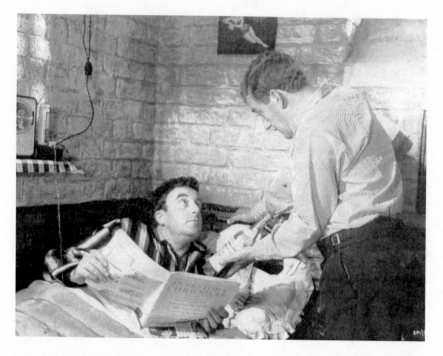

Lennie (Bernard Cribbins) offers a bottle of the best champagne to Dodger, catching up on his investment portfolio in his jail cell outfitted with all mod cons.

the rock quarry for "rehabilitation." The guards drink tea and sleep on duty; Jenkins, the head guard, knocks politely before entering a cell.

He's also very chummy with Dodger and company, whose luxurious cell is furnished with all the amenities of home. Dodger's cell not only receives daily milk and newspaper deliveries but is equipped with a stove, radio, and cuckoo clock, not to mention "Strangeways" the cat and "Wilbur," an obese homing pigeon that must walk to its destination.

But the boys' relaxed incarceration is brought to a screeching halt by the arrival of Sidney "Sour" Crout (Jeffries), a sneering, shrill disciplinarian imported from Rockhampton Prison to replace Jenkins. ("He's just about the most wicked screw who ever crept down a prison corridor!" is Dodger's apt description of Crout.)

Crout's boot-camp mentality not only strikes fear into the Huntleigh population but threatens to disrupt a £2 million "inside" job planned by Dodger and "Soapy" Stevens (Hyde-White). Stevens masterminded the boys' last job and had the only alibi. Now disguised as their kindly vicar, he's finagled the use of the warden's office where he and Dodger hatch their scheme.

The plan is to intercept a shipment of priceless jewels bound for London. The boys will sneak out at night, rob the jewels from a police convoy, and make it back to their cell in time for the morning bed check—all with the perfect alibi. Lending a hand will be Lennie's mother (Handl) and her curvaceous daughter Ethel (Fraser), who also is Dodger's fiancée.

Two-Way Stretch reunited part of the *I'm All Right, Jack* cast with less spectacular results. Not only were Sellers and Lodge on hand, but Irene Handle and Liz Fraser reprised their mother-daughter relationship. The film was clearly dominated, however, by Lionel Jeffries, cleverly lampooning every authoritarian stereotype in Crout's cartoonish Teutonic demeanor. The embodiment of right-wing autocracy with head shaved and mustache neatly clipped, Crout evolves into the Huntleigh laughingstock, the fool swallowed up by his small-minded megalomania. (Crout also is a precursor of Jeffries's turn as bumbling police inspector "Nosey" Parker in *The Wrong Arm of the Law*.)

"Lionel Jeffries, as poor, malevolent Crout, suffers his various comeuppances in a way that will warm the hearts of all right-thinking men," *Newsweek* trumpeted.[4] Jeffries obviously had fun with the role and delivered a colorful performance. Bernard Cribbins, who along with Jeffries would reappear in *The Wrong Arm of the Law*, also deserves mention for his funny portrayal of the nervous Lennie.

Sellers delivered an acceptable performance, certainly nothing extraordinary and a somewhat disappointing follow up to Fred Kite. Still the critics, perhaps awash in post-*Jack* sentiment, were enthusiastic in their praise. "Peter Sellers, flashing a magnificently dishonest smile, is top-hole as the chief jailbird and plotter," crowed Roger Angell of *The New Yorker*,[5] while *Newsweek* called Sellers's performance "another gem of expert underplaying."[6]

12
Never Let Go

Cast:

Lionel Meadows	.....	Peter Sellers
John Cummings	.....	Richard Todd
Anne Cummings	.....	Elizabeth Sellars
Tommy Towers	......	Adam Faith
Cliff	....	David Lodge

STUDIO: Rank
RELEASE DATE: June 2, 1960
RUNNING TIME: 91 minutes (black and white)
DIRECTED BY: John Guillermin
PRODUCED BY: Peter De Sarigny
WRITTEN BY: Alun Falconer
PHOTOGRAPHY: Christopher Challis
MUSIC: John Barry

It is a time-honored show-business given that underneath the comic's clownish façade lurks the soul of a dramatic actor. But it is rare in filmdom when an accomplished comedian makes a successful transition to straight drama.

Pioneering television funnyman Jackie Gleason copped an Oscar nomination for his 1961 performance as Minnesota Fats in Robert Rossen's *The Hustler* but failed miserably in the title role of *Gigot* the following year. Movie audiences are notoriously fickle, preferring to see their favorite stars in familiar roles. Although typecasting is the bane of most actors' existence, it also can mean the difference between working and the unemployment line.

Peter Sellers found himself in 1960 itching to try something different from the comic roles that had launched his film career on its rapid ascent. Sellers already had proven in *I'm All Right, Jack* that he could straddle the fine line between comedy and pathos. Now he was eager to show his audience and harshest critics that he could sustain a dramatic role throughout the course of a feature-length film. With this in mind, Sellers agreed to play gangster Lionel Meadows in John Guillermin's X-rated thriller *Never Let Go*. Filmed in Britain, *Never Let Go* failed dismally and quickly sank into oblivion. But Sellers was lucky in one respect: His prolific cinematic output—four films in 1960 alone—helped mask these errors in judgment that would eventually send his career into a decade-long tailspin.

Although relegated to a late-night television graveyard, *Never Let Go* remains one of Sellers's more compelling films in light of his melodramatic turn as Meadows. It is also Sellers's only dramatic performance ever released to the general public. *The Blockhouse*, a second drama in which he appeared thirteen years later, never saw the light of the projection booth and is now available only on videocassette.

Never Let Go materialized at a crucial turning point in Sellers's career. Although he demonstrated considerable box-office clout with *I'm All Right, Jack* and *The Mouse That Roared*, Sellers's international reputation would not be secure until he followed *Never Let Go* with *The Millionairess* in which he costarred with Sophia Loren. Still, for a man obsessed with his public image, the role of Lionel Meadows was a curious career move.

Rife with dated clichés and stereotypes, *Never Let Go* tells the tale of

John Cummings (Richard Todd), a wimpy, high-strung middle-aged cosmetics salesman who buys a Ford Anglia car in hopes of boosting his slumping sales figures at a London department store.

A father of two with a ludicrously saccharine domestic life (he and his wife embrace passionately every time he enters their apartment), Cummings's fragile world suddenly crumbles when his uninsured Anglia is stolen. Desperately trying to hold on to his job and ignoring the pleadings of his wife, Cummings embarks on a fanatic search for the stolen Anglia. Acting on a reluctant tip from Alfie, the frightened old newspaper vendor who witnessed the incident, Cummings tracks down and questions Tommy Towers (early 1960s pop star Adam Faith), the requisite "mixed-up youth" who hangs out in pubs with his motorcycle gang, blasting the jukebox and pestering customers.

Towers naturally pleads ignorance to Cummings's accusations, but not before he admits to working for thuggish Lionel Meadows, owner of Meadows Garage and suspected ringleader of a stolen-car syndicate. In the best B-movie tradition, Meadows not only lives in fashionable digs above his garage but keeps his own personal concubine: Jackie, another young, confused kid who doubles as Towers's girlfriend when she's not being verbally or physically abused by Meadows.

Convinced that his Anglia is somewhere in Meadows's garage and armed with a posse of local police, Cummings confronts Meadows, who naturally denies any knowledge of Cummings's Anglia and insists he runs a "legitimate business." But Cummings refuses to accept Meadows's explanation, and from this point on, the *Never Let Go* narrative takes a sharp turn for the absurd from which it never quite rebounds.

Cummings, showing either unbelievable naiveté or thickheaded logic (it's hard to tell), returns to the garage later that day, loudly breaks in, and comes face-to-face with a sneering Meadows and his beefy mob henchman Cliff (David Lodge). Meadows holds his fury long enough to allow Cummings a peek around the shop—the Anglia, of course, is being held elsewhere. But when Cummings refuses to leave, Cliff beats the tar out of the annoying salesman, who gets no sympathy from the exasperated police inspector (Noel Willman) conducting an undercover investigation into Meadows's business dealings.

Like an unreachable itch, Cummings refuses to go away and let the police establish their own case against Meadows. Instead, he pesters Towers and Jackie (who by this time has fled Meadows and taken refuge with her boyfriend) into telling him more about Meadows's operation and even talks the police into raiding one of Meadows's business associates.

Meadows by this time has had enough, and after attacking Cummings in his apartment, lies in wait for the pesky salesman to return one last time to Meadows Garage seeking his beloved Anglia.

All very melodramatic fodder, done without any sense of style or narrative rhythm. Guillermin's direction is flat and unimaginative, and the film's murky photography creates a lifeless atmosphere. Plagued by Alun Falconer's tepid screenplay and peopled with one-dimensional characters, *Never Let Go* never gets going. Todd and Willman in particular deliver wooden, unemotional performances. Willman recites his machine-gun police patter without a hint of inflection, while Todd, setting his jaw in determination, draws a blank, colorless slate.

We never feel Cummings's rage toward Meadows or his lot in life, nor do we empathize with the self-loathing that Cummings confesses to his wife. The respected actress Elizabeth Sellars, wearing cocktail dresses and a perfectly coiffed hairdo in Falconer's vision of the "perfect wife," is reduced to a weepy, whiny shrew.

Sellers's stock portrayal of Meadows as a slick dime-store hood is pure low-budget Hollywood, and the novelty quickly wears thin. Yet Meadows emerges as the film's most interesting character, perhaps because of the raw energy and sheer force with which Sellers embellished his creation.

Not very physically or athletically inclined, Sellers cuts a meanacing figure throughout and demonstrates great dexterity in the film's penultimate scene—the final showdown between Meadows and Cummings. Sellers's legendary temper suited him well here. Meadows, lying in wait for Cummings when the salesman breaks into the garage for the second time, hisses, bellows, and works himself into a frothy, towering rage. But the scene's choreographed physicality obviously was in a register alien to the flabby East End mama's boy who was still in constant communication with Peg. Yet Meadows's slugfest with Cummings rings true within the exaggerated confines of Falconer's narrative.

"Winner Todd's face is slashed, but he has his car," *Newsweek* noted. "Loser Sellers is dragged off to jail, scarred, grimy, his face squashed but in his glazed eyes there is an unmistakable glow of triumph. At last, he has made a serious picture. It was a serious mistake."[1]

Some of his intimates saw Meadows as Sellers's on-screen alter ego, an outlet for the actor's violent inner turmoil. With his first marriage (to Australian actress Anne Hayes) nearing its end and troubled by his constant insecurities, Sellers was careening out of control with only his therapeutic film work as an emotional outlet. To film critic Alexander Walker, Sellers chose the role of Meadows "to match his black moods, perhaps to release his undirected inner pressures. With hair too thick, mustache too trim, jawbone seemingly extended physically by sheer willpower into jutting menace, he appeared on screen as a cone of suppressed fury always threatening eruption."[2]

Sellers apparently remained in character even after he returned home from the set. His contention that he was "taken over" by his characters

Mobster Lionel Meadows threatens "mixed up" Tommy Towers (Adam Faith) in the X-rated *Never Let Go*, Sellers's only dramatic performance released to the general public.

during the course of a film was harmless enough when a Tully Bascombe or Dodger Lane emerged at the dinner table. For Sellers's wife, Anne, however, his transformation into Lionel Meadows reached frightening proportions. "The trouble with Peter is that he really lives these characters," she said. "The worst time was when he was making *Never Let Go*. He would come back from the studios each night and shout at us in a nasty way."[3]

Although *Never Let Go* marked Sellers's first cinematic flop, it was seen by very few and passed almost unnoticed through British film corridors. Sandwiched between *The Battle of the Sexes* and *The Millionairess*, *Never Let Go* was quickly forgotten. In hindsight, however, it exposed the first chink in Sellers's armor of seeming invincibility and was an early harbinger of the bad times that his questionable screen judgment would shortly engender.

13
The Millionairess

Cast:

Dr. Kabir	Peter Sellers
Epifania	Sophia Loren
Sagamore	Alastair Sim
Joe	Vittorio de Sica

STUDIO: 20th Century–Fox
RELEASE DATE: October 8, 1960
RUNNING TIME: 90 minutes (Cinemascope/ De Luxe)
DIRECTED BY: Anthony Asquith
PRODUCED BY: Pierre Rouve
WRITTEN BY: Wolf Mankowitz (from the play by George Bernard Shaw)
PHOTOGRAPHY: Jack Hildyard
MUSIC: Georges Van Parys

During World War II, Sellers spent a large chunk of time in India where he met Spike Milligan (born in that country) and cultivated a great respect for the Indian people and culture. After the war, Milligan and Sellers incorporated India's tongue-twisting dialect into the "Goon Show" with two of their more popular characters—Singhiz Lalkaka (played by Sellers) and Babu Banajee (Milligan).

"They became incredibly popular those two, and all kinds of things happened after that," Sellers said. "I was invited to speak at the Oxford Union, the Indian Society once, and a very kind gentleman introduced me and said that it was due to me that members of the Indian race were allowed to get past the garden fence with their carpets . . . because people sounded like Spike and I."[1]

After the "Goon Show" Sellers voiced his Brahmin accents on various comedy albums. But it wasn't until 1960 and *The Millionairess* that he was able to translate his Indian character to film. Adapted by Wolf Mankowitz from George Bernard Shaw's satirical play about the world's richest woman—whose money can't purchase the affection of a saintly Egyptian doctor toiling in London's East End—*The Millionairess* was molded to fit Sellers's on-screen persona. The doctor's character remained essentially the same, but his nationality was changed to accommodate Sellers's ethnic preference.

In many ways, *The Millionairess* marked a watershed in Sellers's nascent film career. While films like *The Ladykillers* and *I'm All Right, Jack* were instrumental in launching his career, they were decidedly British in comedic sensibility and targeted to an Anglophile audience. *The Millionairess*, on the other hand, was Sellers's first multinational production, not only paying him the impressive fee of $115,000 (a hefty raise from his previous $40,000 asking price)[2] but casting him for the first time in a romantic leading-man light and opposite a star of international repute—Sophia Loren.

But along with Sellers's newfound leading-man persona came trouble, as the comedian apparently mistook Loren's affections for something more serious. To say that Sellers developed a huge crush on Loren would be an understatement; his immediate infatuation with the beautiful Italian actress soon grew into an unbridled love that would eventually destroy his marriage. "It was the very last thing I thought would happen," he said. "This was my first really big international film and Sophia Loren was the biggest star I'd been cast with. I was genuinely scared ... overwhelmed, really, is the word. I was just hoping for a good professional relationship, you know—what else man? I was two stone overweight. I wasn't the most attractive man in the world, let's face it. Then it just happened. I think she must have liked the fact that I was so unassuming. She liked my simplicity. I made her laugh. We were very happy together."[3]

(Loren's memoirs, published in 1976, made no mention of Sellers or their alleged affair. Reportedly furious with this deletion, Sellers nonetheless put on his best public face. "I do find that strange," he replied nonchalantly. "After all, our relationship was one of the things that helped break up my first marriage. I was always rushing off to Italy to be with Sophia. It's odd that someone who apparently meant so much in her life—or so she said—should not figure in her life story. Still, perhaps she has her reasons."[4])

The two stars cavorted on the set while recording a phonograph album (*Peter Sellers and Sophia Loren*) containing the single "Goodness Gracious Me!" excluded from the film's soundtrack but a best-seller nonetheless. When $200,000 worth of jewels were stolen from Loren, they were quickly replaced by Sellers with a large valuable gem. "Peter would come and hold Sophia's hand like a boy finding his way into his first affair," said Producer Dmitri de Grunwald. "The nice way of describing her attitude is to say she was kind to him. The other way is to say that her attitude gave him greater hope than was warranted."[5]

But for all its romance, real or imagined, and sparkling chemistry between Sellers and Loren, *The Millionairess* was an artistic and critical disappointment. Loren, bravely tackling her first comedic role, played the alluring Epifania Parega, Italian heiress to her beloved father's inestimably wealthy estate. Epifania's late father—seen in a multitude of intimidating watercolors gracing the Parega estate (and bearing a striking resemblance to Sellers, who voiced the Neapolitan benefactor)—established strict guidelines for his daughter's future husband—namely, the man who marries Epifania must first pass a test of turning £500 into £15,000 within three months.

Epifania's first husband, a philandering lothario, fails the test miserably, and the hot-blooded Epifania files for divorce with her sarcastic lawyer, Sagamore (Alastair Sim). Feeling she's failed her father, Epifania tries a halfhearted suicide attempt by jumping into the Thames, where she's forced to save herself after being ignored by Dr. Kabir, a cheerful Indian doctor out for a ride in his rowboat.

Epifania is furious. After all, *nobody* has ever had the nerve to ignore her. Consequently, her curiosity and libido are piqued by the little doctor who so casually brushed her off. How convenient, then, when she gets a second chance to ensnare Kabir's attentions. Out for a Thameside walk with her psychiatrist Adrian Bland (Dennis Price)—engaged by Sagamore to dissuade Epifania from marrying and consequently putting him out of business—Epifania pushes him into the river when he makes disparaging comments about her father. Who should come to the psychiatrist's rescue but Kabir, who not only saves Bland but also rescues Epifania when she jumps into the water upon spying the doctor.

Taken by Kabir to a fisherman's shack for a physical examination, Epifania is rebuffed in her attempts to seduce the doctor, who is unimpressed with her wealth but smitten with her physical beauty (and strong pulse). ("I am of the aristocracy of money," she tells Kabir. "Ah, well, that is a disease for which I do not prescribe," he replies.)

Epifania can't understand how Kabir can refuse her charms and money, but the doctor is devoted only to the poor souls inhabiting his East End clinic—an institution he envelopes with his spiritual character and strength. When he finds himself attracted to Epifania, his will growing weaker, Kabir knows he must avoid the buxom beauty or risk falling from his self-imposed state of grace.

But Epifania is obsessed with transforming Kabir into her lover and purchases the entire city block in which his Calcutta-backed clinic is situated. Hoping to lure Kabir into her clutches, Epifania invites him to tour her glittery new Parega Clinic, housing the latest in sophisticated high-tech equipment. When he refuses her offer to run the clinic—"Power must come from within, otherwise it destroys," he tells her—Kabir is asked by Epifania to become her husband.

There's a hitch, however. Not only does Kabir want to remain single, trying valiantly to ignore his overpowering romantic impulses, but he tells Epifania that his mother, on her deathbed, imposed wifely guidelines on her son remarkably similar to old man Parega's rules: Should Kabir find himself attracted to a woman, she must first take 500 rupees (35 shillings) and earn a living for three months before being worthy of marriage.

Epifania, undaunted by the challenge, alights in search of a job and lands in Joe's (Vittorio de Sica) outdated pasta shop where she unionizes the workers, imports modern machinery, and quickly turns an enormous profit. But though she proves herself worthy of Kabir's affections, the doctor fails to reciprocate. Forced to tackle the Parega test, he tries hard to give away Epifania's £500 (*Please take one as you leave* reads a sign in his clinic directly over the £500 stack of money). Unable to reconcile the materialistic aspect of his seemingly trivial pursuit, Kabir finally gives the money to a drunken colleague after an all-night party.

Epifania, disappointed in Kabir's cavalier attitude and disgusted with men and money, decides to join a nunnery. Sagamore, meanwhile, visits Kabir and tells him he's inherited Epifania's riches through an obscure codicil to the Parega inheritance clause. Kabir, of course, refuses the money; however, thinking Epifania is about to commit suicide (again), he rushes to save her and finally pledges his love, selling his share of her inheritance for £15,000 and fulfilling his husbandly requirement.

Although burdened with a talky, preachy script and Anthony Asquith's laborious direction, *The Millionairess* was a moderate success in England (less so in America), proving that Sellers could stretch his comedic persona to encompass a romantic leading man. His endearing, well-rounded portrayal of Kabir—a high-minded Brahmin toeing the line of vulnerability—silenced those who thought Sellers's vocal abilities his sole talent. Loren, through no real fault of her own, tried valiantly but failed to ring laughs out of the bitchy Epifania. She was, however, alluringly seductive in her scenes with Sellers.

Sellers had by this time already launched into his oft-repeated statements of becoming a prisoner to the whims of his scripted characters. Once again, this eerie force made its presence felt in Sellers's body during shooting of *The Millionairess*. "I felt I had actually been an Indian in some past life," he said afterward. "Once, during filming, an Indian supporting player came up to me and said, without joking, that I was the new messiah and ought to go to India and lead her people into a happier future. I even began to feel I had developed the power to heal people along with the role. It was frightening."[6] (Sellers reprised his Indian doctor role a year later when he made a cameo appearance in *The Road to Hong Kong* starring Bob Hope and Bing Crosby.)

The Millionairess was the fourth Sellers film released in 1960, and though he should have been pleased with these circumstances, Sellers sank into a lethargy for which a hectic work schedule seemed the only cure. Not only did the completion of *The Millionairess* signal the end of his "affair" with Loren, but his marriage to Anne was now on the rocks and soon to run aground. But however much he mooned, Sellers couldn't overlook this fact: *The Millionairess*, notwithstanding its lukewarm critical reception,

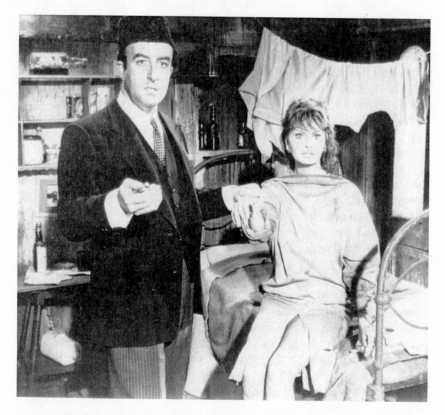

**Dr. Kabir takes Epifania's (Sophia Loren) emphatic pulse after her second
suicide attempt. (Courtesy National Film Archive, London.)**

firmly established the "overweight" British comic as an international
star.

"Very few moviegoers will be able to resist Actor Sellers. Not even
canny old Alastair Sim, who mugs it up as the heroine's lawyer, can steal
a frame from this subtle performer who hardly seems to move his face at
all," enthused *Time* magazine. "Comedian Sellers indeed is not a performer, but an actor in the best sense of the word; not a professional show-
off who attracts attention to what he is doing, but an artist who reveals what
he is. And what Sellers is, solely and invariably, is the character he is portraying."[7]

Variety wrote that "Sellers plays the doctor and it's another challenge
in a career in which he is determined not to be typed. Though he plays it
straight, apart from an offbeat accent, he still manages to bring in some
typical Sellers comedy touches which help to make it a fascinating character
study. He even injects a few emotional throwaways which are fine."[8]

Although Sellers was scheduled to follow *The Millionairess* with a starring role in *Memoirs of a Cross-Eyed Man*—produced under the auspices of his newly-formed partnership with Mankowitz and costarring Diane Cilento—the project fell through when Sellers abruptly dissolved Sellers-Mankowitz Ltd. (enraging Mankowitz and causing an irreparable rift between him and Sellers).

Freed of his close brush with a self-imposed corporate hierarchy, Sellers now decided he was ready to direct, and star in, his first feature. At de Grunwald's urging, he chose Marcel Pagnol's stage play *Mr. Topaze* (entitled *I Like Money* in America) as his entrée into the director's chair. The story of an idealistic French schoolteacher corrupted by a gang of seedy businessmen, *Mr. Topaze* flopped at the box office, with criticism leveled at Sellers's performance and lackluster direction.

"The sad news about the new Peter Sellers comedy, *I Like Money*, is that it has a single defect—it isn't funny ... the picture creaks along in a gentle, harmless, increasingly tiresome, and at last quite maddening way, and none of Mr. Sellers' resources of tact and charm can do more than mitigate one's irritation with it," wrote Brendan Gill in the *New Yorker*. "That the brilliant actor Peter Sellers finds himself in this predicament is largely the fault of the farm from brilliant director Peter Sellers, who lets every sequence drag and, when it comes to mugging, lets every actor except himself get away with murder."[9]

"He was not directing so much as acting the role of director," de Grunwald said. "Acting now came into all his relationships, on the screen or off it."[10]

Mr. Topaze extinguished whatever ambitions Sellers held as a director. Although he would again direct several more times throughout his career, hiring directors then firing them midway through a project, Sellers was now content to reclaim his status as a film star and nothing else.

14
Only Two Can Play

Cast:
John Lewis .... Peter Sellers
Jean Lewis .... Virginia Maskell
Elizabeth Gruffyd-
   Williams .... Mai Zetterling

Guyan . . . . Kenneth Griffiths
Sidney Probert . . . . Richard Attenbor-
                                          ough

STUDIO: British Lion/Vale
RELEASE DATE: January 11, 1962
RUNNING TIME: 106 minutes (black and white)
DIRECTED BY: Sidney Gilliat
PRODUCED BY: Frank Launder and Sidney
   Gilliat
WRITTEN BY: Bryan Forbes (from the novel
   That Uncertain Feeling by Kingsley Amis)
PHOTOGRAPHY: John Wilcox
MUSIC: Richard Rodney Bennett

After the indifferent reception of *Mr. Topaze,* Sellers returned to the
comfortable confines of homespun ensemble comedy, garnering enthusiastic reviews and delivering an eloquent, nuanced performance in *Only Two
Can Play.*

Bryan Forbes's faithful adaptation of Kingsley Amis's novel *That Uncertain Feeling, Only Two Can Play* featured Sellers as libidinous Welsh
librarian John Lewis, part-time drama critic and father of two, battling the
seven-year itch in the small town of Aberdarcy. Lewis lives in a cramped,
garishly-wallpapered apartment with nosy neighbors. Bored with his op-
pressive domestic existence, he seeks refuge in lascivious daydreams. Not
only does he ogle women while commuting to work, but his flirtations ex-
tend to the library, much to the consternation of Guyan (Kenneth Griffiths), his uptight henpecked co-worker and neighbor.

Lewis meets his match in Elizabeth Gruffyd-Williams (Mai Zetterling), the horny Swedish-born wife of local politico Vernon Gruffyd-Williams. She's producing *Bowen Thomas: Tailor of Llandilo,* a play written by
boorish thespian Sidney Probert (Richard Attenborough). Her visit to the
library—and interest in a volume entitled *Precise History of Codpieces*—
quickly catches Lewis's attention. The two opposites immediately attract.
While Lewis falls for Liz's elegance, the antithesis of his unassuming wife,
Jean, bossy Liz sees in Lewis the perfect complement for her unflinchingly
vain ego.

But Liz represents more than just a romantic conquest for Lewis. Her
husband is helping to choose the new assistant librarian, a position promising prestige and a bigger paycheck. Lewis, itching to climb the Aberdarcy
social ladder, applies for the job and embarks on a hilariously unconsummated affair with Liz. When he learns that Liz fixed the job in his favor,
Lewis (somewhat unbelievably) is surprised and angrily ends the relationship, only to learn that his wife was running around with Probert.

Only Two Can Play offered a fine showcase for Sellers's acting talents, even though he was at the time voicing discontent at the roles he was being offered. "Everyone says the same thing, 'Peter, I've got a lovely Little Man part for you, nice and downtrodden,'" he told Joseph Morgenstern of the New York *Herald Tribune.* "I invariably say that I want to do other things, and they say, 'But Peter, don't fall into the trap,' the trap being in their estimation that maybe I was cut out by nature to be a little man and am in mortal danger of eluding my destiny."[1]

Regardless of his personal feelings, Sellers worked hard to underplay Forbes's broad farce. Investing Lewis with a soft Welsh accent and ironic sarcasm, Sellers scored a hit with the critics and his fans, who flocked to *Only Two Can Play* and propelled the film into the box-office stratosphere.

It was a welcome relief to Sellers after his three previous disappointments. "Sellers . . . concentrates on comic acting rather than comic imitation and gives his subtlest performance to date," wrote Stanley Kauffmann,[2] while *Newsweek* gushed that "British comic Peter Sellers manipulates the English language with a similar sort of wizadry. Consider the simple word 'do.' Pronounced by Sellers in reply to a sexpot who has announced she may drop in to see him again soon, it zooms out with a deceptive air of innocence; it makes several circles of innuendo, and it winds up lurking somewhere behind him. . . ."[3]

Although no one could have suspected at the time, *Only Two Can Play* also provided an early glimpse of the slapstick brilliance Sellers would bring to fruition during the long-running *Pink Panther* series. Lewis's clumsy attempts at bedding Liz—the "wan don who thinks he is a Don Juan"[4]—were played for laughs in two scenes affording Sellers the chance to flex his clownish muscles.

Lewis's first stab at unconnubial bliss occurs roughly thirty minutes into the film, shortly after he and Liz exchange a passionate first kiss at the Gruffuyd-Williams's black-tie dinner party celebrating *Bowen Thomas* (and the insufferable Sidney Probert, to whom we're introduced). Walking home from the library a few days later, Lewis stops to survey two nubile tennis players (the clip used to open the film) when Liz comes screeching around the corner and offers him a ride home. Arriving at the flat—Lewis smugly acknowledges Guyan's questioning gaze as they pass him on the road—Liz invites herself upstairs where a frazzled Jean is busy with the kiddies.

Jean suspects something amiss but declines Liz's invitation to accompany the pair out for a drink. ("I'll leave something out for you," she warns Lewis. "Cold.") But Liz doesn't have drinks on her mind as she brings Lewis to her house for the requisite "nightcap" and lets him know that her husband is out for the evening. This sets up the film's funniest sequence, a ten-minute romp in which everything conceivable backfires on the star-crossed lovers. Lewis almost emasculates himself testing out "the master's" exercise equipment, has a bit of trouble carrying Liz into the bedroom, and gets his jacket off just in time to see Vernon's headlights flashing into the room.

But Vernon hasn't returned alone. He's brought the boys back for a drink. Liz (literally) kicks Lewis out of bed, gives him a quick peck on the cheek, and orders him to sneak out the front door undetected. Lewis creeps down the stairs, makes sure the coast is clear, and . . . is just about to taste freedom when he hears more voices coming through the front door. He frantically races back to the foyer, takes the men's coats, and in solemn but-lerlike tones, informs them that "Mr. Gruffyd-Williams is in the lounge" before dropping the coats and running out the front door.

But wait. There are still more voices on the way in, and Lewis the butler suddenly segues into Lewis the blue-collar plumber as he runs into the kitchen and comes face-to-face with "Charlie" (John Le Mesurier), Vernon's friend, cracking ice for the drinks.

"Good evening, I was just, uh, checking up whether everything was all right," the "plumber" tells an incredulous Charlie. "You know, I don't like leaving a job when everything's not all right, really." He blows into a rubber hose attached to the sink ("You won't have any more trouble with that") gingerly pats the sinktop, and scurries toward the back door.

But it's not the backyard Lewis steps into—it's the boiler room, out of which a slew of boxes come tumbling onto the unsuspecting plumber. "Oooh, golden hot it is, warming up a tree," Lewis says, stroking the boiler nervously while regaining his composure and plotting his next move. "Don't worry about this, you see," he says, pointing to the boxes, "because the heat will draw it all back in." And with those nonsensical words of wisdom, Lewis makes his exit, leaving Charlie, mallet in hand, dumbfounded. (This isn't the last time the two shall meet. Charlie also sits on the library board and—much to Lewis's horror—is one of the interviewers for the assistant librarian position. Needless to say, he questions Lewis repeatedly about plumbing.)

Their romantic aspirations on hold, Lewis and Liz try again a few days later—this time in the front seat of Liz's car. It's opening night for *Bowen Thomas*, and confusion reigns backstage. A petrified Guyan, bearing a lit torch as "Death," suddenly forgets his lines and incurs Probert's wrath. The backstage chaos sets the perfect smoke screen for Lewis, covering the play for the *Aberdarcy Chronicle*. While the impatient crowd grows restless, he sneaks out of the theater with Liz before Act I, just as Guyan's torch ig-nites the curtain and (subsequently) the entire theater.

Liz drives to a wooded secluded area, parks the car, and alluringly takes off her earrings. Down goes the front seat at the push of a dashboard button, and with it our two lovebirds. But wait. What's that cow doing pok-ing its head into the car? Liz screams, the cow moos loudly, and Lewis

Lothario librarian John Lewis and the woman in his life, Elizabeth Gruffyd-Williams (Mai Zetterling).

panics, fumbling with the dashboard controls and simultaneously igniting the cacophonous radio, the windshield wipers, and the headlights. There's a shotgun blast (an angry farmer suspecting adolescent horseplay), and the dynamic duo tear off into dark underbrush, swerving past a herd of cattle and narrowly making it out alive.

Sellers completed *Only Two Can Play* at a time in his life that in many ways complemented John Lewis's frustrations. His eleven-year marriage to Anne, plagued by his many infidelities, was nearing its rocky end, and his mind-set meshed snugly with the sarcastic irony Forbes injected into the character of John Lewis. But while Lewis harnessed his emotions and finally resolved his inner turmoil, Sellers predictably found fault with *Only Two Can Play* before and after the film was completed.

According to John Boulting, to whom he often turned for guidance, Sellers began complaining the very first day of location filming in Cardiff. He logged a late-night phone call to Boulting and whined about costar Virginia Maskell. "It was already 11:30 p.m. and the call lasted till 2:15 a.m.," Boulting said. "'John,' Sellers said, 'I'm in a terrible spot here. This girl Maskell, I've had her in my caravan. We went through two or three scenes together and she hasn't the right Welsh accent and can't act for toffee.'"[5]

Although he received the best reviews since *I'm All Right, Jack,* Sellers's penchant for self-loathing, usually directed at his own performances, took a drastic turn once the film was completed. "I don't know what we can do," he complained to the Boultings. "It'll set my career back ten years, back to the beginning again." The Boultings, accustomed to Sellers's fits of despair, offered to buy his 10 percent cut of the film's profits; Sellers expressed immediate interest and agreed to a £17,500 buyout. Of course the Boultings never seriously considered keeping Sellers's share of the profits. Fueled by enthusiastic reviews, *Only Two Can Play* was setting British box-office records, and the brothers offered to pay Sellers his fair share, which had accumulated to roughly £120,000. Sellers never replied to the offer.[6]

Only Two Can Play did receive a small share of negative criticism. Peter Harcourt, in *Sight and Sound,* thought the film "descends to the disheartening cliché of British-American sexual comedy, an essentially emasculated comedy of titillation, depending for its effect upon the conditioned reflex in all of us with which we respond to a blue joke. The laughter, more often than not, is tinged with embarrassment ... the film's essential failure ... can be localized in Peter Sellers's protectively deadpan performance as John Lewis. With his wife, he attempts to create for us a suitably three-dimensional character; with Mrs. Gruffyd-Williams (rather crudely played by Mai Zetterling), he is merely a figure of farce."[7]

"Funny as Sellers' performance is, there is something faintly sad and disappointing about the picture itself," *Newsweek* thought. "*Only Two Can Play* ... is an exhibition game, not the real thing. The very fact that Sellers plays it so well leaves one hoping that, next time, the stakes will be a little higher."[8]

For the most part, however, Sellers and company were lauded for their work. "The romp moves along with a sure touch (that of Director Sidney Gilliat) but it is not entirely farce," Hollis Alpert opined in *Saturday Review.* "The young librarian's home scenes have believability and point, as well as touch of pathos ... he is an 'angry,' but a subdued one, educated, but without the opportunity to put the education to good use. Sellers makes him both funny and convincing...."[9]

"Bryan Forbes has written a witty screenplay from the Amis novel, and Sidney Gilliat has directed his fine cast exceedingly well, with appropriate lightness and also with appropriate sympathy for the husband and wife who really love each other but have grown restive in their drab apartment and dull routine," *Commonweal* thought. "Virginia Maskell is quite effective as the wife ... the supporting cast is also good—especially in this case Kenneth Griffiths, as Peter's less worthy co-worker who is determinedly competing for the sub-librarian job, and Richard Attenborough, who is just right in his few scenes as a Welsh literary idol who hopes to push his cause with Peter's wife."[10]

The Nation enthusiastically recommended the film with this proclamation: "Sex is as good a subject for humor as the race has discovered, and Peter Sellers is as cunning and precise a comedian as our time has produced. It is predictable, therefore, that he can whip a froth of laughter out of the providings of an overactive libido...."[11]

15
Waltz of the Toreadors

Cast:

General Leo Fitzjohn ..	Peter Sellers
Emily Fitzjohn	Margaret Leighton
Ghislaine	Dany Robin
Dr. Grogan	Cyril Cusack
Robert	John Fraser

STUDIO: Rank
RELEASE DATE: April 12, 1962
RUNNING TIME: 105 minutes (Technicolor)
DIRECTED BY: John Guillermin
PRODUCED BY: Peter de Sarigny
WRITTEN BY: Wolf Mankowitz
PHOTOGRAPHY: John Wilcox
MUSIC: Richard Addinsell

After taking Clare Quilty to dizzying surrealistic heights, Sellers returned to more earthy pursuits as skirt-chasing General Leo Fitzjohn in *Waltz of the Toreadors*. Sellers "borrowed" Fitzjohn's voice (and, one imagines, his pompous military bearing) from "Goon Show" Major Dennis Bloodnok, decorated with the Military Cross for emptying trash cans during battle. Like Bloodnok, Fitzjohn was an old fool; unlike the major, however, this horny old boy pressed plenty of young female flesh to his lips.

With the magic of makeup, Sellers, 37, was transformed into the sixtyish Fitzjohn, complete with grey walrus mustache and healthy paunch. Playing someone visually older than himself wasn't much of a problem for Sellers, as he had proved in *The Smallest Show on Earth*.

Wolf Mankowitz adapted *Waltz of the Toreadors* from Jean Anouilh's successful Broadway play starring Sir Ralph Richardson and Mildred Natwick. Mankowitz's screenplay offered little originality or enjoyment. More interesting was the film's behind-the-scenes intrigue.

Several years earlier, Mankowitz had vowed never again to speak to Sellers. A burly man with a dry sense of humor, Mankowitz grew close to Sellers during the latter's alleged romance with Sophia Loren on *The Millionairess:* Sellers-Mankowitz Productions was established shortly thereafter to find vehicles in which Sellers would star or direct. The men hoped to form a consortium much like the fabled United Artists team and had interested Anthony Newley, Diane Cilento, Sean Connery, Albert Finney, and Peter O'Toole in the enterprise.[1]

But Sellers-Mankowitz Productions never saw the light of day. On the morning Mankowitz was to pitch the idea to the consortium, he received a letter from Sellers. "He was withdrawing from the entire deal," Mankowitz recalled. "I was utterly crushed and incensed. The letter said, 'I have been thinking all night about this company. I have decided that I have to be free of commitments to follow the direction my career takes.'"[2]

Mankowitz was present on *Waltz of the Toreadors* in name only, yet Sellers found other ways to make life on the set miserable. His chief distraction, it seemed, was his deteriorating marriage, and he frantically sent for David Lodge to ease the situation. "Peter was in his trailer while everyone cooled their heels outside, including the cavalry horses needed for the scene, and producer Julian Wintle went out of his mind as the costs climbed hourly," Lodge recalled. "Peter had a great heap of old-fashioned pennies in front of him—this is before our coinage went decimal—and he said, very piteously, 'Dave, luv, take the money and go down to the phone booth and get through to Anne. Tell her I'm sorry.' But Anne wasn't going to forgive him for whatever had just happened. I couldn't tell Peter that in his state of mind. So I reported back, 'She says she'll talk to you tonight, so get on with your work now.'"[3]

While Sellers battled real-life marital woes, his on-screen alter ego wasn't faring much better in the marriage department. General Fitzjohn's problems dated back seventeen years when, as a dashing young major in the British army, he met beautiful French damsel Ghislaine (Dany Robin) at an officers' ball. The two instantly fell in love and danced to the strains of "The Waltz of the Toreadors"—under the scrutinizing eye of Fitzjohn's wife, Emily (Margaret Leighton).

Fitzjohn and Ghislaine sustained their relationship, even though Fitzjohn was unhappily married with two very homely daughters (one of whom is played by a young Prunella Scales, better known today as Sybil Fawlty, wife of insufferable Innkeeper Basil Fawlty in John Cleese's classic British sitcom "Fawlty Towers").

Ghislaine, saving herself for "the right man," remained a virgin, while the philandering Fitzjohn chased every skirt he could. Yet each year he traveled to Paris under the pretense of attending an officers's meeting. Only then could he be alone with his beloved Ghislaine.

The Ghislaine-Fitzjohn courtship is recounted in flashback form by the lovers themselves, reunited when Ghislaine travels to Fitzjohn's castle. Tired of their once-a-year rendezvous, she demands that Fitzjohn leave his wife, consummate their relationship, and take her for his wife. But Fitzjohn is reluctant to part with his comfortable lifestyle, particularly the nubile chambermaids in his employ.

And there's Emily. How would he break the news to her? She has been a crotchety invalid for the last ten years, demanding constant attention and making Fitzjohn's life miserable. Though Fitzjohn hates his wife — convinced her sickness is contrived — he still cannot sever the ties that bind.

Not yet, anyway.

Not with Robert (John Fraser), his young protégé, making a concerted effort to win Ghislaine's affections after saving her from a halfhearted suicide attempt. But Ghislaine isn't interested in Robert — she wants only Fitzjohn, who finally tears himself away from the castle (and Emily) and joins his love at the local inn. They plan to run away in the morning and lead a life of bliss.

But their happiness is short-lived. Fitzjohn encounters a plethora of slapstick obstacles trying to reach Ghislaine's room. With this small feat finally accomplished, their tryst is interrupted. Fitzjohn is forced to hide on the balcony, which collapses, depositing him into a full rain barrel from which he is plucked and brought back to his castle.

And so it goes until the film's finale, one farcical situation piled on top of another until Mankowitz's busy screenplay runs out of ideas. Sure enough, Ghislaine falls in love with Robert, and they marry. We learn that Fitzjohn is really Robert's father (though Emily is not his mother), which would have been a pleasant surprise had it not come near the end of this exhausting film. Clearly this revelation is mean to clean up the film's loose narrative ends, but it is has little impact on the rickety plot and is quickly glossed over by Mankowitz and Director John Guillermin.

Waltz of the Toreadors's major problem lies in Guillermin's indecisive direction. Should the film be played as a sex farce or romantic melodrama? Guillermin can't seem to decide. While the *Waltz of the Toreadors* plot could have reached a satisfying middle ground between these two variables, it too often jumps back and forth, leaving a confused, disjointed feeling.

An example of this thematic inconsistency occurs in the film's final scene. Fitzjohn returns to his castle, resigned to Ghislaine's marriage and his deadbeat wife. Suddenly, totally out of character, he decides to commit suicide. He loads his revolver, points the gun to his head, and is just about the pull the trigger when he's interrupted by the new chambermaid. All thoughts of suicide disappear. Fitzjohn drops the gun and grabs the young girl, saved from oblivion by his carnal desires and the merry lure of a new sexual conquest.

General Fitzjohn ponders his fate as Dr. Grogan (Cyril Cusack) looks on.

Although *Waltz of the Toreadors* fared poorly at the box office, Sellers et al. largely were spared the critics' wrath, which focused primarily on the film's plot contrivances. "As a screenplay—written by Wolf Mankowitz and directed by John Guillermin—Anouilh's fine-feathered strutter has been saponified, caponified, shorn of its more splendid plumes of wit and stuffed with a mighty chunk of superogatory and rashly overcolored celluloid that might have been more sensibly and even profitably employed to blow up the bank that financed this picture," *Time* lengthily opined.[4]

"*Waltz* has its funny moments, but is more like a Mack Sennett comedy than French cream puff, *Commonweal* wrote.[5] *Newsweek* thought Mankowitz's adaptation "by turns saccharine and slapstick and for Peter Sellers as the general . . . a losing battle."[6]

16
Lolita

Cast:
Humbert Humbert ... James Mason

Lolita Haze . . . . Sue Lyon
Charlotte Haze . . . . . . Shelley Winters
Clare Quilty . . . . Peter Sellers

STUDIO: MGM/Seven Arts
RELEASE DATE: June 14, 1962
RUNNING TIME: 152 minutes (black and white)
DIRECTED BY: Stanley Kubrick
PRODUCED BY: James B. Harris
WRITTEN BY: Vladimir Nabokov (from his
  novel)
PHOTOGRAPHY: Oswald Morris
MUSIC: Nelson Riddle

Stanley Kubrick's *Lolita* represents Sellers's greatest screen triumph yet remains the comedian's most underrated (and misinterpreted) performance.

In 1962, thirty-four-year-old Stanley Kubrick was being hailed as one of Hollywood's rising young directors. A former *Look* magazine photographer with a passion for chess, Kubrick had written and directed several low-budget, critically acclaimed films in the 1950s (*Fear and Desire, The Killing, Killer's Kiss*) before reaching the cinematic mainstream with *Spartacus* in 1960.

An independent spirit uncomfortable working within the studio system's strict hierarchy, Kubrick was well versed in Hollywood power politics, and knew he needed studio backing to finance his next project, an adaptation of Vladimir Nabokov's controversial novel *Lolita.*

Kubrick bought the *Lolita* screen rights for $150,000, and the $1.9 million film was underwritten by a group of Canadian investors who stipulated that shooting take place in England (much to Sellers's delight; he hated America) to hold down production costs.[1] MGM agreed to distribute the film.

Laced with black humor, *Lolita* documents the fall of Frenchman Humbert Humbert, a middle-aged literature professor obsessed with nymphets, or, in Humbert's vocabulary, "prepubescent girls poised on the verge of womanhood." Invited to teach in America, Humbert arrives in Ramsdale, New Hampshire, where he meets twelve-year-old Dolores "Lolita" Haze, the sultry daughter of boorish society gadfly Charlotte Haze.

Smitten with Lolita and hoping to initiate her into the joys of sex, Humbert's hopes are momentarily dashed when Charlotte sends her precocious daughter off to Camp Climax for a summer of supervised fun. Desperate to remain close to "Lo," Humbert swallows his pride, woos Charlotte, and marries "the Haze woman" (as he snidely refers to Charlotte in his diary). His gamble pays off when Charlotte is killed in a freak automobile accident, leaving Lolita in Humbert's care.

Humbert retrieves Lolita from Camp Climax and takes her on an automobile journey across America, fulfilling his sexual fantasies in cheap motel rooms yet hounded by the phantasmagorical figure of lecherous television playwright Clare Quilty, Lolita's secret lover.

Quilty "steals" Lolita from Humbert but eventually casts her off. A few years pass, and Lolita, now married, writes to Humbert for money. He visits Lo, gives her the money, and she tells him about Quilty. Humbert then drives to Quilty's mansion and murders the playwright.

Nabokov's novel generated a storm of controversy upon its publication in 1955, scaling the top of the best-seller list and transforming *Lolita* from a fictional character into a racy symbol of America's nascent sexual revolution. Nabokov's frank treatment of a taboo subject and his definitive freewheeling literary style were fodder for big-screen treatment. The feel-good Eisenhower Era precluded Hollywood from gambling on such a risky venture, but by 1962 John Kennedy had liberated the White House, and a more relaxed atmosphere pervaded the cinema (fueled, no doubt, by influential foreign films like Fellini's *La Dolce Vita*). Still, certain "morality" groups like the Legion of Decency exerted pressure upon MGM and Kubrick not to undertake the project.

Nabokov himself was at first reluctant to adapt his work to the screen. "It was perfectly all right for me to imagine a 12-year-old Lolita. She only existed in my head," he said. "But to make a 12-year-old girl play such a part in public would be sinful and immoral, and I will never consent to it."[2] When Kubrick offered him the opportunity to write the *Lolita* screenplay, however, Nabokov relented.

Kubrick and Nabokov collaborated on the screenplay and submitted a first draft to Hollywood's Production Code Board, which advised the writers not to specify Lolita's age or detail any explicit love scenes between Lolita and Humbert. The board approved the second *Lolita* draft.[3]

Who wrote what in the final *Lolita* screenplay remains a matter of speculation. *Lolita* Producer James B. Harris said he and Kubrick rewrote Nabokov's work. "On our arrival in London, we weren't satisfied with the lengthy screenplay that Nabokov had written," Harris said. "We shut ourselves in one room for a month and rewrote it scene by scene."[4]

Bowing to the enormous public pressure—and after a year-long talent search—Kubrick cast the fourteen-year-old television actress Sue Lyon in the crucial title role, a concession for which he would be roundly criticized upon the film's release. "The film ducks the duty of specifying Lolita's age and gives the part to a girl of 14 who looks around 17," *Time* complained. "Making her film debut, teenage Lyon is simply overmatched by the demands of her part."[5] "Sue Lyon," noted Brendan Gill in the *New Yorker*, "has the look of a young woman, not a child."[6] "Then there is the matter of Sue Lyon's age: she looks fourteen or fifteen, but the book says Lolita was twelve when Humbert first arrived at the Haze house," wrote *London Magazine*'s James Price. "Here again the film depends upon the likelihood of our having read the book."[7]

Distinguished British film star James Mason agreed to play Humbert (after Laurence Olivier and Noel Coward reportedly turned the part down), and Shelley Winters signed on as Charlotte Haze.

As for the enigmatic Clare Quilty, Kubrick knew of only one man for the job. Having established his Quiltylike chameleon persona, Peter Sellers was an interesting choice to tackle Quilty's wraithlike character. That Quilty dons various vocal disguises in haunting Humbert made the part more alluring for Sellers.

Kubrick was already impressed with Sellers's transformation into meek Mr. Martin in *The Battle of the Sexes* and must have envisioned the Sellers-Quilty connection when he happened upon *The Best of Sellers,* one of the many comedy albums Sellers waxed in the early 1960s. (Kubrick slyly took this connection a step further in *Lolita* by hanging Quilty's album cover in Lolita's bedroom. The cover bears a striking resemblance to Sellers's album covers of the period.)[8]

Sellers, as was his custom when offered a role he thought over his head, fretted over Quilty's apparent insignificance in the *Lolita* story line. Like Roy Boulting before him, Kubrick used his most persuasive arguments to talk Sellers into accepting the role. "Sellers at first sensed it was outside his experience, as Fred Kite had been, and grew nervous," wrote Alexander Walker. "Kubrick dined at his home three or four times, noting that Sellers' depressive states now probably outnumbered his manic ones."[9]

With Sellers's commitment safely in hand, Kubrick knew the comedian needed to "get" Quilty's voice before fleshing out the rest of the character and asked jazz impresario Norman Granz to record Quilty's dialogue. The tape then was given to Sellers for his vocal interpretation.

> In *Lolita,* Stanley wanted me to speak with a New York accent. He said, "Listen, a friend who's a jazz impresario, Norman Granz, has a really perfect sound." Sellers said. So he put this tape on, and it was hysterical. You heard a voice, speaking too loud, saying (in lisping Clare Quilty voice), "Hi there, Stanley, this is Norman. Jesus Christ, this is a whole script, for God's sakes. I mean, you really do ask for some strange things." Then you hear some rustling of paper, and he starts reading the *Lolita* script. And that's where Quilty came from.[10]

When he inked his *Lolita* contract, the workaholic Sellers had already made British radio history with the "Goon Show" and appeared in nineteen films within an eleven-year span. While Milligan's scripts and the "Goon Show" atmosphere fed Sellers's improvisatory hunger, the actor's impulsive creativity had yet to be fully harnessed on film. Vehicles like *The*

Naked Truth and *I'm All Right, Jack* were few and far between. *Lolita* would change all that and in one fell swoop alter the course of Sellers's career.

Stanley Kubrick had a reputation as an "actor's director" and a willingness to experiment that delighted Sellers. The two men would spend hours on the *Lolita* set shooting Quilty's scenes. Kubrick, impressed with Sellers's improvisations, kept several cameras trained on him for fear of missing an inspired moment.

> When Peter was called to the set he would usually arrive walking very slowly and staring morosely. I clear the crew from the stage and we would begin rehearsing. As the work progressed, he would begin to respond to something or other in the scene, his mood would visibly brighten and we would begin to have fun. Improvisational ideas began to click and the rehearsal started to feel good. On many of these occasions, I think, Peter reached what can only be described as a state of comic ecstasy.[11]

As for Sellers, he was equally impressed with Kubrick's directing methods. "I enjoyed working with Stanley Kubrick. He's somebody who's supposedly difficult," Sellers said. "Kubrick is the prime example of the bright, probing, talented director who will always say, 'I think we should do it this way, but does anyone have any suggestions? What do *you* think?' Others are not that intelligent."[12]

Nabokov's screenplay remained true to his novel with a few exceptions, most notably the addition of the German psychiatrist Dr. Zempf to Quilty's Humbert-baiting repertoire. Kubrick shifted Quilty's death scene from the book's epilogue to the film's prologue, thereby unfolding the *Lolita* narrative as a flashback.[13] This was yet another major departure for which Kubrick received mixed reviews. "The murder scene retains from the book its extraordinary mixture of sadism and painful comedy," said James Price.[14]

As did its literary predecessor, Nabokov's *Lolita* screenplay focused on the psychosexual relationship between Humbert and Lolita, with Quilty lurking on the periphery, shadowing Humbert's every move. Nabokov had written Quilty into his novel as a phantom figure, an overpowering yet fleeting presence whose physical characteristics aren't revealed until *Lolita*'s concluding scene.

Kubrick wasted no time in unmasking Quilty by shifting his death from end to beginning in a powerful scene between Sellers and Mason that establishes the film's melancholy tone.

Four years have passed since Humbert's arrival in Ramsdale when he drives to Quilty's baroque mansion, bent on revenge. Entering the house and circling the large inner room like a nervous cat stalking its prey, Humbert shouts for Quilty several times until the playwright, hidden corpselike under a sheet in a drunken stupor, replies fuzzily. (Quilty's first line of dialogue—"No I'm Spartacus, you come to free the slaves or something?"— is an inside joke, referring to Kubrick's 1960 film. The dialogue or imagery in Kubrick's opening shots often echo his previous work.[15])

Quilty emerges in his pajamas, the sheet wrapped togalike around his body, his slippered feet shuffling unsteadily toward Humbert. Not recognizing Humbert, he challenges his visitor (whom he alternately refers to as "Jack Brewster," "Captain" or "Mac") to a game of "Roman Ping-Pong like two civilized senators."

Humbert, donning his fingerprint-proof gloves, can only stare and listen in disbelief as the disheveled Quilty babbles about inhospitable guests, telephone calls, and the volley styles of different Ping-Pong champions. His voice quivering with hurt and rage, Humbert grills Quilty about Lolita, banging his paddle on the table to silence the depraved playwright. Sure, Quilty says, he remembers Lolita—"Maybe she made some telephone calls, who cares." This vapid recollection is all Humbert needs. He draws his gun, trains it on the nervous Quilty, and follows the condemned man, who's "just dying for a drink," as he shuffles toward his destiny into the next room.

The ensuing exchange between Sellers and Mason—in which Quilty reads and ridicules his death sentence, written by Humbert—is a typically bizarre Nabokovian scene that demonstrates the razor-thin line Sellers credibly straddles between *Lolita*'s low comedy and high drama. Sellers obviously improvised parts of the scene, adding bits of Goonish dialogue to Nabokov's scripted innuendo as Quilty, staring down the barrel of Humbert's pistol, brazenly ignores his fate.

Humbert: Quilty, I want you to concentrate—you're going to die. Try to understand what is happening to you.

Quilty: You are either Austrian or a German refugee. This is a gentile's house—you'd better run along.

Humbert: Think of what you did, Quilty, and think of what is happening to you now.

Quilty (in redneck accent): Hee-hee-hee . . . gee, that's a—that's a durling little gun you got there. That's a durling little thing. How much a guy like you want for a durling little gun like that?

Humbert (holds note out to Quilty): Read it!

Quilty: What's this, the deed to the ranch?

Humbert: It's your death sentence. Read it.

Quilty: I can't read, er, mister. Never did none of that there book learning, ya know.

Humbert: Read it, Quilty.

Quilty: Mmm? "Because you took advantage of a sinner. Because you took advantage. Because you took . . . Because you took advantage of my disadvantage." Gee, that's a dang-blasted durn good poem you done

there.... "When I stood Adam-Naked..." Adam-Naked, you should be ashamed of yourself, Captain. "Before a Federal Law and all its stinging stars." Tarnation, you old horned toad, that's a mighty pretty ... that's a pretty poem. "Because you took advantage"—gee, it's getting a bit repetitious, isn't it—"Because"—here's another one—"Because you cheated me. Because you took her at an age, when young lads..."
> *Humbert* (snatches paper from Quilty): That's enough!
> *Quilty:* Say, what you took it away for, mister? That was getting kind of smutty there! (staccato burst of laughter)

Sellers catches Quilty's sudden horror when Humbert fires his first shot, ripping through the boxing gloves Quilty has donned ("I wanna die like a champion!") and penetrating the playwright's alcohol-induced bravado ("Gee, right in the boxing glove ... you want to be more careful with that thing").

Quilty the hunter has become the hunted, frantically looking for an escape route as he slumps onto a piano bench.

> *Quilty* (nervously wiping his brow): Listen, Captain, why don't you stop trifling with life and death? I'm a playwright. You know, I know all about this sort of tragedy and comedy and fantasy and everything. I've got fifty-two successful scenarios to my credit, added to which my father's a policeman. Listen, you look like a music lover to me. (Turns to the piano, constantly looking over his shoulder at Humbert.) Why don't you let me play you a little thing I wrote last week? (starts playing Chopin's "Polonaise.") Nice sort of opening that, eh? We could dream up some lyrics, maybe. You and I ... dream them up together, you know, share in the profits. Do you think that'll make the hit parade? Uh, the moon was blue, and so are you and I tonight ... she's mine ... yours ... she's ... she's yours tonight....
> [Quilty picks up a glass, takes a drink, then smashes the glass and runs from the room. Humbert follows him calmly, takes aim, and fires, hitting Quilty as he runs up the stairs.]
> *Quilty* (grabbing his leg): Gee! Gee, that hurt me, that ... you really hurt me. Listen, if you're trying to scare me, you did a pretty good job already. My leg'll be black and blue tomorrow. (starts to drag himself up the stairs, grimacing in pain as Humbert reloads his gun.) You know how this house is ... roomy and cool ... you see how cool it is. (cries out in pain.) I intend moving to England or Florence forever ... You can move in ... I've got some nice friends, you know, who could come and keep you company here. You could use them as pieces of furniture.

Quilty drags himself to the top of the stairs and continues babbling as Humbert takes aim and fires his gun three times, killing Quilty through the watercolor portrait of a beautiful woman.

"Quilty goes bleeding up the stairs and the audience laughs to the bitter end," wrote James Price.[16] But there really isn't much laughter in Kubrick's 150-minute opus once Humbert's breathy voice-over narration

Quilty reads his death sentence.

segues into the film's thematic framework. *Lolita*'s pacing is labored and downright tortuous at times, and Nabokov's screenplay meanders in search of a connective thread. The film runs out of dramatic steam shortly after Humbert meets Lolita and Charlotte dies in the car accident. Strong performances from Mason, Lyon, and Winters keep *Lolita* from drowning altogether.

As Quilty, Sellers's surreal reappearance as "a lurking threat, a pursuing shadow, the spy of a society that hunts witches but whose own corruption surpasses that of its victims,"[17] jolted Nabokov's narrative from its lethargy: Quilty's forced encounter with Charlotte at Lolita's high school dance ("Didn't you have a daughter with a lovely name ... yeah, a lovely lyrical lilting name?"); the "normal" Southern cop smothering the nervous Humbert with innuendo at the hotel ("I wish I had a lovely pretty tall lovely little girl like that"); and Dr. Zempf, the Teutonic school board psychiatrist grilling Humbert about Lolita's "acute repression of the libido" and threatening to "investigate thoroughly the home situation."

Without Sellers's inspired characterization, *Lolita* would be nothing more than a slightly perverse love story. At the time, Kubrick was damned with faint praise for using Sellers to inject some "inspired foolery"[18] into the somber film.

Generally, though, the critics applauded Sellers. "Peter Sellers, as

Quilty ... rips off two freestyle impersonations which are the best thing he's done since *I'm All Right, Jack*," wrote *Esquire*'s Dwight McDonald. "They are frankly cadenzas which, as cadenzas do, interrupt the composition, or plot, but they are funny and what's wrong with a cadenza—or right with a plot?"[19] Sellers, said *Nation*'s Robert Hatch, "is given enough space to create a chilling sketch of the American operator crazed by his own know-how."[20]

"Peter Sellers is staggeringly accurate as the American Quilty and Quilty-as-a German," critic Stanley Kauffmann wrote in the *New Republic*. "In accent parts he still gives the feeling of a brilliant mimic rather than an actor: he always seems to be alone, like an entertainer, no matter how many others are with him; but he *is* brilliant."[21]

Time, noting "several wondrous Sellers disguises," said Sellers's "funniest camouflage is as a transplanted psychiatrist who knows all about 've Amerrikans' and can break the spine of the English language or rake the arms of a chair with his Teutonic ardor. Whenever Sellers leaves, the life of the picture exits with him."[22] *Newsweek*, however, thought that "Sellers and Miss Winters are too often caught doing imitations...."[23]

Notwithstanding its many faults, *Lolita* showcased Sellers's powerful screen presence. Under Kubrick's direction, Sellers transcended the stock comedic roles into which he was pigeonholed by the British film industry and delivered what would be the best performance of his thirty-year film career.

17

The Wrong Arm of the Law

Cast:

Pearly Gates	Peter Sellers
Nervous O'Toole	Bernard Cribbins
"Nosey" Parker	Lionel Jeffries
Val	Nanette Newman
Assistant Commissioner	John Le Mesurier
Superintendent Forest	Martin Boddey

STUDIO: Romulus
RELEASE DATE: March 14, 1963
RUNNING TIME: 94 minutes (black and white)

DIRECTED BY: Cliff Owen
PRODUCED BY: Aubery Baring and M. Smedley Aston
WRITTEN BY: John Warren and Len Heath
PHOTOGRAPHY: Ernest Steward
MUSIC: Richard Rodney Bennett

The Wrong Arm of the Law, released in 1963, marks Peter Sellers's last hurrah for the nationalistic British cinema. Four Sellers films had been released in 1962, the last of which, *The Dock Brief* (also known as *Trial and Error*), had Sellers playing a tired old barrister defending Milquetoast wife killer Richard Attenborough—and single-handedly blowing his client's case. Adapted from John Mortimer's radio and stage play, *The Dock Brief* was mildly successful but didn't stretch Sellers's talents to great extent.

"Sellers has the opportunity of showing many moods and much of his work is good," wrote *Variety.* "But there is a danger that he is being overexposed and some of the tricks are beginning to show up. He is in peril of giving a string of excellent imitations and impersonations rather than a sustained performance."[1]

But Sellers was still in high demand, and the offers poured in. Since his 1951 debut in *Penny Points to Paradise,* he had appeared in twelve films, all produced in Britain. Although *I'm All Right, Jack* poised Sellers on the cusp of international stardom, he was still reluctant to leave the safe confines of British cinema.

Sellers achieved instant celebrity after *The Pink Panther* premiered in January 1964. Unbeknownst to the comedian, however, *The Wrong Arm of the Law* would be his final "little man" film targeted specifically at his loyal British audience. Sellers couldn't have chosen a better vehicle with which to segue into the big time. *The Wrong Arm of the Law* provided him not only a Goonish plot and excellent supporting cast but the chance to polish a French accent later to be fractured by Inspector Jacques Clouseau.

The writing team of John Warren and Len Heath—also responsible for *Two-Way Stretch*—provided *The Wrong Arm of the Law*'s script and with it their penchant for colorful names, snappy dialogue, and racy British humor. Besides its script, the picture recalled *Two-Way Stretch* in its central casting, which reunited Sellers with Lionel Jeffries and Bernard Cribbins. All three reprised their *Two-Way Stretch* roles in everything but name.

Sellers obviously enjoyed dipping into his bottomless bag of voices to limn the Cockney criminal syndicate ringleader Pearly Gates, who doubles as "Monsieur Jules," the effete French owner of a posh London gown shop ("the old rag shop" as Pearly lovingly calls his front). Pearly slips through the law's fingers as much as he switches personalities, and he's proud of his booming enterprises.

But there's trouble in paradise. A gang of Australian crooks dressed as coppers are heisting booty from gangs all over London—it's the old "IPO" (impersonating police officers) caper! The Gates gang insist they're being victimized by the coppers, but Pearly thinks he's being double-crossed by his own men—some thanks for the way he's treated his boys! Doesn't he show them training and educational films like *Rififi* and *The Day They Robbed the Bank of England?* And don't they get four nights' holiday on the Costa Brava and free luncheon vouchers?

What Pearly doesn't know is that his sexy live-in girlfriend, Valerie (Nanette Newman), is on the Aussies' payroll. She's using Pearly's pillow talk to glean information about his gang's upcoming jobs.

Meanwhile, on the other side of town, Nervous O'Toole's men are singing the same IPO song. Nervous—he of the facial tic and fear of germs—shares London's crime on a rotating basis with Pearly. (The Gates gang works the city Monday thru Friday; the O'Toole gang, on weekends.) Nervous suspects Pearly's gang as the IPO mob and vice versa. When the two ringleaders hold a summit in the back of Nervous's car and plead ignorance to the caper, they realize they've got a serious problem on their larcenous hands.

It's time to convene a "special extraordinary meeting" of the syndicate, where it's decided to take the unprecedented step of enlisting Scotland Yard's help in nabbing the IPOs. Pearly, nominated as the syndicate's representative, approaches buffoonish Inspector Fred "Nosey" Parker (Jeffries), known more for his proboscis than his crime-solving acumen. Parker is the sort of sycophantic clod who succeeds in spite of himself. Aiding and abetting the likes of Pearly Gates is out of the question—that is, until Pearly paints the sweet picture of Parker's promotion to chief inspector once he nails the IPOs.

Pearly arranges to meet Parker, the assistant commissioner (John Le Mesurier), and Superintendent Forest (Martin Boddey) on a calliope at the Battersea Fun Fair, and there a deal is struck: Pearly will call off the troops for twenty-four hours, allowing London's finest to scour the city for the IPO mob's phony police car.

The plan fails, of course, because of Nosey's incompetence, but Pearly hashes another "can't miss" scheme: Why not stage a fake robbery complete with real cash to nab the IPOs? Scotland Yard agrees, but "loans" Nosey to Pearly as insurance the money will be safely returned. After explaining his plan to Nosey, Pearly opens a drawer and tosses "two hundred knicker" at Nosey, who immediately accuses Pearly of trying to bribe an officer of the law (as he does several times throughout the film).

"What are you talking about, bribe you—that's your expenses, boy, you're working for me now, you know," Pearly tells the disheartened Nosey. "The assistant commissioner said so. He sent me your insurance cards. You're on my payroll now."

In *The Dock Brief* (1962), Sellers played a washed-up barrister defending wife killer Richard Attenborough.

Bribe or no bribe, Nosey fingers the money greedily. "I say, a month's wages all in one go," he says, snorting with delight.

"Well, use it to set yourself up somewhere in some nice little drum," Pearly instructs his employee. "Get yourself kitted out with some decent clobber!"

Nosey certainly does live it up, dressing to the nines (in a tuxedo, no less) and renting rooms in a swank London high rise. It's there that Pearly brings Siggy Schmoltz (Tutte Lemkow), the renowned German crook imported to authenticate the robbery. Siggy's job is to cut through the police van so Pearly and Nosey can "steal" the money and be chased by the IPO mob. The plan calls for Pearly and Nosey to lead the IPOs into a trap of plainclothes coppers and "duff 'em up." But Pearly has other plans of his own—namely, a fueled airplane waiting to take him to parts unknown once he absconds with the money.

Leave it to Nosey to throw a wrench into Pearly's plans.

Pearly is alone with the briefcase full of money, ready to speed off for the airport, when in jumps the ever-suspicious Nosey to "keep an eye on" Pearly. But Pearly is stealing that money, Nosey and all, and as he speeds

Pearly, Siggy Schmoltz (Tutte Lemkow), and "Nosey" Parker argue about their "can't miss" plan.

toward the airport, Nosey, finally realizing what's happening, handcuffs himself to the briefcase.

Pearly doesn't miss a beat; he offers to cut Nosey in on the deal. "Two hundred fifty thousand pounds tax-free, boy, do you know what that would mean to you, Nosey . . . you'd be away from it all boy, your missus, her sister . . ."

"Her mother," Nosey interjects. "Right, step on it, the super's just behind us."

But unlike his cinematic cousin Dodger Lane—beaten at his own game by slippery fingers—Pearly actually escapes with the booty (still tethered to Nosey's wrist). And it doesn't much matter that Val is hidden aboard the airplane; she'll provide some entertainment for the dynamic threesome.

But back at Scotland Yard the assistant commissioner and Forest just can't understand it. Parker? After twenty-five years on the force? Well at least he won't be showing his face in these parts again, not after fleeing the country with the likes of Pearly Gates and all that loot.

Which is all fake, of course.

Cut to a remote desert island and a hastily painted sign: *Maison Jules.* Pearly, Monsieur Jules, is showing his latest line, "moderately priced at three bowls of raw fish or a dozen coconuts." It isn't exactly Maison Jules, but why complain? After all, the work is being done by Nosey, now reduced to working a foot-powered sewing machine.

But Nosey's grumbling doesn't sit well with Pearly, who explains his self-imposed labor laws. "Listen, mate, if you want a day off for the fertility rites, you'll have to get weavin.'"

Jeffries once again shines in his role as the comic buffoon, and his scenes with Sellers rank as the film's high points. In praising Jeffries's performance, *Newsweek* said: "Inspector Fred ("Nosey") Parker, who qualifies handily as the stupidest flatfoot on screen since Edgar Kennedy turned in his badge, couldn't catch a hangnail in a square mile of linsey-woolsey."[2]

Sellers, no doubt determined to match Jeffries's performance after the *Two-Way Stretch* debacle, is equally engaging.

Surrounded by familiar faces—including Graham Stark—Sellers appears relaxed and confident, strutting his campy sense of the absurd and getting lots of mileage out of Warren and Heath's farcical script.

"[Sellers] has been making, it seems a film a week, and he has never once been bad," *Newsweek* opined. "In *The Wrong Arm of the Law*, which is one of those unpretentious, machine-tooled British comedies, he absolutely shines."[3]

Brendan Gill of the *New Yorker* wrote that "*The Wrong Arm of the Law* is a good Peter Sellers picture, and high time too. As Pearly he's a tough Cockney, and as M. Jules he's an effeminate dandy, and it goes without saying that Mr. Sellers has a fine time darting back and forth between these two opposing natures."

With his British screen career now behind him, Sellers set his sights on America, navigating a collision course with director Blake Edwards and preparing for *The Pink Panther*.

18
Heavens Above!

Cast:

The Reverend John Smallwood	Peter Sellers
Lady Despard	Isabel Jeans
Archdeacon Aspinall	Cecil Parker
Matthew	Brock Peters
Harry Smith	Eric Sykes
Rene Smith	Irene Handl

STUDIO: British Lion/Charter
RELEASE DATE: May 21, 1963
RUNNING TIME: 118 minutes (black and white)
DIRECTED BY: John Boulting
PRODUCED BY: Roy Boulting
WRITTEN BY: Frank Harvey and John Boulting
PHOTOGRAPHY: Max Greene
MUSIC: Richard Rodney Bennett

Peter Sellers tackled more than fifty roles in his long career, only a handful of which touched upon aspects of his personal life. *Heavens Above!* was the first Sellers film to tear a page from the actor's past. In his portrayal of the kindly Reverend John Smallwood, Sellers didn't need to "get" the voice or agonize over how to play the character. All he needed was to draw upon his childhood school days.

Although money in the Sellers family was scarce in the 1930s, Peg insisted on private schooling for her spoiled son. That Peter was half Jewish didn't seem to bother Peg; she enrolled him in St. Aloysius College, run by an order of Roman Catholic teachers, when he was eleven years old. Young Peter wasn't the best of students and would say later that he felt out of place because of his Jewish background. But what he didn't realize at the time is that his close relationship with one teacher in particular, a Brother Cornelius, would pay handsome dividends later in his career.

> Sellers was standing in front of a mirror working up his characterization of a Church of England vicar for the Boulting Brothers comedy, *Heavens Above!* in 1963, when he suddenly realized that he had involuntarily copied the wise owl of a face, the spectacles, and the hair that was brushed stiffly up at the sides—his old teacher was staring back at him![1]

The script also arrived on Sellers's doorstep during one of the many "black" periods in his personal life. His father, Bill, was stricken by a heart attack and died in 1962 at the age of 62, leaving Sellers remorseful over his distant relationship with his father and concerned, fleetingly, about his own health. And his stormy eleven-year marriage to Anne had finally ended. Anne, it turned out, had fallen in love with (and later married) Ted Levy, a South African architect hired by Sellers to refurbish his home.

But *Heavens Above!* offered Sellers a temporary refuge from his disastrous personal life. Not only could he reminisce about his schoolboy days, but he'd be working again with the Boultings for the first time since *I'm All Right, Jack.* John Boulting would direct the film while Roy handled the producing chores. And like *Jack, Heavens Above!* was scripted by John Boulting and Frank Harvey, who this time chipped away the holy façade of the Church of England.

For all its pretensions, however, *Heavens Above!* didn't quite live up to expectations. It tried hitting too many targets and quite often missed, declining into a silly farce saved from obscurity only by Sellers's touching performance.

"If *Heavens Above!* were the only film the Boultings had ever made (brother Roy produces, brother John directs), it could be dismissed as pretty feeble farce on what sounds a promising subject for comedy," wrote Isabel Quigly in *The Spectator*. "But they have made other films you can't fail to take into account, better films that have established a Boulting image reflected, however dimly, in this one."[2]

The Boultings were obviously trying to duplicate *Jack*'s lampooning of the British labor movement, substituting the Church of England as the sacred cow ripe for desecration. But while *Jack*'s satire was subtly layered, *Heaven's Above!* pounded its audience over the head with a preachy mallet. Similarities in the Boultings' editing techniques and witty asides were prevalent, but that's where it all ended.

Sellers played the Reverend John Smallwood, an unorthodox prison chaplain mistakenly transferred to Orbiston Pava to become that town's vicar. It seems Orbiston Pava residents are more interested in rock and roll, the movies, and fornication than in churchgoing. The town's main industry is something called Tranquilax, the world's only sedative-stimulant-laxative. Tranquilax is owned by the Despard family whose matron, Lady Despard (Isabel Jeans), rules the town like a benevolent queen.

Smallwood has his work cut out for him, but he's invigorated by the challenge. He's not prepared, however, for the negative backlash he creates by naming the black trash man (Brock Peters) vicar's warden and telling his cynical congregation he's going to "reopen negotiations with the kingdom of God."

If that weren't bad enough, this loony parson even moves the filthy, flea-ridden Harry Smith family into the vicarage. The Smiths were evicted from their gypsylike trailer when Tranquilax decided to expand its operation. Now the Smith children, all twenty of them, urinate in the street and milk goats on the front lawn. Orbiston Pava is up in arms, and it's up to Lady Despard to talk some sense into the Reverend Smallwood. After all, didn't he return her generous contribution to the church organ fund?

But Smallwood will hear none of Lady Despard's suggestions, telling her in unflattering terms her money could be more charitably spent. In one of *Heaven Above!*'s forced contrivances, selfish Lady Despard suddenly changes her mind and offers to donate produce to the local merchants, who in turn will pass it to the hungry, free of charge. But when the merchants refuse Lady Despard's offer—citing a negative profit margin—she turns to Smallwood, who establishes a food distribution center in the church, to the consternation of the local shopkeepers.

Meanwhile the archdeacon (Cecil Parker), apprised of the "clerical error" that brought the wrong John Smallwood to Orbiston Pava, cooks up a scheme to have Smallwood declared mentally incompetent and the "other" John Smallwood (a bucktoothed Ian Carmichael) installed in his place.

But the plan goes awry when the "other" Smallwood accidentally talks with the psychiatrist. Not aware of the Orbiston Pava situation, the doctor declares Smallwood a paranoid schizophrenic when he angrily denounces the *other* Smallwood who mistakenly took his place. (The two Smallwoods, unaware of the other's name, actually meet face-to-face while waiting to see the psychiatrist.)

Back at the church, the Smiths—supposedly made "good" Christians by their baptism and Bible classes—are stealing the free food and selling it elsewhere. And Smallwood makes national headlines when he blasts Tranquilax from the pulpit, causing the company to lay off dozens of workers. The shopkeepers, already angry at Smallwood, close their shops in sympathy with the "redundant" Tranquilax workers, creating a demand for free food that Smallwood's church is not equipped to handle. To make matters worse for Smallwood, Lady Despard, acting on a "sign" from her late capitalist husband, stops the church's food shipment.

Smallwood is finally forced out of town by the angry mob. But he again makes headlines when the church, intent on keeping Smallwood out of sight, names him Bishop of Outer Space and assigns him to a remote North Atlantic island to bless rockets and comfort astronauts.

Harvey and Boulting's narrative should have ended here; the film's conflict has been neatly resolved and its thematic framework milked for intermittent laughs.

The Boultings were never known for their subtlety, but their sledgehammer approach on *Heavens Above!* quickly wears thin. So not only is Smallwood the first Bishop of Outer Space, he's the first Bishop *in* outer space when he mugs an astronaut, dons his space suit, and is launched into orbit singing church hymns.

Although it boasted a solid cast, including Eric Sykes and Irene Handl, *Heavens Above!* failed to generate much interest at the box office. The Boultings' satiric edge had dulled. John Smallwood was no Fred Kite, try as they might to make him so, and the Church of England certainly proved a trickier object of ridicule than Britain's labor movement.

Much of the film's satire was forced and in some cases downright sophomoric. Smallwood falls into an open grave on his way to a church meeting, proclaiming, "It's great practice for Judgment Day." Four vicars on their way to see the bishop are told, "The last supper is now being served." One of Lady Despard's dogs urinates on Smallwood's leg. A person waiting for food outside Smallwood's church surveys the huge crowd

Smallwood and Lady Despard (Isabel Jeans) give free food to the masses.

and proclaims, "Next thing, we'll have the blasted Jews queuing up." And so on.

Sellers, notwithstanding his own schizophrenic religious background, gave a low-keyed, buoyant performance, emphasizing Smallwood's zealous commitment to his holy cause. Smallwood could easily have evolved into an object of ridicule (shades of Fred Kite). Sellers, much to his credit, invested Smallwood with a noble bearing that withstood the sharpest arrows slung by Harvey and the Boultings.

Esquire, however, thought both the film and Sellers's performance laborious and unfunny. "As the labor leader [in *I'm All Right, Jack*], Sellers gave a subtle interpretation of an individual, but his clergyman is broadly played as a type. And a Sellers type at that; by now, he has spread his talent so thin in so many films that he seems unable to keep his characterizations separate. Furthermore, the satire is heavy-handed and illogical."[3]

19
The Pink Panther

Cast:

Inspector Jacques Clouseau	....	Peter Sellers
Sir Charles Litton	....	David Niven
Simone Clouseau	....	Capucine
Princess Dala	....	Claudia Cardinale
George Litton	....	Robert Wagner

STUDIO: United Artists
RELEASE DATE: January 9, 1964
RUNNING TIME: 113 minutes (Technirama)
DIRECTED BY: Blake Edwards
PRODUCED BY: Martin Jurow
WRITTEN BY: Blake Edwards and Maurice Richlin
PHOTOGRAPHY: Philip Lathrop
MUSIC: Henry Mancini

Next to his juggling of religions, clairvoyance played an increasingly larger role in Sellers's life as his career and accompanying insecurities grew. London psychic Maurice Woodruff was often consulted to chart the comedian's career path and advise Sellers on everything from his love life to "communication" with departed loved ones. But even Sellers couldn't have foreseen the circumstances surrounding his most famous role.

Blake Edwards, casting his newest comedy romp, *The Pink Panther*, wanted Peter Ustinov for the role of accident-prone Sûreté Inspector Jacques Clouseau. Ustinov agreed but later withdrew his offer, allegedly upset that Ava Gardner couldn't be coaxed into doing the film.[1] Ustinov was later slapped with a $175,000 breach-of-contract suit by the Mirisch Company, which charged that the film's production schedule had to be reorganized "at a considerable expense" to accommodate Edwards's second choice for Clouseau, Peter Sellers.[2]

Fresh from filming *The Wrong Arm of the Law*, Sellers was eager to escape his constricting British roles, and *The Pink Panther*, with its alluring international cast, lush Hollywood theme music, and exotic locales, strongly indicated worldwide box-office appeal. Not only would Sellers share the screen with established stars David Niven, Capucine, and Claudia Cardinale, but *The Pink Panther* promised some lighthearted fun before Sellers began work on his next project—Stanley Kubrick's "nightmare comedy" *Dr. Strangelove*.

Sellers was originally to appear as a cabdriver in Jules Dassin's *Topkapi* and was set to begin filming when a female acquaintance warned him about costar Maximillian Schell's alleged "unprofessional" behavior on the set. Sellers broached the subject to Dassin and consequently lost the role.[3] Ustinov, ironically, was later tapped by Dassin and won an Academy Award for his *Topkapi* role. For *The Pink Panther,* Sellers agreed to an offer of £90,000 for five weeks' work on location in Rome and Cortina.[4] But more than money, *The Pink Panther* afforded Sellers the chance to realize a long-standing ambition: performing slapstick on the big screen.

An ardent admirer of French screen clown Jacques Tati, Sellers had shown remarkable physical dexterity in earlier works like *tom thumb* and *Only Two Can Play.* But never was he given as free a slapstick rein as in *The Pink Panther,* and he found a welcome ally in Director Blake Edwards. Much to Sellers's delight, Edwards was a free-thinking director, receptive to ideas in much the same way Stanley Kubrick was during *Lolita*'s filming. Although Sellers and Edwards would embark on a fourteen-year love-hate relationship after wrapping *The Pink Panther,* their initial encounter proved nothing but friendly.

"For years I'd been getting bits of what I wanted into films, as writer or director ... but I had never had an area in which to exploit my ideas to the full," Edwards said. "Then along came Peter, a walking storehouse of madness, a ham with an almost surrealist approach to the insanity of things, and we found an immediate affinity.

"We talked about Clouseau, kidding him, ridiculing him, until he became a third person. As we kidded around with the character, the slapstick and the gags came naturally. Then we looked at each other and said, 'Let's do it'—just like that—and we did."[5]

Sellers reversed his usual modus operandi in "getting" the character of Clouseau. Since Clouseau's accent didn't pose any serious problems—it was a more refined version of Monsieur Jules from *The Wrong Arm of the Law*—Sellers literally clothed his interpretation of Clouseau from the outside in. While flying to Rome's Cinecitta Studios to begin filming *The Pink Panther,* Sellers began stitching together the fabric of Jacques Clouseau.

> Suddenly something came to me—Captain Webb matches. That's an old British brand of safety matches. On its package is a guy in a long, straight, striped, old-fashioned bathing costume, with a big stiff mustache standing out on his face. I thought that one of the things some Frenchmen have is this sort of ostentatious show of virility.
>
> So I think Clouseau will have a nice big mustache and I shall play him with great dignity because I feel that he thinks he is probably one of the greatest detectives in the world. From what I gather from the script, he is a complete idiot, but he would never want anyone else to know that.
>
> I suggest this to Blake Edwards when we meet at the Rome airport. I then tell him of an experience I had in Paris, where I saw a concierge who was very quick on the old uptake and handled Americans and all kinds of tourists

with aplomb. He'd say (in a Clouseau-like accent), "Yes, yes, sir, *I'll* tell
you what I am going to do." He was a fool who was shrewd around fools.
Blake loved that character.[6]

More than any other film in his career, *The Pink Panther* showcased
Sellers's impeccable comedic timing. Inspired by Edwards's inventiveness,
which turned every animate and inanimate object Clouseau encountered
into his nemesis, Sellers delivered a nearly flawless performance in an ab-
breviated role.

Although it seems improbable today in light of its four hugely successful sequels, Sellers wasn't the star of *The Pink Panther;* he took second
billing behind David Niven. But while his screen time was limited to a supporting role, Sellers dominated the *Panther*'s thin story line and stamped
his comedic trademark into the film's fabric. It was a performance that
would eventually ensure Sellers a place in cinematic history and leave
Niven, on the rebound after a string of second-rate pictures, somewhat
disappointed. "That first *Panther* really was supposed to be his picture, and
when they suddenly brought in Sellers instead of Ustinov he could see it
being taken away from him scene by scene," *Panther* costar Robert Wagner
said of Niven. "He just sat back and watched Sellers take it from him,
because he knew there was nothing he could do...."[7]

In contrast to later *Panther* films featuring progressively asinine plots,
Edwards's original 1963 version was rather simple in scope and ambition.
And unlike most of its successors, *The Pink Panther* narrative relates directly
to its namesake—a priceless pink diamond with a panther-shaped flaw running through its center.

The diamond, labeled the Pink Panther, is introduced in the film's
opening sequence as a gift to the Indian king of a mythical country. The
king shows the diamond to his daughter, young Princess Dala, to whom the
gem will someday belong. We're then introduced to the international *Panther* cast through a series of quick vignettes.

In Rome there's "the Phantom," who steals valuable gems before leaving his trademark white glove at the crime scene. In Hollywood, young
American George Litton (Wagner) poses for a phony college graduation
picture before being chased by two hoods. And in Paris, a disguised woman
hands the Phantom's gems to a fence before being chased by police.

That woman is Simone Clouseau (Capucine), none other than the
wife of Sûreté Inspector Jacques Clouseau. "We must find that woman!"
Clouseau snaps at his subordinate, putting his hand on a spinning globe
and falling flat on his face. "Yes, yes, what was that you said?" Clouseau
demands, springing up from the floor.

Although Sellers couldn't have known at the time, this first glimpse of

Clouseau would set the tone not only for *The Pink Panther* but also for the successive *Panther* films. Said Edwards:

> When we got on the set, we had a sequence introducing the inspector. He was saying "We must find that woman." Looking at it, I didn't see that we were incorporating any phyical humor and I felt that if we're going to do it, we'd better do it in the first scene. I saw a giant globe on the set, so I suggested Peter spin the globe at first. After he made the declaration, "We must find that woman," he would lean on the globe and it would fling him out of the frame. The die was cast. Peter is not really a physical comedian in the sense that Chaplin or Keaton were; he is not that kind of an acrobat and he is not trained that way. But he has a mind that thinks that way.[8]

Even before filming began, however, Sellers knew how he would introduce Clouseau to the world. "I'll play Clouseau with great dignity, because he thinks of himself as one of the world's best detectives," he said. "The original script makes him out to be a complete idiot. I think a forgivable vanity would humanize him and make him kind of touching. It's as if filmgoers are kept one fall ahead of him."[9]

Unable to find "that woman," Clouseau travels with Simone to the snowy mountains of Cortina where Princess Dala (Cardinale) is on a skiing holiday. So is international playboy Sir Charles Litton (Niven), an egotistical womanizer who doubles as the Phantom in his spare time. Unbeknownst to Clouseau, Litton and Simone are lovers, and they've hatched a scheme to snatch the Pink Panther from Princess Dala.

But their plan is thrown awry by George Litton, Sir Charles's long-lost American nephew who decides to drop in for an unexpected (and unexplained) visit. George takes a shine to Simone after she mistakenly jumps into his bed (thinking he is Charles). Simone must now hide her affair with Charles not only from Clouseau but from George. This sets the stage for several hackneyed "lover hiding under the bed" scenes cleverly staged by Edwards and deftly executed by Capucine, Niven, and Wagner.

The Pink Panther progresses slowly, and not much happens in the way of character or plot development; if nothing else, the film shows off the beautiful Cortina scenery. ("Has Skis, Needs Lift" is how *Time* described the film.[10])

After nearly seducing the "virgin" princess, Sir Charles sets his sights on the Panther diamond. But the gem isn't in Cortina; it's hidden in Princess Dala's safe back home. So naturally the princess decides to have a costume party in her home and invite the whole Cortina beautiful-people crowd. This gives Sir Charles his chance to steal the gem, but he has competition—from George, who has discovered Charles's secret and is himself eyeing the Pink Panther.

But first they have to get through Clouseau's crack armed guard.

Clouseau is disguised for the occasion in medieval armor, affording him the opportunity to flail about helplessly and accidentally ignite a huge fireworks display inside Princess Dala's house. Once the smoke clears, the Panther is discovered to be missing, and Charles and George are both arrested on suspicion of theft. Clouseau visits the men in their prison cell, and in the midst of gleefully savoring his apparent triumph, sticks his gloved fists into two bowls of porridge.

Perhaps the only surprise in the Edwards-Richlin screenplay is the way *The Pink Panther* ends—with Clouseau being carted off to jail after being framed for the robbery by Princess Dala. (Called to the witness stand at the Litton trial, Clouseau wipes his brow, only to find the Pink Panther dangling from the end of his handkerchief. Dala's "people" have claimed the jewel is rightfully theirs, and the princess herself "stole" the Pink Panther. She's talked into framing Clouseau by Simone, who is aware that Dala has a soft spot for Charles and wouldn't want to see him go to jail. Curiously, none of the four *Panther* sequels refer to Clouseau's imprisonment.)

Niven, Wagner, Capucine, and Cardinale breezed through their roles effortlessly, not having much to do in the way of acting. Edwards was obviously more interested in creating situations for Clouseau, and this he did with apparent relish. Clouseau casually leans on a piping-hot fireplace mantle, screams in agony, and thrusts his burned hand into a full beer stein. Making a conversational point, Clouseau thrusts his finger directly into the nostril of a man standing behind him. Walking into the lobby of his Cortina hotel, Clouseau trips and falls directly on Sir Charles's bruised leg.

Since *The Pink Panther* was ostensibly a bedroom farce, Clouseau predictably encounters rough times in the boudoir as well. Not only is he frustrated in his attempts to locate the Phantom, but his attempts to make love to his uninterested wife turn into a continuous adventure. With Simone waiting for him in bed, Clouseau wrestles with his bathrobe, finally pulling it down around his legs. Simone slides through Clouseau's legs as he tries to kiss her, leaving him with a mouthful of pillow. Simone sends Clouseau into the bathroom for sleeping pills; off-camera, we hear him spill the pills on the bathroom floor right before he walks back into the darkened bedroom and crushes his beloved Stradivarius. And the list goes on.

"The clumsiness was part of what Blake wanted him to be. Because of this dignity, Blake wanted him to be, shall we say, accident-prone," Sellers said. "That's why when something happens to him, he gets up from the floor and says to his assistant, who's been completely silent, 'What was that you said?' The assistant says, 'Nothing, sir.' And he can only say, 'Eh, yeah, I see.' That's how his mind works."[11]

Critically, *The Pink Panther* and Sellers received mixed reviews, although the film cleaned up at the box office. The film's detractors seemed more impressed with Henry Mancini's catchy score and the animated Pink

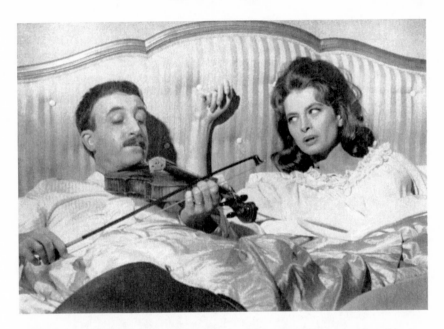

Clouseau relaxes in bed with his beloved Stradivarius, much to the consternation of wife Simone (Capucine).

Panther credits than with Sellers and company; others thought Sellers's performance added some much-needed depth to Edwards and Richlin's flimsily constructed narrative. "Seldom has any comedian seemed to work so persistently and hard at trying to be violently funny with weak material," wrote critic Bosley Crowther. "And the measure of it as humor is the way Mr. Sellers has to work to make it frenetically funny, which indeed, it occasionally is.... Here, for a while, Mr. Sellers makes his stupid detective quite a joke ... but the humor drains out of it, quickly."[12]

"As a twittery, accident-prone French detective, Sellers trips over carpets, steps into a Stradivarius, and pratfalls through love scenes with his wife," *Time* wrote. "Some of Sellers's sight gags are funny, but not funny enough to keep this over-waxed comedy from schussing steadily downhill at the recherche Italian ski resort where *Panther*'s high-priced actors search in vain for a lift."[13]

Newsweek wrote that "Director Blake Edwards is about as funny as the instruction on form 1040, and no matter how hard Sellers falls on his prat, there is little he can do to redeem this wearisome film."[14]

Arthur Knight, writing in *Saturday Review,* was more generous.

Most of the time the pace is headlong and hilarious, with each scene clipped short to stab right into the action of the next. In fact, apart from an interminable seduction scene that seems to have slipped in from another picture also starring David Niven and Claudia Cardinale, *The Pink Panther* is a happy concatenation of fresh dialogue and suave variations on old sight gags.... And Sellers never fails. His look of quiet reproach as a doorknob comes off in his hand, his polite fumblings with a particularly recalcitrant knot to a dressing gown while Capucine looks on cool and inviting in her bed, his superb aplomb despite every conceivable disaster become masterful understatements of materials that most comics have been overplaying since the birth of the movies."[15]

20
Dr. Strangelove

Cast:

Captain Lionel Mandrake/President Merkin Muffley/Dr. Strangelove	Peter Sellers
General Buck Turgidson	George C. Scott
General Jack D. Ripper	Sterling Hayden
Major King Kong	Slim Pickens
Ambassador de Sadesky	Peter Bull
Colonel Bat Guano ...	Keenan Wynn
Miss Foreign Affairs ..	Tracey Reed

STUDIO: Columbia
RELEASE DATE: January 30, 1964
RUNNING TIME: 93 minutes (black and white)
DIRECTED BY: Stanley Kubrick
PRODUCED BY: Victor Lyndon
WRITTEN BY: Stanley Kubrick, Terry Southern, and Peter George (from the novel *Two Hours to Doom* by Peter George)
PHOTOGRAPHY: Gilbert Taylor
MUSIC: Laurie Johnson

Sellers returned to England in 1963 to begin work on Stanley Kubrick's *Dr. Strangelove, or How I Learned to Stop Worrying and Love the Bomb*, one of the most provocative films in cinematic history.

Kubrick had been impressed with Sellers's work habits and creative receptiveness during the filming of *Lolita* and shortly thereafter offered

Sellers no less than four roles in *Dr. Strangelove,* still two years in the offing. Kubrick said:

> When you are inspired and professionally accomplished as Peter, the only limit to the importance of your work is your willingness to take chances. I believe Peter will take the most incredible chances with a characterization, and he is receptive to comic ideas most of his contemporaries would think unfunny and meaningless. This has, in my view, made his best work absolutely unique and important.[1]

Sellers later said Kubrick even offered him the role of General Buck Turgidson, eventually played by George C. Scott. "Some days Stanley would be sittin' outside my front door saying, 'What about Buck Schmuck? You've got to play Buck Schmuck.' And I'd say, 'I physically can't do it! I don't like the role anyway, Stan.'"[2] (Sellers was also slated to play redneck pilot Major King Kong. But after fretting about Kong's accent and how to limn the part, Sellers broke his ankle, and the role was given to Slim Pickens.)

Kubrick had purchased the rights to a dramatic novel, *Two Hours to Doom,* written by RAF officer Peter George, who published the novel in England under the pseudonym Peter Bryant. Released as *Red Alert* in America, the novel told the story of an insane American general, Quinten, suffering from a terminal disease, who orders an unprovoked nuclear attack on Russia. The president, trying to avert total nuclear annihilation, gets on the hotline to the Russian premier and offers to destroy Atlantic City to prove the attack the work of a lunatic.

But when Kubrick, George, and underground satirist Terry Southern began work on their adaptation of *Red Alert,* it soon became apparent that *Dr. Strangelove* had all the elements of a scathing black comedy. America was recovering from the failed Bay of Pigs invasion, tensions were mounting at the Berlin Wall, and cold war temperatures had reached the freezing point. Kubrick, George, and Southern decided to shift the tone of *Dr. Strangelove* drastically while retaining the narrative focus of George's starkly written novel, which underwent a transformation from the sublime to the ridiculous. The result was Kubrick's self-proclaimed "nightmare comedy" poking fun at the horrifying prospect of total nuclear destruction. "But after a month or so I began to realize that all the things I was throwing out were the things which were the most truthful," Kubrick said. "After all, what could be more absurd than the very idea of two mega-powers willing to wipe out all human life because of an accident, spiced up by political differences that will seem as meaningless to people in a hundred years from now as the theological conflicts of the Middle Ages appear to us today?"[3]

(Shortly after filming began on *Dr. Strangelove,* Max Youngstein's Entertainment Corporation of America announced plans to film a novel entitled *Fail-Safe*, written by political science professors Eugene Burdick [coauthor of *The Ugly American*] and Harvey Wheeler. *Fail-Safe* bore remarkable plot similarities to *Red Alert*, and when Kubrick learned of Youngstein's plans, he filed a lawsuit trying to stop the film's production. Wheeler filed a countersuit. Directed by Sidney Lumet and released in 1964, *Fail Safe* starred Henry Fonda, Walter Matthau, and Larry Hagman. Unlike *Dr. Strangelove*—to which it was inevitably compared—*Fail Safe* treated its subject matter in a deadly serious vein.)

As he did with *Lolita*, Kubrick chose to film *Dr. Strangelove* in England, this time at Shepperton Studios, to reduce production costs, although Sellers's fee alone had risen to the $1-million range (prompting Kubrick to joke he was getting "three for the price of six").

Kubrick established *Dr. Strangelove*'s irreverent, bawdy tone and omnipresent sexual imagery (no doubt inspired by Southern) in the film's opening montage, where bomber jets phallically refuel in midair to the strains of "Try a Little Tenderness." Meanwhile, down below, all hell is breaking loose on Burpelson Air Force Base. That's where macho cigar-chomping General Jack D. Ripper (Sterling Hayden), convinced of a Soviet plot to "sap and impurify all of our precious bodily fluids" through fluoridation, has ordered his thirty-four-plane bomb wing to attack Russia and drop its 1,400-megaton atomic payload on the primary target site at Laputa (near–Spanish for "whore").

One of the bombers under Ripper's command is piloted by Major "King" Kong (Pickens), who disdains Ripper's orders ("Well I've been to one World's Fair, a picnic and a rodeo and that's the stupidest thing I ever heard come over a set of earphones!"), but nonetheless dons his ten-gallon cowboy hat and tries to allay his men's fears.

> Well, boys, I reckon this is it. Nucular combat toe-to-toe with the Rooskies.... Look, boys, I ain't much of a ham at makin' speeches. But I got a pretty fair idea that somethin' doggone important's going on back there. And I got a fair idea the kind of personal emotions that some of you fellas may be thinkin'. Heck, I reckon you wouldn't even be human beins if you didn't have some pretty strong personal feelings about nucular combat. I want you to remember one thing: the folks back home is a countin' on ya' and by golly we ain't about to let 'em down! Tell ya' somethin' else; this thing turns out to be half as important as I figure it just might be, I'd say that you're all in line for some important promotions and personal citations when this thing's over with. That goes for ever last one of ya' regardless of your race, color or your creed. Now let's get this thing on the hump, we got some flyin' to do!

The bomber's theme song, "When Johnny Comes Marching Home," plays unremittingly whenever Kong and crew, including a young James Earl Jones, are onscreen.

**General Jack Ripper (Sterling Hayden) expounds on his theory of fluorida-
tion and "precious bodily fluids" while Captain Mandrake listens in horror.**

Ripper's plan is opposed by his second-in-command, RAF Group
Captain Lionel Mandrake (Sellers), who learns to his horror that Ripper
developed his fluoridation theory upon experiencing a "profound loss of
essence"—read impotence—during a strenuous bout of lovemaking. Mandrake's efforts to talk Ripper into issuing the bomb wing's recall code are
imperiled when the general pulls a gun and holds Mandrake hostage.

Not only has Ripper's demented plan brought the United States and
Russia to the brink of war, but it's interrupted the sexual exploits of General
Buck Turgidson (Scott), a crew-cut libidinous war hawk summoned from
a tryst with *Playboy* centerfold "Miss Foreign Affairs" (Tracey Reed) to the
Pentagon's "War Room" by President Merkin Muffley (Sellers), a balding
Adlai Stevenson type. Muffley has also invited Soviet Ambassador Alexei
de Sadesky (Peter Bull) into the War Room, much to Turgidson's disdain
("I don't know exactly how to put this, sir, but are you aware what a serious
breach of security that would be?! I mean, he'll see everything, he'll see the
Big Board!"). But Muffley is trying to help divert worldwide destruction
and needs de Sadesky to track down Russian Premier Dmitri Kissoff, himself engaged in a bit of drunken revelry ("You would never have found him
through his office, Mr. President. Our premier is a man of the people but
he is also a man, if you follow my meaning," de Sadesky explains).

While Muffley and Kissoff confer on the "hot line," Ripper and Mandrake are fighting off invading American forces sent from a nearby air force base to capture Ripper and get the recall code. When his "boys" at Burpelson surrender, Ripper, fearing he'll be tortured for the code, commits suicide.

Mandrake finds a notepad on which Ripper has repeatedly scribbled the phrases *Peace on Earth* and *Purity of Essence*—a twisted permutation of the recall code—and is about to phone the president when he's "captured" by Colonel Bat Guano (Keenan Wynn), a gung-ho gun-happy moron who suspects Mandrake of unsavory behavior. "I think you're some kind of deviated pervert," Guano figures, "and I think General Ripper found out about your perversion, and that you were organizing some kind of mutiny of perverts."

After finally convincing Guano that he needs to make the urgent pay-telephone call to Muffley, but lacking the necessary change, Mandrake goads the dimwitted colonel into shooting a Coca-Cola machine for its coinage ("Okay, I'm gonna get your money to ya'," Guano tells Mandrake. "But if you don't get the president of the United States on that phone, you know what's gonna happen to you? You're gonna have to answer to the Coca-Cola company").

Back in the War Room, de Sadesky breaks the news of the Russian-built "Doomsday Machine," a device designed to destroy all human and animal life on earth while enshrouding the planet in a ninety-three-year radioactive cloud should Russia be attacked in a nuclear war. The Doomsday Machine also is triggered to go off should any attempts be made to disengage the device.

President Muffley calls on his director of weapons research and development, the wheelchair-bound ex–Nazi, Dr. Strangelove (Sellers again), who confirms the Doomsday Machine's validity. Hidden behind sunglasses and burdened with a spring-loaded mechanical arm that has a life of its own, Strangelove dreams of life after the impending apocalypse, an underground bunker world in which there would be "ten females to each male"—chosen, of course, for their genetic superiority—and "little to do" save procreate.

Meanwhile, Kong's plane fails to respond to Mandrake's phoned-in recall code because of damaged equipment. Kong himself, trying to fix a faulty bomb-release mechanism, rides an atomic bomb into oblivion, straddling it, hollering like a rodeo cowboy atop a bucking bronco, and triggering the Doomsday Machine.

Before filming began, Sellers feared his *Strangelove* roles would be seen as a casting gimmick, a "Guinness" that would hinder his attempts to be taken seriously as an actor and detract from the film's underlying message. But under Kubrick's masterful direction, Sellers fashioned three brilliant performances, each distinctly different from the others. It was as if three different actors were playing each of Sellers's roles. Unfortunately, it was an artistic apex from which Sellers would descend shortly thereafter.

Mandrake—he of the mustachioed stiff upper lip—was Sellers's affectionate tribute to British military chivalry, the kind of good-old-boy officer he frequently impersonated during his days in the RAF ("Oh hell," Mandrake replies nonchalantly when Ripper informs him of the "shooting war" with the Russians). Mandrake also inspired a classic piece of improvised Sellers dialogue. Ordered by Ripper to help him fend off the invading army, Mandrake suddenly begs off, citing an old war injury.

> *Ripper:* Mandrake, come here.
> *Mandrake:* Are you calling me, Jack?
> *Ripper:* Come over here and help me with this belt.
> *Mandrake:* I, uh, I haven't had much experience, you know, with those machines, Jack, I only ever pressed a button in my old Spitfire....
> *Ripper:* Mandrake, in the name of the majesty and the Continental Congress, come here and feed me this belt, boy.
> *Mandrake:* Jack I'd love to come, but what's happened, you see, the string in my leg's gone.
> *Ripper:* The what?
> *Mandrake:* The string. I never told you but you see, got a gammy leg, oh dear, gone and shot off....

Mandrake's reaction while watching Ripper unwind to the point of manic incoherency was also a study in hilarity. While Ripper babbles about "precious bodily fluids" and "purity of essence," Mandrake, nervously and neatly folding a piece of paper, can't restrain a staccato burst of laughter. He's met the insane enemy face-to-face: General Ripper.

If Mandrake is the lone voice of reason, then Dr. Strangelove (who changed his name from Merkwuerdigichliebe when he became a citizen) is his Teutonic antithesis. With his Nazilike ardor ("Deterrence is the art of producing in the mind of the enemy, the *fear* to attack!") and mechanical arm involuntarily rising to a *sieg heil*, Sellers played Strangelove with a campy glee.

Although it was thought that Strangelove was loosely based on Henry Kissinger, both Kubrick and Sellers later dispelled this speculation. "Neither Peter nor I had ever seen Kissinger before the film was shot," Kubrick said. "It was an amazing coincidence.... Strangelove's accent was probably inspired by the physicist Edward Teller, who became known as the father of the H-bomb, though Teller's origins are Hungarian and his accent isn't really that close to what Peter did."[4]

Sellers provided a surprisingly mundane explanation of Strangelove's vocal origins.

On the set, we had a special stills guy called Weegee, who is now dead. He was very famous, and he took a lot of pictures for *Life* magazine in the old days. When all the hoods used to get riddled with bullets, he was always the first photographer there, and he'd get as good a shot as possible for the Mafia, and he got $25 from *Life*. He used to talk in a strange little voice like, "Hey, Peter, I really have an idea for a shot here." So I put a German accent on top of Weegee's.[5]

Sellers also provided some insight into the creation of the Strangelove character.

Strangelove was never modeled after Kissinger—that's a popular misconception. It was always Wernher Von Braun. But the one gloved hand that kept rising up to salute, well, the man *was* a Nazi. That idea just came to me—it was entirely spontaneous. And Stanley stopped everything and shot the gesture with three cameras. Before then nobody had seen it but him and, of course, it caused "falling bricks" afterward. There was all kind of stuff that we cut out, too. Strangelove started jerking off with the hand. We knew we'd have to take that out, but Stan said, "Aw, do it anyway."

(Apparently Sellers's Strangelove antics affected the cast. In the film's final scene, when Strangelove tries to keep his mechanical arm from rising, eventually whacking it back into place with his "good" arm, the scowling de Sadesky breaks into a fleeting smile. Kubrick either neglected to notice Peter Bull's understandable indiscretion or elected to retain the shot, fearing he couldn't recapture Sellers's inspired moment.)

But it was the role of Merkin Muffley that underscored Sellers's comedic range. While Mandrake and Strangelove were cartoonish inventions, Muffley called for Sellers to play it somewhat straight yet retain the film's blackly comedic overtones. Nowhere is this better illustrated than in the famous "phone call" sequence when a shaken Muffley calls Kissoff to inform him of Ripper's actions:

Well now, what happened is, one of our base commanders, he had a sort of, well he went a little funny in the head. You know, just a little *funny,* and he went and did a silly thing. Well, I'll tell you what he did. He ordered his planes to attack your country. Well let me finish, Dmitri. Let me finish, Dmitri. Well, listen, how do you think I feel about it? Can you imagine how I feel about it, Dmitri? Why do you think I'm calling you just to say hello? [Pause] Of course I like to speak to you, of course I like to say hello! Not now but any time, Dmitri. I'm just calling up to tell you something terrible has happened. It's a friendly call, of course it's a friendly call! Listen if it wasn't friendly, you probably wouldn't have even got it. They will not reach their targets for at least another hour. I am positive, Dmitri. Listen, I've been over all of this with your ambassador, it is not a trick. Well, I'll tell you. We'd like to give your air staff a complete rundown on the targets,

flight plans and defensive systems of the planes. Yes, I mean if we're unable to recall the planes, then I'd say that, well, we're just gonna have to help you destroy them, Dmitri. I know they're our boys. . . .
I'm sorry too, Dmitri. I'm very sorry. All right, you're sorrier than I am, but I am sorry as well. I am as sorry as you are, Dmitri. Don't say that you're more sorry than I am, because I'm capable of being just as sorry as you are. So we're both sorry, all right? All right.

(Sellers conceptualized Muffley as a spineless, sniveling wimp and originally armed the president with a nose inhaler and limp-wristed gestures. Kubrick disliked this interpretation and reshot Muffley's scenes, this time having Sellers play the president in a more self-assured manner.[6])

But while *Dr. Strangelove* rested squarely on Sellers's shoulders, members of the film's high-caliber supporting cast—particularly George C. Scott and Sterling Hayden—each carved out his own niche with a classic performance.

Scott's wild-eyed, depraved Turgidson was an unforgettable creation. Whether gleefully ranting about the Bomb's overkill potential ("I'm not saying we wouldn't get our hair mussed, but I do say no more than ten to twenty million killed, tops, depending on the breaks!") or anticipating a "mine shaft gap" between the United States and Russia, Turgidson was the epicenter of Kubrick's nightmarish vision—madness infecting every level of American society.

Scott's exaggerated facial and physical expressions were matched by his surprising comedic deftness, and he kept pace with Sellers in the War Room while stealing a few scenes from the film's star. Scott perfectly limned Turgidson's combination of childish whining, military pompousness, and jingoism while transforming the general into a cartoonish parody of military excess.

As Jack D. Ripper, the imposing Hayden cuttingly conveyed Kubrick's sentiments on the cold-war paranoia running rampant at the time of *Dr. Strangelove*'s release. With his mantra of "precious bodily fluids" and fluoridated obsessions of Soviet world domination, Ripper was yet another in *Strangelove*'s chorus of insanity.

> *Ripper:* Mandrake?
> *Mandrake:* Yes, Jack?
> *Ripper:* Have you ever seen a Commie drink a glass of water?
> *Mandrake:* Well, I can't say I have, Jack.
> *Ripper:* Vodka, that's what they drink, isn't it? Never water.
> *Mandrake:* Well, I believe that's what they drink, Jack.
> *Ripper:* On no account will a Commie ever drink water, and not without good reason.
> *Mandrake:* I, uh, can't quite see what you're getting at, Jack.
> *Ripper:* Water, that's what I'm getting at, water. Mandrake, water is the source of all life. Seven-tenths of this earth's surface is water. Why, do you

realize that seventy percent of you is water? And as human beings, you and I need fresh pure water to replenish our precious bodily fluids. Are you beginning to understand?

Mandrake (laughing in horror): Yes....

Ripper: Mandrake, have you ever wondered why I drink only distilled water or rainwater and only pure grain alcohol?

Mandrake: Well, it did occur to me, Jack, yes.

Ripper: Have you ever heard of a thing called fluoridation, fluoridation of water?

Mandrake: Yes I have heard of that, Jack.

Ripper: Know what it is? Do you realize that fluoridation is the most monstrously conceived and dangerous Communist plot we have ever had to face?

Although *Dr. Strangelove*'s now-familiar ending ("Mein Fuhrer, I can walk!") is a cinema classic, it wasn't how Kubrick originally intended to finish his film. The director shot an entirely different "pie fight" conclusion that if used would have completely altered the film's tone. Sellers explained:

> The pie fight started with the Russian ambassador photographing the Big Board again, and George Scott rushes over and chases the scared ambassador behind the buffet table. The Russian says, "You vill pay for dis!" And he picks up a large pie and goes to hurl it at George C. Scott. He ducks and it hits me, the president, full in the face.
>
> Scott says, "Gentlemen, our beloved president has been struck down in the prime of life by pie! We demand merciful retaliation." And of course the whole army, air force and navy hate each other anyway and they start on the ambassador first, and then they start on each other.
>
> Strangelove eventually turns out like—you know when you see a bug and you spray it until it's slimy and can't move? Well, just everybody pelted him until he couldn't get up. And he's trying to get back on his chair and the more he grabbed it the further it went away from him.
>
> In this sea of muck, cake and whatever-have-you, George Scott and the president are seen in a corner like little kids making mud pies. Their minds are gone. Suddenly, you see a heaving mess drag himself out and it's Strangelove. And he gets a gun and fires it in the air and says, "Gentlemen, gentlemen, don't you realize what will happen to us all in a moment? This pie is nonprotective! We must go down to the shelter as quickly as possible. Don't worry about showers, we have plenty down there. Through the mine shaft!"
>
> And as they all go out of the room you hear the song "We'll Meet Again."[7]

Kubrick decided not to use this ending because of its length (it took a week to shoot) and irrelevance to the rest of the *Dr. Strangelove* plot.

Not surprisingly, *Dr. Strangelove* generated a media frenzy upon its release in January 1964. Never before had such a foreboding topic been handled in such an unconventional manner, let alone discussed at all—the earnest approach of Stanley Kramer's *On the Beach* (1959) being one of Hollywood's exceptions.

"Sellers, playing three important roles, unerringly finds what's askew in a character and settles any vestige of doubt about his status as the screen's first comedian," *Time* wrote in its enthusiastic review. "But Sellers excels as Dr. Strangelove, a dehumanized German scientist employed by the U.S. Deadly alternatives don't faze Strangelove—his only problem is a wayward arm fed by such lethal impulses that it sometimes tries to strangle its owner, or springs out from his withered body in a Nazi *heil.*"[8]

"The film's images of a world divided against itself create similar feeling [*sic*] of discord in the audience, so that even the splitting of Peter Sellers's personality into three, and of Dr. Strangelove's further sub-division (one half of his personality trying desperately to prevent his metal arm from jerking to the Nazi salute) becomes normal and acceptable," James Price wrote in *The London Magazine.* "And instead of referring us to a standard of normalcy, as another film-maker might have done, Kubrick refers us to a standard of madness: Strangelove himself, madness personified."[9]

The *New Statesman*'s John Coleman praised Kubrick's "mesmeric" film for its script and performances by Scott, Wynn, and Hayden. "And Sellers—what about his *three* performances? Pleasantly, the playing around him is rich enough for once to assimilate his genius," Coleman wrote. "I can't feel, apart from its box-office power, that it was a particularly good idea to have him trebling up: it makes for attentiveness in the wrong direction when he's ostensibly talking to himself (President Muffley to Dr. Strangelove, his nuclear expert) and that's a pity. But he does his stints with, by now, predictable brilliance—a meek, worried leader of men, fussily placating Kissov [*sic*] over the hot line; the sinister German doctor, with a black-gloved hand forever struggling up into Nazi salutes and clutchings, leading a life of its own (the broadest of his roles, but the film gets broader as it rushes to a close); the lovingly complex embodiment of an English officer and gentleman, a bit cracked himself, reining in a tendency to a scream at the society he's lumbered with."[10]

But whatever the final critical verdict, Hollywood deemed Sellers's three performances suitable enough to warrant Oscar consideration. He was nominated for best actor, and Kubrick was nominated for best director. The film itself received nominations for best picture and best script. Although *My Fair Lady* swept the 1964 Academy Awards, with Sellers beaten out by Rex Harrison and Kubrick by George Cukor, there was no doubt Sellers had reached the apex of his career.

21
The World of Henry Orient

Cast:

Valerie Boyd	....	Tippy Walker
Marian Gilbert	......	Merrie Spaeth
Henry Orient	....	Peter Sellers
Mrs. Dunworthy	.....	Paula Prentiss
Isadore Boyd	....	Angela Lansbury
Frank Boyd	....	Tom Bosley

STUDIO: United Artists
RELEASE DATE: March 20, 1964
RUNNING TIME: 106 minutes (Panavision/ De
  Luxe)
DIRECTED BY: George Roy Hill
PRODUCED BY: Jerome Hellman
WRITTEN BY: Nora and Nunally Johnson
  (from a novel by Nora Johnson)
PHOTOGRAPHY: Boris Kaufman, Arthur J.
  Ornitz
MUSIC: Elmer Bernstein

After wrapping *Dr. Strangelove* in mid-1963, Sellers made a rare foray into America to film what amounted to an extended comedic cameo in *The World of Henry Orient*. Helmed by the young director George Roy Hill (who would later direct *The Sting*), *Henry Orient* remains one of Sellers's least-known roles. And for good reason: Although he received top billing, Sellers clearly was upstaged by teenage costars Merri Spaeth and Tippy Walker.

In fact, Sellers's *Henry Orient* screen time was limited to incidental reappearances; much like *Lolita*'s Quilty, Sellers's Henry Orient served as the narrative core around which screenwriter Nora Johnson and her father, Nunally Johnson, constructed their quirky lighthearted tale.

But while Kubrick and Sellers were able to integrate Quilty's enigmatic personality into *Lolita*'s thematic structure, the Johnsons' screenplay didn't. afford Sellers and Hill such a luxury. As the *Henry Orient* story line progresses—and grows more disjointed—the character of Henry Orient becomes superfluous to the film's message. It's almost as if Sellers were acting in a completely different film, and his tired mugging was largely ignored in the wake of the film's disappointing box-office performance.

Walker and Spaeth were the real stars of *Orient*, and both girls were delightful to watch in their first big-screen appearances. Their roles as Marian and Val bore a close resemblance to their off-screen lives.

Elizabeth Tipton "Tippy" Walker, the daughter of a Rye, New York, businessman, was seventeen during the filming of *Henry Orient*. An adoring

Beatles fan with a particularly soft spot for John Lennon, she attended the prestigious Masters School in nearby Dobbs Ferry and had just landed a modeling job in Manhattan when she was spied by Producer Jerome Hellman. A natural blond, Tippy dyed her hair brown for the film.

Lisping fifteen-year-old Merrie Spaeth, the blond daughter of a Philadelphia ophthalmologist, was recommended to Pan Arts by a teacher at the posh Germantown Friends School.[1]

The girls played Valerie Boyd and Marian Gilbert, eighth-grade students attending a swank Manhattan girls school. The girls, both new students without many friends, meet one windy afternoon and quickly become inseparable, plunging into a fantasy world of secret languages and imagined "lost loves" played out against the exciting backdrop of New York City.

The world is Val and Marian's oyster, as it can be only for two bright, mischievous fourteen-year-olds. But more than their everyday pursuits, the girls find a common bond in their disappointing home lives. Val's jet-setting parents see their daughter only on holidays. Their absence has created a huge void in Val's life, which she's filled with terrific flights of fancy. Feeling ignored, she's bounced from school to school and been labeled an "unmanageable" discipline problem. Visits to a psychiatrist—at her parents' insistence—don't seem to help matters. Marian, whose parents are divorced, lives with her mother (Phyllis Thaxter) and "Boothie" (Bibi Osterwald), a family friend and divorcée.

But the girls' attentions are diverted to more important pursuits one blustery fall day when they go "adventuring" in Central Park. Pretending to be two "beautiful white nurses" about to be "ravaged" by the natives, Marian and Val stumble upon a man and woman necking under a tree. The man, speaking in a soft Italian accent, is about to make his move when up pop the bubble gum-chewing girls, staring impishly at the couple before scampering away.

Cut to a barber shop where that same man is describing the scene in the park. "And then two small bladders came out of their mouths, and just when she was beginning to hum, too," he says in flat Brooklynese. The man is none other than avant-garde pianist Henry Orient, a vain Don Juan as phony as his affected accent. The "she" to whom he refers is a certain Mrs. Dunworthy (Prentiss), a married woman forever paranoid her husband will discover her unconsummated trysts with Orient.

As if trying to bed the uncooperative Mrs. Dunworthy wasn't enough, Orient soon has to contend with Val and Marian, who seem to be following his every move around New York. At first it's only a coincidence when Val knocks Orient flat on his back outside a restaurant. But when Val and Marian attend Orient's Carnegie Hall concert and realize the "man with the piercing eyes" and Orient are one and the same, they become obsessed with

Avant-garde concert pianist Henry Orient is hassled in Central Park by thrill-seeking teenagers Valerie (Tippy Walker) *(left)* and pigtailed Marian (Merrie Spaeth).

the pianist. Even if he does need "practice on his scales," according to Val.

Val—seeking the love she doesn't get from her parents—immediately decides she's in love with Orient, and with Marian's encouragement weaves an elaborate fantasy world around her "dreamy dream of dreams." She compiles a Henry Orient scrapbook, complete with Orient's "first love letter" to her, and buys his two record albums. As would any lover, Val even maps out Orient's daily routine, complete with his wake-up time and food preferences.

Soon the girls are even calling Orient on the telephone (hanging up, of course) and keeping a vigil in front of his apartment building. And they aren't making Orient's love life any easier. Mrs. Dunworthy thinks the girls are spies hired by her husband, and their shenanigans, including a detailed ruse involving the New York Police Department, throw the cowardly Orient into fits of hysterics over the dreaded Mr. Dunworthy.

Henry Orient's fun mood takes a turn for the worse, however, with the introduction of Val's parents into the story line. Up to this point, the Johnsons' screenplay neatly ties together *Henry Orient*'s loose ends of comedy and sentimentality. But the film sinks heavily into maudlin waters when Isadore and Frank Boyd visit New York for the Christmas holidays.

The bickering Boyds are an obviously unhappy couple. While Frank (Tom Bosley) seems to be a decent sort, Isadore (Angela Lansbury) is an insatiable, selfish flirt, virtually ignoring her daughter in pursuit of her next romantic conquest. Soon after the Boyds whisk Val from her town house into their suite of hotel rooms, Val discovers her mother's affair with a young gentleman friend (pianist Peter Duchin). Isadore, angry at Val and seeking a measure of revenge, discovers the Henry Orient scrapbook and punishes her daughter.

In an extended sequence that takes too much time, Val runs away to Marian's house; meanwhile, Isadore phones Orient, demanding to know if he's been dating her daughter. They meet in a restaurant, and Orient— after wooing Isadore by telling her she's the "perfect" Renoir, "all golden"— takes her back to his apartment. Unbeknownst to Isadore, Val and Marian have finally decided to confront Orient face-to-face. But hardly have they entered his building when out walks Isadore from Orient's apartment. Val is crushed by her mother's tryst with Orient, but everything ends happily when Frank decides to divorce Isadore, give up his traveling, and get a "real home" for him and Val.

While Sellers's role was limited to forced frivolity (especially in the Carnegie Hall sequence), the comedian was living a Henry Orient–like existence off the set. One incident in particular illustrated both his being "taken over" by his on-screen persona and his neurotic, bizarre mental state.

Sellers had received a fan letter from a female admirer and invited the young woman to New York during the filming. Sellers drove to the airport with his secretary, Hattie Stevenson, and chauffeur, Bert Mortimer, and hid out of sight so he could inspect the girl when she stepped off the plane. Imagining a romantic interlude, Sellers was aghast when the woman turned out to be obese. But he arranged for her to have a room in the Plaza Hotel (the same hotel in which Sellers was staying) and promised her over the telephone he would meet her when she had sufficiently slimmed down. After three weeks and a crash diet, the woman had lost thirty pounds, was presented with an impressive engagement ring, and received a marriage proposition from Sellers. Sellers eventually grew bored with the game, and the woman was sent packing.[2]

In contrast to Sellers's erratic behavior both on and off the screen, Walker and Spaeth were the pictures of wholesomeness and the only bright spots in *Henry Orient*. Both girls were absolutely believable and delivered effortless, buoyant performances, managing to rise above the Johnsons' inconsistent screenplay and Hill's choppy direction. One could imagine them in real life doing all the girlish things they did in *Henry Orient*: jumping over fire hydrants, pretending to be ultrasophisticated, and engulfing themselves in an impenetrable fantasy world to ward off life's inequities.

"What makes the film about 10 times better than it sounds is its cast," wrote the *Spectator*'s Isabel Quigly. "I never expected to see Sellers acted off the screen, and by a pair of unknown fourteen-year-olds at that; but he is and it's they who carry the film—at least its socio-sentimental two-thirds."[3]

Bosley Crowther wrote in the *New York Times* that Walker and Spaeth were "full of gloriously fresh vitality. They are full of school-girl eccentricities, urges to romanticize and fabricate fanciful dream worlds into which they can happily roam."[4]

The *New Republic* critic Stanley Kauffman thought Sellers played Orient with "uncanny accuracy" but complained that Val and Marian's adventures "are maimed by lushness and sentimentality elsewhere. The home of the one girl who has a home is so magazine-perfect, the mother is so patently out of soapopera and her wisecracking companion out of Moss Hart, the bandleader Peter Duchin is miscast with such feeble cleverness as a lover, the whole is dragged on so long and spread so wide to make a 'major' production, that the small spell which this film might have cast is denied it."[5]

"Sellers whoops it up in fine style, kidding the role with an accent that comes and goes and with a broad burlesque of the temperamental man and his amorous affairs," wrote *Commonweal*'s Philip T. Hartung. "The girls are the show and they're simply wonderful."[6]

The *New Yorker*'s Brendan Gill, citing Hill's "debonair" direction, wrote that "the giggly girls are played full tilt by Tippy Walker and Merrie Spaeth ... and Henry Orient is played by Peter Sellers, who, though he often appears to have his mind on other things, runs through a couple of genuinely comic scenes with Paula Prentiss...."[7]

22
A Shot in the Dark

Cast:

Inspector Jacques Clouseau	Peter Sellers
Maria Gambrelli	Elke Sommer
Chief Inspector Drey-fus	Herbert Lom

Benjamin Ballon ..... George Sanders
Hercule .... Graham Stark
Cato .... Burt Kwouk

STUDIO: United Artists
RELEASE DATE: June 24, 1964
RUNNING TIME: 101 minutes (Panavision/De
  Luxe)
DIRECTED BY: Blake Edwards
PRODUCED BY: Blake Edwards
WRITTEN BY: Blake Edwards and William
  Peter Blatty
PHOTOGRAPHY: Christopher Challis
MUSIC: Henry Mancini

After completing *The Pink Panther*, Edwards thought he had seen the last of Peter Sellers. But Edwards was still under contract to the Mirisches, and when preproduction problems arose on their next vehicle, *A Shot in the Dark*, the brothers asked Edwards to replace Director Anatole Litvak. Edwards agreed to do so only with "drastic revision." As shooting approached, he decided to tailor the picture to feature Clouseau.

"If they wanted me to save them, I'd have to take something with which I was familiar to begin with," Edwards said. "I needed a detective."[1] So Edwards contacted Sellers, who enthusiastically agreed to reprise his bumbling detective.

A Shot in the Dark began shooting in London near the end of 1963 and was released only a few months after *The Pink Panther* premiered in Britain. It became the year's fourth-highest-grossing film in Britain.

Notwithstanding Sellers, *A Shot in the Dark* bore little resemblance to its forebear. Not only were David Niven, Capucine, and Claudia Cardinale noticeably absent, replaced by Sellers pals Graham Stark and David Lodge, but the sterility of a London studio now replaced the exotic locations that were featured so prominently in *The Pink Panther*.

Even *The Pink Panther*'s namesake was absent from Edwards's script, cowritten by William Peter Blatty (future author of *The Exorcist*). *A Shot in the Dark*'s plot, loosely based on the stage plays of Harry Kurnitz and Marcel Achard, revolved around a murder, not a stolen gem, and all vestiges of *The Pink Panther* were erased. Married in the first film, Clouseau made no mention of his wife and now lived in a bachelor apartment. Nor was the jail sentence he received at the end of *The Pink Panther* mentioned by Clouseau or anyone else.

Sellers also altered Clouseau's French accent, so proper in *The Pink Panther* but starting its improbable rollercoaster ride around the English language in *A Shot in the Dark*. Said Sellers:

It's not pure French, because you have to be careful with the French accent, apart from Maurice Chevalier's. I wanted to get some other sound. You'll find, if you look at the original *Panther,* that the sound changed for *A Shot in the Dark,* and he started to say a word like "bump" in a pursed way, similar to speech patterns based on the actual French language.[2]

But while *A Shot in the Dark* took a chance by deviating from a proven formula, it also introduced Herbert Lom and Burt Kwouk, who would stamp their indelible images into the series and become an integral part of its success. Lom, who had starred with Sellers a decade earlier in *The Ladykillers* and more recently in *Mr. Topaze,* was recruited to play Chief Inspector Charles Dreyfus, he of the nervous tic and pathological hatred of Clouseau. Dreyfus was a key figure in *A Shot in the Dark,* and his character would grow progressively madder with each *Panther* installment. (Although he couldn't at the time have foreseen the *Panther* series's future plot contrivances, Edwards eerily forecast the *Revenge of the Pink Panther* plot when he had Dreyfus tell his assistant, "Give me ten men like Clouseau and I could destroy the world!")

Not only did Lom provide comic buffoonery nearly on a par with Clouseau, but like Sellers's, his timing was immaculate. Whether Dreyfus was quietly slicing off his thumb with a guillotine-shaped cigar cutter, stabbing himself with a letter opener, or twitching uncontrollably, Lom was hilarious as an otherwise normal man driven to the point of insanity by Clouseau's very existence.

A Shot in the Dark provided the first glimpse of Clouseau's domestic life, which proved as catastrophic and strange as the logic Clouseau used to conduct his investigation of the Ballon murders. Chief among Clouseau's bizarre antics were his ongoing karate fights with Cato, his oriental manservant, played by Burt Kwouk. Trained by Clouseau in the element of surprise, Cato sprang from behind doors, from the top of Clouseau's canopy bed, and even as Clouseau bathed in the tub. Although Kwouk had very little dialogue in *A Shot in the Dark*—his role was subsequently enlarged—he was one of the film's more memorable characters.

Also deserving of special mention is Graham Stark, who deadpanned his way through *A Shot in the Dark* as Hercule, Clouseau's bemused assistant. Obviously sharper than his blustery boss, Hercule is forced to suffer Clouseau's foolhardy theories. Stark helped to brighten Sellers's mood on the set, and the longtime friends engaged in some inspired improvisation during a watch-synchronizing scene between Clouseau and Hercule, a scene that found its way into Edwards's completed film.

"Blake Edwards said to me, 'Now, Graham, you turn to Peter and both of you synchronize your watches,'" Stark explained. "Then he added, 'By the way, how exactly do you synchronize watches?' The ensuing sequence wasn't even rehearsed: it was totally ad-libbed, Peter and I

Cato (Burt Kwouk) strikes again as Clouseau packs for the Foreign Legion.

knew each other so well. Blake supplied the inspiration, Sellers the performance."[3]

But the fun mood on the set soon turned sour. Sellers and Edwards, who had gotten along famously during *The Pink Panther,* began to bicker. Both men were headstrong perfectionists whose egos clashed repeatedly. In an interview published after Sellers's death, Edwards explained the inherent difficulties many directors faced when working with the temperamental Sellers.

We came right back with *A Shot in the Dark,* and things were fine for the first half of filming, but then the shit hit the fan. Sellers became a monster. He just got bored with the part and became angry, sullen and unprofessional. He wouldn't show up for work and he began looking for anyone and everyone to blame, never for a moment stopping to see whether or not he should himself . . . for his own madness, his own craziness. He worried about everything. There wasn't a movie Sellers made . . . that he didn't think was a total disaster by the time it was finished. He'd want to buy it and chuck it out.[4]

If Sellers was bored, it certainly didn't show in his performance. *A Shot in the Dark* afforded him the opportunity to expand Clouseau's character and slapstick range, and Sellers tackled his assignment at full throttle. (Ironically, it also gave him the chance to work with George Sanders, whose throaty voice had been Sellers's inspiration for the "Goon Show's" Hercules Grytpype-Thynne.)

Edwards and Sellers established the film's tone—and the imaginative pratfalls awaiting the unsuspecting Clouseau—almost immediately when Clouseau is sent to investigate a murder at the home of millionaire Benjamin Ballon (George Sanders). Arriving at the Ballon residence, Clouseau steps out of his car and falls directly into a fountain in front of his resigned assistant. And it's all downhill from there. Sloshing around inside Ballon's mansion, the unflappable Clouseau begins his investigation by inspecting the murder weapon, a small pistol, with a pen ("my own personal pistol pen"), then splattering ink on Henri, the head butler.

Taken aback with the beauty of Maria Gambrelli (Elke Sommer), the curvaceous chambermaid accused of shooting her Spanish lover, Clouseau absentmindedly sniffs a jar of cold cream, which leaves a white glob on the end of his nose, then begins questioning Maria. "There is still something here I do not quite understand," he says pensively, suavely sticking the pen in his mouth and sucking out the ink. Maria, feeling Clouseau's wet clothes, tells him he should change or he might catch pneumonia. "Yes, I probably will," he says stoically. "But it's all part of life's rich pageant, you know."

Offering Maria a cigarette, Clouseau puts his lighter, still aflame, back into his trench coat. "Goodness, it's a bit stuffy in here," he says. Maria notices his smoking trench coat, and Clouseau, in a panic, rips his coat off and rushes to the open window. In barges Commissioner Dreyfus, who flings open the door and knocks Clouseau out of the window and down to the gravel driveway below.

Clouseau is not hurt. A cartoonish character, he is able to withstand any physical calamity and emerge unscarred. And *A Shot in the Dark* certainly presented Clouseau with a plethora of sticky situations. Retrieving Maria's dossier from his filing cabinet, Clouseau rips his pants. Maria, grabbing Clouseau's arm, rips the sleeve off his jacket. Clouseau's hand

Clouseau arrives at the mansion of millionaire Benjamin Ballon (George Sanders) to investigate the murder.

gets painfully jammed in a spinning globe. Playing billiards with Ballon, Clouseau rips a hole through the table's felt surface, then engages in hand-to-hand combat with a rack of cue sticks. Clouseau and Maria, escaping naked from a nudist colony, get stuck in a downtown Paris traffic jam and are surrounded by gawking pedestrians.

What ensured the film's success and provided its comedy wasn't its flimsy plot but the predicaments in which Clouseau became entangled. Sellers's genius in the early *Panther* films was in limning Clouseau as a complete fool to everyone but himself. No matter how dire or ridiculous the situation, Clouseau always insists he "planned it" that way.

A Shot in the Dark perfectly illustrates this in its penultimate scene, a parody of the standard whodunit genre in which the "brilliant" detective unmasks the "real" killer. Clouseau has gathered the entire Ballon household into the drawing room while Hercule waits in the basement, ready to extinguish the lights to allow Clouseau time to "make his move," whatever that may be (we never find out). Explaining his long-winded theory about the killer, Clouseau manages to wreak havoc on everything and everyone in the room: He falls backward through a set of closed doors, tramples on the women's feet, knocks heads with Ballon, topples a coffee table, and almost gets into a karate fight with Henri. About to name the killer, Clouseau leans back on a sofa—and falls off.

"What happened?" he asks confusedly, springing to his feet. "You fell off the sofa, you stupid fool," Madame Ballon (Tracy Reed) says. "I know I fell off the sofa, madame, there's no need to tell me! Everything I do is carefully planned, madame, I know that."

Through all these clumsy maneuvers, Clouseau puts on the airs of a man with a mission, a man with a method to his madness.

"With an output of comic invention that goes far beyond the matter or the style of the comparatively sophisticated trifle that was played here on the stage three years ago, Blake Edwards and William Peter Blatty have fashioned an out-and-out farce that puts no tax at all on the mentality but just plunges from gag to gag," Bosley Crowther wrote in the *New York Times*. "And they have got Mr. Sellers to plunge with it in the joyously free and facile way that he has so carefully developed as his own special comedy technique."[5]

Saturday Review's Hollis Alpert, not wholly impressed with Edwards's film or Sellers's performance, wrote that "the laughs are fairly constant, but unfortunately Edwards now and then remembers that play he has adapted and things tend to bog down."[6]

The *New Yorker* wrote that Sellers "has a trace of Chaplin's appeal, a touch of the grand fakery of W. C. Fields, and yet he is somehow *sui generis*, which is quite a trick in these days of prefabricated comics. . . . Mr. Sellers does a remarkable job of representing a modest sleuth in a nudist camp with nothing between him and utter embarrassment except a guitar."[7]

Newsweek, while finding the film "twice as funny" as *The Pink Panther*, criticized Clouseau as, "a simple Keystone Cop with no subtlety nor the capacity of building from small gag to larger gags. In fact, the funniest lines in the picture are those of Herbert Lom, who plays Chief Inspector Charles Dreyfus."[8]

Part III:
The Lost Decade
(1965–1974)

23
What's New, Pussycat?

Cast:

Dr. Fritz Fassbender ..	Peter Sellers
Michael Jones	Peter O'Toole
Victor Shakopopolis ..	Woody Allen
Carol Werner	Romy Schneider
Rita	Ursula Andress
Liz	Paula Prentiss
Renee	Capucine

STUDIO: United Artists
RELEASE DATE: June 23, 1965
RUNNING TIME: 108 minutes (Technicolor)
DIRECTED BY: Clive Donner
PRODUCED BY: Charles K. Feldman
WRITTEN BY: Woody Allen
PHOTOGRAPHY: Jean Badal
MUSIC: Burt Bacharach

A young new wife and two uncompleted films almost spelled the end of Sellers's life, both physically and professionally.

Now thirty-eight, Sellers met twenty-one-year-old Swedish starlet Britt Ekland, recently put under contract by 20th Century–Fox, in London's Dorchester Hotel while filming *A Shot in the Dark* at Pinewood Studios. Sellers was immediately infatuated with the petite blond, who spoke little English, and after a whirlwind romance proposed ten days later. The couple were married on February 19, 1964, at the registrar's office in Guildford.

But there was no time for a honeymoon, and trouble soon arose. While Ekland was to begin work on *Guns at Batasi,* in which she played a Swedish UN worker, Sellers flew immediately to the United States where he was to star in his first Hollywood feature, *Kiss Me, Stupid.* A bedroom farce directed by his idol Billy Wilder. *Kiss Me, Stupid* had Sellers playing an insanely jealous piano teacher trying to keep his wife from falling under the spell of womanizing pop singer Dean Martin. Kim Novak was also featured in the film, cowritten by I. A. L. Diamond.

For Sellers, it was an uncomfortable situation of art imitating life, for while he acted his part on the film set, privately he fretted over Ekland and her *Batasi* costar John Leyton. When production on *Guns at Batasi* broke for a short Easter recess, Sellers persuaded Ekland to fly to Hollywood where he was installed in a plush mansion belonging to 20th Century–Fox President Spyros Skouras.[1] When she arrived, Ekland found that Sellers had filled her closets with a completely new wardrobe, and as her new husband lavished her with gifts, he also persuaded Ekland to abandon the *Batasi* set, breaking her contract.

Ekland and Sellers were slapped with a $1.5 million breach-of-contract suit by Fox, forced to reshoot Ekland's scenes with replacement Mia Farrow. To make matters worse, Sellers quickly grew disenchanted with Wilder's gregarious "open set" policy, which was upsetting his concentration.

A three-pack-a-day smoker, Sellers had been secretly preparing for his upcoming role as James Bond in *Casino Royale* by embarking on a strenuous exercise program after returning from the *Kiss Me, Stupid* set. But perhaps more dangerously, he had begun using the heart stimulant amyl nitrate in his sexual relationship with Ekland. After an amyl nitrate–enhanced bout of lovemaking on the night of April 5, 1964, Sellers complained of fiery chest pains and was taken the next day to Cedars of Lebanon Hospital, where he was diagnosed as having suffered a mild heart attack.

After resting comfortably most of the day, his condition suddenly took a turn for the worse. At about 4:30 A.M. Tuesday, April 7, Sellers's heart stopped beating for roughly a minute and a half before being resuscitated. Fearing another massive coronary, Sellers's doctors transported him to the hospital's intensive-care unit, where—electric shocks from a pacemaker machine notwithstanding—his heart stopped completely another seven times during the early morning hours. His condition was diagnosed as acute myocardial infarction with a complete heart block.

Technically, Sellers had died eight times.

"I just thought I kept dozing off" was how Sellers described his heart stoppages. "Then I'd hear that Klaxon go off and I'd wake up and see four or five guys standing around my bed. So I'd say, 'Hey, what are you cats doing here?' I didn't know it, but I wasn't dozing off—I was dying. You'd feel okay, chatting with these chaps, then you'd suddenly feel, 'Ah—here we go again—' and that was death. I shan't fear it again."[2]

But while Ekland was told to expect the worst and media around the world prepared their obituaries, Sellers's heartbeat miraculously stabilized. After spending another week in the intensive-care unit, he was moved back upstairs for another four weeks before being discharged and told to rest for at least a year.

"What we shall do is this," he said. "I live in one of the most beautiful parts of England. I have bought myself a red setter, to take long walks with. I also have a pair of matched palominos, for riding. I've ordered a nice, fast, new car—my 84th, a blue Ferrari. And I want to take Britt to a discotheque one evening and have a 'hippy, hippy shake.' I want to try out all these silly new steps I've been seeing on TV, like the Watusi. I've even invented my own new dance. I call mine The Gas Stove."[3]

After signing his name and cementing his handprints at Grauman's Chinese Theater in Hollywood, Sellers headed home to England. But hyperactive as ever and bored with the rigors of domestic life, he soon yearned to return to work. "The inactivity was killing me," he said. "The old adrenalin was rushing around again and I was full of energy and there was nothing burning it up."[4]

Sellers did find time, however, to complain bitterly to film critic Alexander Walker about his *Kiss Me, Stupid* experience and Hollywood in general.

> I've had Hollywood in a big way, luv. America I would go back to gladly tomorrow, but as far as filmland is concerned I've taken the round trip for good. The noise, and to coin a phrase, the people. At the studios they give you every creature comfort except the satisfaction of being able to get the best work out of yourself. I used to go down to film *Kiss Me, Stupid* with Billy Wilder and find a Cooks Tour of hangers-on and sightseers standing just off the set right in my line of vision. Friends and relatives of people in the Front Office come to kibitz on Peter Sellers, actor.[5]

Sellers's remarks sent an immediate wave of resentment rippling through Hollywood, and he received a succinct cable shortly thereafter: "Talk about unprofessional rat finks." Signed by Wilder, Dean Martin, and Novak, among others, it reflected Hollywood's growing hostility toward Sellers and his unpredictable behavior.

In October, deemed well enough for some light work, Sellers flew to New York to film a three-day television role in *Carol for Another Christmas* for the United Nations. Around the same time he was offered $300,000 plus 10 percent of the producer's gross to star in Producer Charles K. Feldman's big-budget sex comedy, *What's New, Pussycat.*

Feldman, last of the spendthrift, cigar-chomping Hollywood producers, had already hired young television writer-turned-standup-comedian Woody Allen to rewrite the film from I. A. L. Diamond's original script. Feldman had seen Allen's standup routine at New York's Blue Angel nightclub and was suitably impressed to offer the unproven comedian $35,000 to write the screenplay and appear in the film opposite Sellers and Warren Beatty,[7] for whom a major part had been written (and from whose phone greeting to young females Feldman borrowed the film's title). When a prior commitment forced Beatty to pull out of the project, Feldman sent the script to Peter O'Toole, who agreed to his first comedic role. Ursula Andress, Paula Prentiss, Capucine, and Romy Schneider rounded out the all-star cast.

"I had never done a film, I was a complete nobody," Allen said of his initial *Pussycat* reaction, which would change drastically throughout the course of filming. "Sellers was an absolute giant and I was delighted he'd consented to do my script and I was going to share the movie with him. To me, nothing else mattered. I'd have been happy to hold his coat."[8] (Allen's first choice for Sellers's role, however, was Groucho Marx.)

For Sellers, worried he'd lost his touch after his heart attack and subsequent recuperation, *What's New, Pussycat* would be a real test. It certainly tested the nerve—and pocketbook—of Feldman, who desperately wanted Sellers for his film and shelled out $360,000 of his own money for an insurance policy covering his star's possible catastrophic loss.[9] He also decided to put Sellers on a short sixteen-day shooting schedule to reduce the strain on his heart.

Television director Clive Donner was hired to helm *Pussycat,* whose theme song, written by young Burt Bacharach, was belted out by an unknown Welsh singer, Tom Jones. After months of preproduction planning and location changes—"It was one of those things of how not to make a film," Allen said[10]—Feldman decided to drop his traveling caravan in Paris where filming began.

Sellers, clad in a black pageboy wig and black velvet suit, played neurotic German psychiatrist Fritz Fassbender, living in fear of his huge Nordic wife (Edra Gale) while trying to solve the problems of philandering fashion magazine editor Michael Jones (O'Toole), engaged to Carol Werner (Schneider) but distracted by a bevy of beautiful women (Capucine, Prentiss, and Andress) lurking around every corner.

Allen's Victor Shakapopolis, a strip-joint wardrobe man, composed one of *Pussycat*'s many subplots as he wandered through life as a perennial loser.

These elements, played for broad farce, composed *Pussycat*'s basic, incomprehensible narrative, spun off from Allen's carefully scripted narrative. Said O'Toole:

> We began with a brilliant, sketchy, Perelmanesque script by Woody Allen, who is a genius. Then things got a little neurotic, with lots of politics and infighting and general treachery and finally—with the ghost of W. C. Fields hovering over our heads—we improvised the whole thing from start to finish. There were areas in the script that were undeveloped, which is the norm with most films: you cast first and write afterwards. I actually wrote with my own fair hand about three-fifths of the script. When I say "wrote" I mean that we'd meet at ten in the morning—Sellers and I and Clive Donner, the director—and sit around talking and hoping. Sellers had the

Fassbender's problems with women are multiplied by the beautiful Renee (Capucine).

> ideas, I did the words and Clive was the arbitrator. We jotted things down on the back of contraceptives and off we went.... We took it on the wing every day, grabbed an idea and built it from there.[11]

Allen was not amused at the butchering of his script—replete with "in" jokes and completely without comic substance—and complained bitterly to Feldman, asking the producer to remove his name from the finished product. "It's like the Milton Berle shows without his genius, the way they produced it," Allen said later. "It was the whole approach to filmmaking that I hate and I've since demonstrated that it isn't my kind of film. But I've never had anything as successful. *Pussycat* was just born to work."[12]

Indeed, *What's New, Pussycat* was the smash comedy of 1965, garnering generally negative reviews but playing to packed houses the world over. "*What's New Pussycat?* is designed as a zany farce, as wayout as can be reached on the screen," wrote *Variety*. "It's all that and more ... it goes overboard in pressing for its goal and consequently suffers from over-contrived treatment. That there are laughs, sometimes plenty of them, there can be no denying ... and the windup is fast and crazy."[13]

For Sellers, fearing he'd lost his touch, *Pussycat* confirmed his drawing power, perhaps grown even stronger in light of his much-publicized marriage to Ekland and subsequent heart attacks. But unbeknownst to Sellers, *Pussycat* also would mark his final dominant performance of the 1960s.

24
The Wrong Box

Cast:

Morris Finsbury	Peter Cook
John Finsbury	Dudley Moore
Joseph Finsbury	Ralph Richardson
Masterman Finsbury	John Mills
Michael Finsbury	Michael Caine
Julie Finsbury	Nanette Newman
Peacock	Wilfred Lawson
Dr. Pratt	Peter Sellers

STUDIO: Columbia
RELEASE DATE: May 26, 1966
RUNNING TIME: 110 minutes (Technicolor)
DIRECTED BY: Bryan Forbes
PRODUCED BY: Bryan Forbes
WRITTEN BY: Larry Gelbart and Burt Shevelove (from the novel by Robert Louis Stevenson)
PHOTOGRAPHY: Gerry Turpin
MUSIC: John Barry

The *After the Fox* debacle (Chapter 25) left a bad taste in Peter Sellers's mouth and certainly didn't improve his standing in the film community. But the *Casino Royale* mess, which cemented Sellers's bad-boy reputation, was a year off, and in 1966 the comedian was still considered to be at the peak of his performing and audience-drawing powers.

Director Bryan Forbes badly wanted Sellers for a cameo appearance as the decrepit back-alley abortionist Dr. Pratt in his Victorian-era comedy, *The Wrong Box,* adapted from the Robert Louis Stevenson–Lloyd Osbourne novel by American comedy writers Larry Gelbart and Burt Shevelove (collaborators on the Broadway hit *A Funny Thing Happened on the Way to the Forum*). But when Forbes balked at Sellers's demand of £25,000 for five days of work, the two reached a compromise: Sellers would perform free, with his fee donated to charity.[1]

The Wrong Box afforded Sellers the chance to return to his early Goonish roots and indulge in some inspired improvisation. And though he always despised his work and fretted over his performance, Sellers for once seemed to enjoy himself on the set. Not, however, without some prodding encouragement from Forbes, who said:

> After a day's shooting, Peter saw the rushes, decreed he was dreadful and wanted it all re-shot—failing that he would quit the picture. "Look, you're my oldest friend," I said, "you have my word you are excellent. I've never lied to you; I'm not lying now." When he saw I was telling the truth, then he came to love and indeed possess Dr. Pratt. He'd go into the voice on every occasion. When he was filming, he kept dropping things on the suit at every meal. When he went home, he slept in it. And to the end of his days every letter he sent me was signed "Pratt, M.D."[2]

Along with Peter Cook and Dudley Moore—making their big-screen debuts after their *Beyond the Fringe* Broadway smash—and Tony Hancock, Sellers was among the hip British comedians used by Forbes in *The Wrong Box*. The film seems quite dated now, but its artsy, silent-movie-style title cards, and irreverent tone were par for the swinging 1960s course. And though its attempts at black humor were rather tame and its humor somewhat forced at times, *The Wrong Box* was a pleasant diversion and proved Sellers could still deliver if placed within the right comedic structure.

Paired with these upstart comedians were legendary British actors Sir Ralph Richardson and John Mills, who starred as Joseph and Masterman Finsbury, brothers and lone survivors of a £100,000 tontine.

The brothers, who live next door to each other, haven't spoken for forty years. The hypochondriacal Masterman hates his brother, Joseph, a boorish know-it-all, and schemes to win the tontine for his adopted grandson Michael (Michael Caine), a novice surgeon in love with his cousin Julia (Nanette Newman), Joseph's adopted niece.

Further complicating matters are Joseph's nephews Morris (Cook) and John (Moore), greedy, conniving cousins out to ensure Joseph's winning the tontine, thereby passing the money on to them.

But it won't be easy.

Masterman, pretending to be on his deathbed, sends for Joseph, who is away on holiday in Bormouth with Morris and John. Masterman plans to kill Joseph upon his arrival, thereby winning the tontine and all its monetary spoils.

Morris and John, thinking Masterman is really dying, gleefully hop on the next London-bound train with Joseph in tow. But the train also happens to be carrying the "Bormouth Strangler" (Tutte Lemkow), wanted by police for a series of grisly murders. Joseph, wandering through the train, encounters the strangler (silently and furiously working a pair of knitting needles) and engages him in a long-winded, one-sided conversation. When Joseph gets up to sneak a smoke in the men's room, the strangler dons Joseph's hat and jacket, and is about to jump off the train when it collides head-on with another locomotive.

Joseph, unharmed, wanders off into the woods and hitches a ride with a passing horseman. But Morris and John, searching for Joseph, find the strangler, or rather his feet, sticking out from a wooden box where he was thrown and killed after the crash. Thinking he's Uncle Joseph, the cousins are thrown into a panic; after all, they can't win the tontine if Joseph dies before his brother. So Morris hatches a diabolical scheme: He and John will crate "Uncle Joseph's" body and send it back to their London home. When Masterman dies in a day or two, they'll tell everyone Joseph suffered a fatal heart attack upon learning of his brother's death.

Of course, this means they'll need a phony death certificate, so Morris pays a visit to the filthy office of Dr. Pratt, who once helped John out of a jam by performing an abortion (or "the thing," as Morris and John call it) for one of his many sexual conquests. But Dr. Pratt's office is now overrun by cats instead of patients.

Sellers wore a false putty-ish nose, stringy wig, and coiled stethoscope as Dr. Pratt, and shuffled about Pratt's office aimlessly spouting gibberish about how he "wasn't always as you see me now" and "sanitizing" his hands by washing them in a sink, then wiping them dry on a cat. Although he appeared in only two scenes, Sellers galvanized *The Wrong Box* with his seedy interpretation of Pratt and had the film's most memorable moment.

After Morris talks the drunken doctor into signing a blank death certificate, he returns to Pratt's office the next day. Pratt, surrounded by his beloved cats (or "moggies"), shakily signs the death certificate, then picks up one of the cats to use as an ink blotter. That particular move was scripted. Sellers, however, was prone to ad-lib, and Forbes described the quickness with which Sellers could improvise if thrown the lifeline of a comical situation:

> He was doing this scene with Peter Cook in the doctor's cat-infested surgery. He had to open a desk drawer, draw out a kitten and say, "You wouldn't like a moggy instead of a death certificate?" Cook had to reply, with considerable patience, "No doctor, I collect eggs." At that point in the filming, Sellers said vaguely, "Eggs? Ah, yes. Ah like an egg meself. But they don't make good pets. Too quiet. You can't call 'em in at night." We just got three frames past this glorious ad-lib when Peter Sellers broke up, Peter Cook broke up, the entire crew—myself included—broke up. It was brilliant. The thing about Peter was that if someone gave him the clues across,

Dr. Pratt and his moggy–ink blotter.

he would work at the part like a crossword puzzle and come up with some staggering solutions to the down words.[3]

The Wrong Box, meanwhile, staggered toward its rickety conclusion with an exhaustive array of plot contrivances thrown in its way. The box containing the Bormouth Strangler is mistakenly delivered to Masterman's house while a box with a nude stone sculpture, destined for Masterman's house, is delivered instead to Joseph's residence. Masterman, meanwhile, tries unsuccessfully to kill Joseph. When Michael discovers the strangler's body in the crate, thinking it's Uncle Joseph, he thinks Masterman really did kill Joseph and hides the body in a piano. Michael then calls an unsavory undertaker to dump the body in the river. When the undertaker rings

rings the bell, Masterman goes to answer the door and falls down a flight of steps. The undertaker, thinking Masterman is the dead body, throws him in a cart and on the way to the river passes Morris, who is sure Masterman is now dead and the tontine his.

And so it goes, one farcical gag after another, until a frenzied conclusion involving a Keystone Kop–style chase led by Tony Hancock.

The Wrong Box opened to generally enthusiastic reviews. *Time* praised the film, noting that "some of the gags crumble on impact, others are stretched out like taffy, but there is enough fun left over to leave most moviegoers happily wallowing in greed, sex, homicide, body snatching and other nefarious diversions."[4]

Other publications, like *The Nation*, thought the film too smug and its comedy "surprisingly brief and infrequent. Everyone seems to have been infected with director Bryan Forbes's patronizing view of slapstick clowning ... too often the cast plays its laughs for laughs, an estranging mannerism which in this case is reinforced by a scent of effeminacy that hangs over the whole picture and works to the particular disadvantage of the females in the company."[5]

Sellers was lauded for his brief performance, the last favorable press he would receive for quite some time. "The film's biggest invention, barely suggested by Stevenson and never even named, let alone introduced in the book, is the venal Dr. Pratt (Sellers)," wrote *Newsweek*, "a scrofulous sawbones who lives amid a chaos of filthy cats ("That's one of the finest ratters in the East End"), performs abortions when he can get them and practices sterile ablutions according to the hygienic principles of Lister before signing, for his 1-shilling fee, a fake death certificate which he blots with a kitten's back."[6]

But Sellers would be in for a letdown following his Goonish portrayal of Dr. Pratt. Although he enthusiastically prepared himself for the coveted role of superagent James Bond in *Casino Royale,* the film would spell one of the worst disasters of his career.

25
After the Fox

Cast:
Aldo Vanucci .... Peter Sellers
Tony Powell .... Victor Mature

Gina	....	Britt Ekland
Okra	....	Akim Tamiroff
Harry	....	Martin Balsam

STUDIO: United Artists
RELEASE DATE: September 29, 1966
RUNNING TIME: 103 minutes (Panavision/
  Technicolor
DIRECTED BY: Vittorio de Sica
PRODUCED BY: John Bryan
WRITTEN BY: Neil Simon and Cesare Zavat-
  tini
PHOTOGRAPHY: Leonida Barboni
MUSIC: Burt Bacharach

Although *What's New, Pussycat?* was far from vintage Sellers, the film was immensely popular. Its financial success allowed Sellers to form his own production company, Brookfield Productions, along with Oscar-winning production designer-turned-producer John Bryan.

Sellers had apparently forgotten the doubts he expressed to Wolf Mankowitz only five years earlier when he pulled out of Sellers-Mankowitz Productions at the last minute. Now glowing with success once again, Sellers pushed his hovering insecurities aside for the moment and moved ahead with Brookfield Productions.

It was decided the company would produce six films under its banner, the first being *After the Fox,*[1] a comedy starring Sellers and wife Britt Ekland. Sellers set his sights on legendary Italian director Vittorio de Sica to helm the project.

De Sica's 1948 film *Bicycle Thieves,* hailed for its neorealism, had earned the director a place in the cinematic history books. Sellers had long admired de Sica and was thrilled to be working with a legend. "The director has given me all sorts of little hints. And he's changing the film too," Sellers said. "He's putting a touch of warmth into what was just a straightforward comedy. He's making me show family feeling, in the Italian style."[2]

With de Sica directing, Sellers starring, a script by prolific television and Broadway writer Neil Simon, and Burt Bacharach's bouncy soundtrack, *After the Fox* was a sure thing.

Or was it?

Shooting began outside Rome, and Sellers, as was his wont, quickly grew disenchanted. De Sica's English was very poor, and he was forced to communicate with his cast through body language—a technique Sellers found irritating and insulting. "He knew he wasn't getting anywhere near to what he believed was possible," Bryan said. "He blamed de Sica's direction and he was probably right. De Sica simply didn't have the feel for this particular stuff."[3]

Further annoying Sellers was the fact that *After the Fox* was being financed by his own company; should the film fail, Sellers would have no one to blame but himself. "This was the first time I noticed Peter thinking about his long-term career instead of just his current performance," said Theo Cowan, Sellers's longtime publicist. "The production troubles—his own company, remember—made him aware how vulnerable he was. If the movie were good, he took credit; if bad, he copped all the blame. It was one of the earliest times that he had a view of himself wider than that of a working actor. He told himself, 'If I have to interfere in the future, I shall interfere—to protect myself as much as the picture.'"[4]

Sellers indeed interfered, trying unsuccessfully to have de Sica fired and replaced three weeks into production. When Bryan resisted, however, Sellers accused him of purposely supporting de Sica and tried to have *him* fired. Paranoid as always, Sellers then accused Bryan of giving him "some very strange looks lately." Needless to say, *After the Fox* was the first and last Brookfield production. Bryan and Sellers quickly severed their business relationship upon the film's completion.[5]

As if there wasn't enough tension on the set, Sellers's stormy relationship with Ekland flared up during shooting. The couple were living in a luxurious villa on the Appian Way, across the street from Simon and his wife and about two hundred yards from Tony Curtis, who was also in Rome shooting a picture.

Sellers was very jealous of Ekland and became furious one day when she happened to glance at an Italian actor on the set. The two had a terrific fight that evening. Sellers threw a chair at Ekland, who fled through a back window in her nightdress to Simon's villa. Simon called Sellers, and the two had a quiet talk before Sellers retrieved Ekland. Their reconciliation didn't last long, however, and they renewed their bickering when the production moved to the seaside island of Ischia.[6]

But try as he might, Sellers couldn't escape *After the Fox* or his role as Aldo Vanucci, a brilliantly cunning Italian criminal nicknamed "the Fox" for his legendary exploits.

Vanucci, a master quick-change artist, is serving a lengthy prison sentence. But it's not all that bad; Vanucci can break out of prison any time he pleases, but he leads a good life behind bars. So good, in fact, that Vanucci's family and friends ask *him* for treats like packaged sausage and fruit. It's during one of these visits that Vanucci learns, much to his horror, of the exploits of Gina (Ekland), his starry-eyed younger sister. Gina, an aspiring actress, is rumored to be walking the streets, and Vanucci, enraged at the thought of men touching his sister, impersonates the prison doctor and breaks out of the slammer to save Gina from a life of sin.

But Gina's only crime is wanting to be a movie starlet; she's playing a hooker as a bit part in a new movie being filmed in town. Vanucci quickly ends Gina's short-lived career and reenters his own line of work. While hiding out in his mother's apartment, Vanucci is approached by Okra (Akim Tamiroff), a self-proclaimed "swarthy-looking man in a fez" who masterminded the "Gold of Cairo" job in which three hundred bars of gold bullion were stolen from an armed truck near the Egyptian pyramids. Okra offers Vanucci half the gold if he can find a way to smuggle the bullion into Italy from a passing ship and elude the long arm of Interpol, working overtime on the case.

Enter Tony Powell (Victor Mature), a fading American film star whose arrival in Rome has set off a virtual mob scene. Witnessing this spectacle, the Fox hits upon a master plan: Why not incorporate the bullion smuggling into a phony motion picture starring Powell? This way, star-struck villagers, thinking they're acting in a "scene," will themselves unload the Gold of Cairo under the protection of the local police force.

What could possibly go wrong?

Posing as "Federico Fabrizi," neorealist Italian director, Vanucci visits Powell's hotel suite and persuades the vain actor—his gray hair dyed a slick black—to star in his "newest" film, *The Gold of Cairo*. Powell's costar, of course, will be Gina, or rather "Gina Romantica," Italy's newest undiscovered sensation. Powell's agent, Harry (Martin Balsam), is skeptical, but Powell knows he isn't getting any younger and could use the international exposure. And to be asked to star in a film by the great Fabrizi, the same Fabrizi who takes daily telephone calls from a distraught "Sophia," is more than Powell could have hoped for at this stage of his moribund career.

So it's off to a seaside village, where Fabrizi/Vanucci will film *The Gold of Cairo*'s one scene, the landing of the gold, helped by the unwitting villagers. The posturing Fabrizi soon has the townsfolk eating out of his phony hand. It doesn't matter that he has no filming permit; the village's dimwitted police chief, encouraged by Fabrizi's admiration of his "good bone structure" and promised a walk-on part in the picture, will take care of this little technicality. And so what if Fabrizi has no script—a "genius" doesn't need written words, only the spontaneous flashes of inspiration that strike Fabrizi at a moment's notice.

For instance, there's Fabrizi's staging of the film's first scene. Forced to stall for time because of engine trouble on the bullion-laden ship, Fabrizi announces a change in the shooting schedule. Pacing the sandy beach deep in thought, he's struck by a novel idea—Tony, wearing his trademark trench coat, and Gina will sit at opposite ends of a long metal table, staring at each other and not saying a word as the ocean laps at their feet. A stroke of brilliance!

"It's about nothing," Fabrizi explains to the curious Tony. "Tony, sweetheart, in the scene we have a great opportunity to make a wonderful comment on the lack of communication in our society. Two extremely

"The Fox," Aldo Vanucci, disguises himself as the prison doctor and escapes from his cell.

beautiful people, sitting alone at a cafe with absolutely nothing to say! You get the significance?"

The second scene is even more intriguing.

> *Fabrizi:* In this scene, instead of doing *nothing,* we do *something!*
> *Tony* (throwing up his hands): What!
> *Fabrizi:* Running, running.
> *Tony:* What are we running from?
> *Fabrizi:* From yourself. You get the symbolic meaning? No matter how fast you run, you can never run away from yourself!

So Tony and Gina are off, running a marathon through the village in the hot midday sun.

And so it goes, Fabrizi directing one incredibly stupid scene after another while Tony, under the impression he's working for a cinematic genius, thinks he's appearing in a "new wave" masterpiece. When the ship finally does arrive in port, Vanucci executes his plan perfectly, and the bullion is loaded into a waiting van. But there's only one problem: Okra has different ideas, and he jumps in the van and drives off with the bullion. Interpol, meanwhile, has been alerted to the bullion's arrival and shows up in force, setting the scene for the requisite monotonous car chase through the mountains of southern Italy.

Vanucci is apprehended, put on trial, and sentenced to five years in prison, but not before *The Gold of Cairo* is screened for the jury and a wild-eyed film critic proclaims the film's brilliance. *After the Fox* ends as it began, with Vanucci once again escaping from prison by impersonating the prison doctor.

Sellers was flat in his early scenes as Vanucci, virtually sleepwalking through the role without any originality. He did show some spark during Vanucci's heated arguments with Gina—an example of art imitating life rather than good acting. But when he transformed Vanucci into Fabrizi, Sellers came alive and pulled out all the stops, embellishing the director with a campy accent and smarmy phoniness. This was not enough, however, to offset the negative criticism Sellers received upon the film's release.

"Sellers throughout seems more concerned with having an abundance of footage than with making something of it," wrote Arthur Knight in *Saturday Review*. "Everyone connected with the film, particularly Sellers, is apparently convinced that to bring down the house all he need do is roll his big, brown eyes. Alas, not so."[7]

Bosley Crowther of the *New York Times* compared Simon's script to "the sort of jocularity you generally find in Jerry Lewis films" and said of Sellers: "I hate to have to say that Mr. Sellers acts on the level of Mr. Lewis, which is to say broadly, bluntly and often quite hoggishly. Not only does he spread himself thick over the first part of the film ... but he brazenly outhams such experts as Akim Tamiroff, Victor Mature and Martin Balsam..."[8]

But it was Victor Mature's wickedly funny performance that saved *After the Fox* from plummeting into obscurity. Simon penned Tony Powell as a broad caricature, the quintessential preening narcissist. Mature certainly played the hammy actor in this vein and, much to his credit, turned Powell into a likable, harmless schlemiel. "*After the Fox* has its moments, mostly when Mature is on screen," wrote *Newsweek*.[9]

After the Fox certainly wasn't a great film, but neither was it an embarrassment. Despite their differences—and obvious clashing of comedic styles—Sellers and de Sica provided some sporadic, lighthearted fun and tried valiantly to overcome Simon's uneven script (altered somewhat by de Sica cohort Cesare Zavattini). Nevertheless, Sellers's problems with de Sica and the film's unflattering critical reception were harbingers of worse times to come.

26
Casino Royale

Cast:
James Bond .... David Niven
Evelyn Tremble ...... Peter Sellers
Vesper .... Ursula Andress
Le Chiffre .... Orson Welles
Mata .... Joanna Pettet
Jimmy Bond .... Woody Allen

STUDIO: Columbia
RELEASE DATE: April 14, 1967
RUNNING TIME: 130 minutes (Panavision/ Technicolor
DIRECTED BY: Joe McGrath, John Huston, Ken Hughes, Val Guest, and Robert Parrish
PRODUCED BY: Charles K. Feldman and Jerry Bresler
WRITTEN BY: Wolf Mankowitz, John Law, and Michael Sayers (from the novel by Ian Fleming)
PHOTOGRAPHY: Jack Hildyard
MUSIC: Burt Bacharach

The on-set hostility he engendered on *After the Fox* paled in comparison to the troubles awaiting Sellers on his next film, *Casino Royale.*

Producer Charles K. Feldman, confident of Sellers's star power after the success of *What's New, Pussycat?*, offered Sellers $1 million to star in an adaptation of Ian Fleming's novel *Casino Royale,* the only James Bond adventure for which producer Albert "Cubby" Broccoli didn't own the rights. Feldman gambled that audiences would be attracted to another anarchic vehicle like *Pussycat* and put his money where his mouth was.

Not only was Sellers signed to a starring role (only three weeks before production began), but David Niven, William Holden, Orson Welles, Ursula Andress, Deborah Kerr, and Woody Allen also inked contracts. (Niven, incidentally, was Fleming's choice for the original James Bond. But Broccoli thought him too old for the part and eventually handed it to thirty-year-old Sean Connery.)

Yet regardless of its impressive cast, *Casino Royale* was a time bomb waiting to explode, even before Sellers's arrival on set. It was obvious from the start that Feldman didn't care much about the film's continuity or narrative coherence. For starters, he hired a bevy of screenwriters, Sellers's enemy Wolf Mankowitz among them, to write different portions of the film without consulting one another. Welles, John Law, Ben Hecht, Michael Sayers, Terry Southern, and Billy Wilder contributed to the completed screenplay, which, not surprisingly, was a jumbled mass of confusion.

"We were not supposed to know the other one was working on the picture!" Welles said. "We would arrive at various hours at Charlie's house with our secret scripts, which he would take and put in the safe on the theory that our ideas were so brilliant that people would try to steal them."[1]

At Sellers's insistence, Feldman also chose inexperienced Joe McGrath, a low-key Scotsman whom Sellers met in the late 1950s, to direct the massive undertaking. McGrath's experience was limited to BBC television, yet he was put in charge of the $12 million production—and eventually fired, only to be replaced by directors Ken Hughes, Val Guest, Robert Parrish, and John Huston, who each directed a different segment of the film.

"A director would say, 'Excuse me just a minute' and he'd go off and a door would open, and in would come another director!" Welles said. "Then at the end of it, having fired several directors—they used to be led off the set—Charlie hired John Huston, and John immediately moved everybody to Ireland because he wanted to do fox hunting."[2]

"I don't know why everybody thinks it's so funny we have so many directors on this picture," Feldman said near the film's completion. "From the start, we had the idea of multiple Bonds, multiple directors, multiple writers, multiple sets—just like *The Longest Day* had. It was the only way I could do it."[3]

But it was Welles's gargantuan presence more than anything else that sounded *Casino Royale*'s death knell when filming began on January 11, 1966. Through no fault of his own, Welles had engendered in Sellers an intense loathing and contempt. The two men had never worked together before, though Sellers showed interest in starring in Welles's 1960 London stage production of *Rhinoceros* (a role tackled by Laurence Olivier), yet Sellers warned McGrath and anyone else within earshot about Welles's penchant for "taking over" a film.

Mankowitz said of Sellers:

> He was a treacherous lunatic and he became more so after *The Million-aires*, which is the film we did together with Sophia Loren. He fell in love with Loren and it drove him right over the top. He went completely barmy. My advice to Charles Feldman was not in any circumstances to get involved with Sellers. But Sellers was at his peak at that time. I told Charlie that Sellers would fuck everything up: he wanted different directors, he wanted to piss around with the script. He knew nothing about anything except going on and doing funny voices, and he wasn't really a great actor. He was terrified of playing with Orson and converted this into an aversion for Orson before he even met Orson.[4]

Sellers's paranoid insecurity manifested itself in Welles's legendary presence, yet he reached new heights of behavioral absurdity on the *Casino Royale* set. Not only did the highly superstitious comedian consider Welles a "bad witch" (Welles was a talented magician who enjoyed performing feats of illusion), but Welles's substantial girth also posed problems for the once-overweight Sellers ("a really fat man masquerading as a thin one," Mankowitz explained).[5]

The fireworks began when Mankowitz and Welles visited Sellers in his Dorchester Hotel suite to discuss script revisions. Mankowitz, himself a heavyweight, commented on Sellers's lean physique, and Sellers, shooting a disapproving glance at the two men, preached that all it took to shed excess poundage was self-discipline.

But according to Welles, the final blow was struck by Princess Margaret, a Sellers intimate who'd known Welles since he directed *Othello* in London. Sellers invited the princess to an on-set luncheon, unaware of her friendship with Welles. "Then Princess Margaret came and walked on the set and passed him by and said, 'Hello, Orson, I haven't seen you for days!'" Welles said. "That was the real end. That's when we couldn't speak lines across to each other. 'Orson, I haven't seen you for days!' absolutely killed him. He went white as a sheet because *he* was going to get to present *me*."[6]

Whatever his reasons, Sellers shocked the entire *Casino Royale* cast and crew by announcing his refusal to appear on camera with Welles, a decision jeopardizing the film's pivotal scene in which Tremble matches wits with Le Chiffre at the baccarat tables. Sellers then disappeared for five days, and it fell on the unfortunate McGrath literally to use mirrors in accomplishing the difficult task of portraying Sellers and Welles within the same frame. Said McGrath:

> This was my first film in Panavision, the letter-box-shaped screen. You could hold a hundred yards of the set in the lens. We had seven hundred extras for the gaming tables sequence, but we had no way of bringing our

two stars together in the same shot! After a day or two of this, he (Welles) raised one big eyebrow and said to me, "Joe, this may take some time." Orson was shooting a film of his own in Madrid, off and on, and looked on his fee from *Casino Royale* as production coin to resume work on his own pet project. He certainly didn't want to linger longer than necessary with us. Moreover, he was eating his head off in the apartment he'd taken near the best restaurant in Mayfair. As the delay got longer, he got fatter.[7]

The circuslike atmosphere continued even after Sellers returned for work. Graham Stark, called to appear in the film out of the blue about four weeks after filming began, described life on the chaotic set: "I found Peter being fed a steady supply of gags on flimsy paper by a relay of writers working away in a caravan just beyond camera range. We shot for six days and it was sheer lunacy."[8]

Woody Allen also found himself tossed into Feldman's sea of confusion. Allen sat in his London hotel room waiting for months to film his insubstantial part, using the time to write his Broadway play *Don't Drink the Water* and the screenplay for *Take the Money and Run,* his first starring role. "My part has been steadily changed, even up to two days ago," a disconsolate Allen told *Look* magazine. "Think of the old pyramid builders, and you have some idea of what Charlie Feldman is like, lavish in the Egyptian tradition of lavish. What he's really trying to do is to eliminate the Bond pictures forever."[9]

Meanwhile, Sellers's relationship with McGrath slowly began to deteriorate until the two men came to blows in Sellers's trailer. McGrath was summarily dismissed from the production on a Friday night and immediately replaced by Robert Parrish. In an uncharacteristic gesture, Sellers later wrote McGrath expressing his disappointment in the finished picture and regret at McGrath's abrupt departure.

"I don't know why he was sorry," McGrath said. "It was obvious he had withdrawn his support. The reason I started the film was because Peter insisted. It must figure that the reason I was dropped was because . . . Peter insisted."[10]

Sellers departed the *Casino Royale* set before his role was completed, citing a time stipulation in his contract.

> I was approached by the producer and asked if I would be prepared to continue and make what they called "a gesture." I was naturally anxious to see my part finished, as I have helped to write it and will be getting an author's screen credit. So I told them, "All right, but we've got to get on with it." We were about to begin one week's extra work when they decided not to continue. It's all very strange . . . a gigantic puzzle, the whole film.[11]

The "puzzle" began, simply enough, with the simple premise of Sir James Bond (Niven) being lured out of retirement to fight SMERSH,

Tremble disguised as you-know-who.

headed by the notorious gambler Le Chiffre (Welles). Since Bond's retirement, the British Secret Service has substituted another 007 in his place,
a hard-drinking womanizer who's left his mark around the world (a passing
reference to Connery's 007).

Now inexplicably afflicted with a stutter, Bond turns down the offer
to return to the fold until his mansion is blown up by the combined secret
services of Britain, America, Russia, and France. "M" (Huston) is killed
in the explosion, and Bond must return to London to fill his former boss's
shoes. But first he stops at M's Scottish castle to visit his widow and the
entirely female McTarry family, only to discover they're SMERSH agents
trying to force him into committing suicide. In fact, it seems that SMERSH
is now employing only female agents to do its dirty work, and the secret service needs an AFSD (antifemale spy device) to withstand the wiles of its
seductive agents.

Meanwhile, Bond recruits his daughter, Mata Bond (a product of his
tryst with Mata Hari), to infiltrate SMERSH's Berlin training compound.
To confuse SMERSH further—and the *Casino Royale* audience—Bond
decides to name *all* agents James Bond. Baccarat expert Evelyn Tremble
(Sellers) is recruited to pose as 007 and engage Le Chiffre in a high-stakes

game of baccarat at Casino Royale. Le Chiffre, saddled with gambling debts, is using SMERSH funds to pay the bookies while cheating at baccarat.

But Tremble's £100,000 victory over Le Chiffre smashes SMERSH, and the entire *Casino Royale* mess ends with Bond's nephew, Jimmy Bond (Woody Allen)—really SMERSH's evil chief, Dr. Noah—killing everybody when he swallows his atomic bacillus and blows up the entire Casino Royale.

Casino Royale was perhaps one of the most blatantly asinine big-budget films ever produced and made absolutely no sense. So desperate were the writers, trying to keep pace with directorial changes, that they ended the narrative with a huge fight scene into which were thrown the U.S. Cavalry, American Indians, George Raft, and Jean-Paul Belmondo. It was a huge mess deserving all the negative press heaped upon its carcass. The film's only saving grace was Burt Bacharach's song "The Look of Love," nominated for an Academy Award.

Sellers turned in an uncharacteristically flat performance, opting to play Tremble in his own voice when he failed to "find" the character. "He was walking through the role giving a vocally featureless performance," McGrath said later. "It was like he was trying to play it a la Cary Grant."[12]

Not surprisingly, *Casino Royale* opened to universally scathing reviews. Feldman, dealt perhaps his biggest career disappointment, died about a year after the film's April 1967 London premiere.

"With so many egos—including five directors—competing for attention, the picture soon degenerates into an incoherent vaudeville," *Time* opined. "Each actor frantically does his bit and then gets offstage to make room for the jugglers."[13]

Esquire's Wilfred Sheed, while panning the overall film, laid the blame squarely on Sellers's doorstep in an insightful review that echoed a sentiment being heard more frequently as Sellers's reputation began to take a beating:

> Mr. Sellers approaches his comic roles very ponderously these days, like a bad magician, full of pauses, small smiles and inscrutable bits of business, and the result is a little ball of lead in the middle of your movie.... It would help immeasurably if Sellers would forget this business of being another Alec Guinness ... and would just bustle things along as a good farceur should.[14]

Although *Casino Royale* did surprisingly well at the box office—aided by its seductive poster depicting a naked tatooed woman—Sellers took the brunt of Columbia Pictures's anger and was unofficially blacklisted by the industry giant. Mike Frankovich, head of Columbia's European film productions, vowed Sellers would never again work for the studio, a statement indicative of how far Sellers's stock had plunged in the film community.[15]

27
The Bobo

Cast:

Juan Bautista	....	Peter Sellers
Olimpia Segura	......	Britt Ekland
Carbonell	....	Adolfo Celi
Matabosch	....	Rossano Brazzi

STUDIO: Warner Brothers
RELEASE DATE: August 17, 1967
RUNNING TIME: 105 minutes (Technicolor)
DIRECTED BY: Robert Parrish
PRODUCED BY: David R. Schwartz
WRITTEN BY: David R. Schwartz (from the novel *Olimpia* by Burt Cole)
PHOTOGRAPHY: Gerry Turpin
MUSIC: Francis Lai

The *Casino Royale* fiasco not only solidified Sellers's soiled Hollywood reputation but seemed to trigger the comedian's self-destructive tendencies. There is no other way to rationalize Sellers's involvement in *The Bobo*, a horrendous embarrassment that featured the comedian as a singing matador. While Sellers had shown increasingly bad judgment following his 1964 heart attack, his film choices were now becoming alarmingly erratic. With *The Bobo*, they reached a new low.

At an almost eerie clip, Sellers was virtually disappearing from the international film scene, his once-commanding per-picture salary diminishing with each successive failure. Gone were the studied, nuanced performances and Goonish fun, replaced by broad, unoriginal caricatures in listless endeavors.

More perplexing, however, were the depths to which Sellers was plunging in search of his worldwide audience that was quickly evaporating. For a performer steeped in the cleverness of Spike Milligan, Stanley Kubrick, and the Boulting Brothers, Sellers seemed to have developed little taste in choosing projects suited to his unique talents.

After patching up his *After the Fox* differences with Vittorio de Sica long enough to make a brief cameo appearance with Shirley MacLaine in *Woman Times Seven*, Sellers remained in Rome and prepared to shoot *The Bobo*. Parts of the film were also lensed in Barcelona, Spain, where its dismal plot unfolded. Sellers's production company, Gina Productions (his third such endeavor), was footing the bill this time, a situation that had caused problems in the past when Sellers fretted over costs and schedules. But this was only the tip of the proverbial iceberg. Sellers soon rented a house on the Appia Antica, setting the stage for more violent showdowns not only with Britt Ekland but with *The Bobo*'s co-producer, Elliot Kastner.

By now it was a bad industry joke that a Peter Sellers film meant trouble, and during *The Bobo* Sellers more than lived up to his unflattering reputation. "I'm a different fellow on the studio floor," he proclaimed in 1967. "I'm a very quiet chap in private life . . . but when I'm working I'm a different cup of tea. Ruthless, yes. Ruthless. You have to be. . . . You must be ruthless just to survive."[1]

One could almost see Sellers's ruthless streak coming, especially when his lawyers wrote to Ekland requesting a divorce just days before the film was scheduled to begin shooting.[2] The Sellers-Ekland marriage had been violently stormy from day one and wasn't helped by the couple's icy relationship during *After the Fox*. Adding more fuel to the fire was Sellers's fragile ego and jealous nature, which weren't assuaged when Ekland lined up film offers that would cast her opposite Hollywood legends Frank Sinatra and Yul Brynner.

Although he had sworn off directing after his *Mr. Topaze* stint, Sellers planned to direct *The Bobo* during the film's preproduction planning. At first he had no intention of casting Ekland as his leading lady, a situation that would soon change and stir up even more marital discord. "I didn't dream of playing Olimpia myself," Ekland said. "I was working steadily, doing a picture with Yul Brynner, and there was talk of a picture with Frank Sinatra to follow. I was very happy with the way things were going for me."[3]

But Sellers had other ideas and a conveniently short memory. Notwithstanding the couple's already rickety marriage and ignoring their *After the Fox* strife, Sellers cast Ekland as his costar. This not only allowed him to keep a jealous eye on his wife but also fed Sellers's insecurities by letting him feel he was controlling Ekland's career.

But after a month the mercurial comedian changed his mind, informing Ekland, without explanation, that the part would no longer be hers.[4] "I knew I had just lost the part of my life," she said. "But I knew Sellers too well to argue or to kick. I knew I had to play it cool."[5] A short time later, after the search for a new leading lady proved fruitless, Sellers informed Ekland the part was once again hers. "Sellers knew inside himself that he didn't want anybody but me," Ekland said later. "But he was furious with me just the same."[6]

While his battles with Ekland were just beginning, Sellers stirred up trouble on yet another front, this time with Kastner. Sellers, who had abdicated his director's chair in favor of Robert Parrish, thought he merited a directing credit and approached Kastner with this suggestion. Kastner disagreed with Sellers's assessment, and their discussions grew more heated, culminating in a fistfight reminiscent of Sellers's brawl with Joe McGrath during *Casino Royale*.

When *The Bobo* was completed, Sellers sent Kastner the following telegram: "Have received your message and I am not surprised. It is typical of you. I have given all there is that any artist can possibly give to you. *The Bobo* is the last time we will work together."[7]

(Of his relationship with Sellers, Parrish said: "You still know that the next day you could easily receive a letter from him that begins, 'Dear Bob: Please never speak to me again,' or, 'I don't like your kids,' or, 'Why do you drive that kind of car? I hate you for it.' He is a man you cannot anticipate with intelligence because there is no intelligent pattern, no apparent reason, no visible cause."[8])

Adding to Sellers's misery and self-loathing during *The Bobo* was the death, at 72, of his beloved Peg, who passed away in January 1967 while Sellers was in Rome. Amazingly, Sellers refused to return to London when Peg was stricken by her fatal heart attack, an unfathomable move he would regret for the rest of his life.

The news of Peg's death and his ongoing battle with Ekland, Kastner, and Parrish certainly didn't bode well for *The Bobo*'s success and couldn't have helped what little concentration Sellers needed to limn singing matador Juan Bautista, who travels to Barcelona seeking fame and fortune.

The untalented Bautista, with his strange hankering for cheese sandwiches, seeks out and pesters local impresario Francisco Carbonell (Adolfo Celi) into booking him into the local theater. Carbonell finally gives in to Bautista's nagging and agrees to give the singing matador his big break on one condition: that he spend one hour, alone in the dark, with Olimpia Segura (Ekland), a vicious, bitchy gold digger with a soft spot for blue Maseratis. Carbonell gives Bautista three days to complete this insurmountable task.

Bautista piques Olimpia's interest by posing as an "emissary" of Count Martin Contreras, a wealthy playboy who in reality lives in Brazil. The count, taken with her beauty, supposedly wants to meet Olimpia for a romantic evening. But he is a busy man and is always called away on urgent business, leaving Bautista to entertain Olimpia.

Bautista fancies himself a great lover, but his three-day deadline is nearing without much success. Having a difficult time breaking through

Olimpia's icy façade, he plots the grand finale to his scheme. Not only does he buy her a mink coat (using a phony check endorsed by the count), but he takes her to dinner at a posh Barcelona restaurant featuring private rooms with soft music, champagne, and a bed.

Olimpia, of course, thinks Bautista is chaperoning her until the count's arrival and makes herself comfortable. When the count fails once again to materialize, Olimpia inexplicably seduces Bautista, and the two new lovers return to Olimpia's apartment. Out go the lights in Olimpia's bedroom, and Bautista is on his way to stardom.

Almost.

There is still the small matter of the phony check, which is returned to Olimpia the next morning along with any promises of the mink coat. Bautista admits to Olimpia the deal he worked out with Carbonell, and Olimpia, furious at being used and bent on revenge, forces the naked Bautista into a bathtub filled with blue dye. But instead of humiliating Bautista, his blue skin inspires him to bigger and better things: Rather than being just the "singing matador," why not become the "singing blue matador"? It's a marketing ploy that just might work, especially now that Carbonell has reneged on his promise when Bautista lied about not consummating his relationship with Olimpia.

The Bobo was savaged by the critics and quickly slipped into oblivion, resurfacing in later years only as late-night television fodder.

"It's amazing how labored and unfunny is the screenplay of this pseudocomic tale," wrote the *New York Times*'s Bosley Crowther. "And it is downright pitiful to see how wistful and without spirit Mr. Sellers is as this pretentiously quixotic fellow who succeeds, but then is too honorable to take advantage of the deal."[9]

"Sellers occasionally evokes vague memories of Chaplin and a promising young screen comedian named Peter Sellers who was awfully funny in some low-budget British farces," wrote *Newsweek*. "Lately, however, his roles have been playing him, a familiar figure afflicted by gigantosis of the production and paralysis of the talent."[10]

For the record, *Life*'s Richard Schickel raved about the film and Sellers's performance.

> Like Chaplin's celebrated little fellow, he faces absurd misfortune with splendid courage. And more. There is in his character a wonderful scramble of guile and innocence, humility and dignity, not to mention a certain wise, romantic rue that is the real instrument of Olimpia's downfall. What is so good about Sellers' performance is that he never insists upon these emotional generalizations at the expense of specific characterization, is never excessively sweet or sour and never, never tries obviously to turn the Bobo into an Everyman, as so many lesser actors have when they have tried to work a vein that is so trickily laced with fool's gold.[11]

"The Blue Singing Matador" meets his next foe.

For Sellers, the film's quick death was probably a blessing in disguise. His performance was awful. The same man who had brilliantly limned three characters in *Dr. Strangelove* only three years before was now reduced to badly lip-synching a singing matador—in blueface. And he had no one to blame but himself.

Ironically, shortly after *The Bobo* was completed but before its public premiere, Sellers confidently told *London Daily Express* columnist Peter Evans that the next decade will see the fruition of all my hopes. It's going to be a very exciting time, no more crap, nothing but what I really want to do. If you want to be known as a sweet guy, a lovely fella, never a hard word all day, arrives on the set on the dot and gets on with his job, does as he is told and goes home smiling polite good-nights to everyone, and have people say, "there goes Peter Sellers, sure he's all right as an actor—but what a sweet, lovely, gentle human being," fine, you know, if you want that, it's easy.

You abdicate your responsibilities as an actor. I want to be something more than an "all right" actor. So I have to protect myself—from the vultures, from the morons, from the mediocre. Especially the mediocre. I know what's best for me. I do. And on that level, sure, I'm difficult. You bet I'm difficult.

But these were more than idle words. They were a self-inflicted epitaph that would hound Sellers over the next ten years and nearly destroy his career.

28
The Party

Cast:

Hrundi V. Bakshi	Peter Sellers
Michele	Claudine Longet
Levinson	Steve Franken
General Clutterbuck	J. Edward McKinley
C. S. Divot	Gavin MacLeod

STUDIO: United Artists
RELEASE DATE: April 5, 1968
RUNNING TIME: 98 minutes (Panavision/De Luxe)
DIRECTED BY: Blake Edwards
PRODUCED BY: Blake Edwards
WRITTEN BY: Blake Edwards, Tom Waldman, and Frank Waldman
PHOTOGRAPHY: Lucien Ballard
MUSIC: Henry Mancini

The year 1967 found Peter Sellers at a dangerous crossroads in his career. Once one of the industry's biggest box-office draws, Sellers was quickly fading from view and sorely needed a hit to keep his career alive and in the public eye. (On the other hand, it was hard to forget Sellers's private life, which was constantly splashed all over the British tabloids.)

By mid-1967, Sellers had completed no less than thirty-three films in sixteen years, an exhausting pace not slowed a whit by his 1964 heart attack. But while Sellers had worked under some of filmdom's biggest studios—Warner Brothers, United Artists, and Columbia—and had earned an Oscar nomination for *Dr. Strangelove,* he had yet actually to work in Hollywood. Sellers didn't necessarily see this as a drawback. The *Kiss Me, Stupid* affair hadn't exactly ingratiated him to the Hollywood community, for which he never felt any great affinity in the first place.

It was with some irony, then, that Sellers finally stepped onto a Hollywood set when he began shooting *The Party,* Blake Edwards's $3 million comedy that attempted to satirize Hollywood's excesses. While both Sellers and Edwards had sworn never to work together again, their downward career paths didn't give them much choice. And despite their differences, both *The Pink Panther* and *A Shot in the Dark* had proven critical and financial successes.

"Even though I knew his potential for making trouble, our last experience had been a good one," Edwards said. "Peter's career had been at a low ebb then ... and those times, he'd be cooperative and wonderful to work with."[1]

Sellers voiced similar sentiments. "To be honest, I thought I'd never work with him again," he said of Edwards. "During *Shot in the Dark* we were quite incompatible. But I'm the last person to condemn temperament in this business. What matters is, can you produce the goods?"[2]

On paper, *The Party* offered Sellers a chance to "produce the goods" and redeem his sputtering career. Not only would Edwards direct and Henry Mancini provide the elegant soundtrack, echoing the *Panther* films, but Sellers was teamed with young French actress Claudine Longet in a bid to reclaim his younger audience.

As in *The Pink Panther* and *A Shot in the Dark,* Edwards left Sellers room to improvise and expand on Bakshi's scripted character. *The Party's* 63-page script was, in fact, short by Hollywood standards, where a 150-page script is the norm. And to gauge the effect on Sellers's performance immediately, Edwards used an instant-playback television system, a crude precursor to the sophisticated videotape recorders used today on most film sets. "It helped enormously because we had no script," Edwards said. "I mean we had an outline but a script person just couldn't sit there and say he does this and that. We were really ad-libbing so we needed to practice and look at it and not later on in the rushes. It gave us an ongoing record that we could change and modify."[3]

The Party gets off to a fast and funny start in its opening sequence with the introduction of Hrundi V. Bakshi, an Indian actor of little talent recruited by Hollywood's General Federal Studios for a supporting role in *Son of Gunga Din*. Bakshi is given to excess in his first big role and can't seem to do anything right. He bugles through a hail of bullets, refusing to die on cue; wears an underwater wristwatch in a murder scene, oblivious to the fact that *Son of Gunga Din* takes place in the 1870s; and worst of all, ruins the film's finale when, stooping to tie his sandal strap, he puts his foot down and discharges a keg of dynamite that destroys a fort.

Kicked off the *Son of Gunga Din* set by lecherous Producer Charlie "C. S." Divot (Gavin MacLeod), it looks like Bakshi's short-lived Hollywood career has bitten the dust. Bakshi's name is prominently mentioned when Divot phones gruff, cigar-chomping studio head General Fred Clutterbuck (J. Edward McKinley) to explain why the film can't be completed on schedule. Clutterbuck vows the actor "will never work again in this town," but in his anger accidentally writes Bakshi's name on a guest list for a dinner party being thrown by his wife. Bakshi receives an invitation and drives to the general's home, soon to become the life of *The Party*.

In his *Panther* films, Edwards worked furiously to devise different slapstick scenarios for Clouseau, constantly trying to top each ridiculous situation with something even more outrageous. *The Party*'s narrative, scripted by Edwards with help from Tom and Frank Waldman, follows this formula without necessarily distinguishing Bakshi from Clouseau. Save for the Hindustani accent, Bakshi is a Clouseau in brownface, remaining resolute in the face of physical and social absurdities and blind to the havoc he wreaks.

Stylistically, Edwards chose to film *The Party*'s first half like a silent movie, with Sellers as his Keaton or Chaplin. The film, wrote Wilfrid Sheed in *Esquire*, "is about as close as we can now get to those two-reelers, and is a lot better than most of them were."[4] Following the opening *Gunga Din* sequence and *The Party*'s plot establishment, Edwards films Bakshi's arrival and subsequent travails at the Clutterbuck homestead with very little dialogue. Bakshi blunders his way through the film's next half hour, with Sellers relying on facial expressions and purely physical humor to convey the Indian actor's escapades.

Nothing goes right for Bakshi as he alights from his car, burns his hand on the red-hot engine, then soils one of his white shoes. Bakshi enters the opulent Clutterbuck home, complete with a miniature pool in its foyer, and nonchalantly dips his muddied shoe in the water. Naturally the shoe comes off, and when Bakshi devises an ingenious plan to fish it out of the water, using the branch of a plastic plant, he succeeds in flinging the shoe into the Clutterbuck kitchen and onto a platter of hors d'oeuvres. Of course no one notices the white shoe, not even the head waiter carrying the platter, who does a double take when Bakshi quickly plucks his shoe from the platter, exclaiming, "Oh, I'm on a diet, but what the hell!"

Bakshi sidles uncomfortably into the living room, trying to find a friendly face while remaining inconspicuous (wearing a vanilla suit, he is one of the only men not dressed in black-tie formal wear). He sits on the couch next to a couple who immediately get up and leave, and laughs at a joke without knowing what he's laughing at ("I must remember that one," he says). Walking over to a group of people listening to a guest tell how he was robbed, Bakshi suddenly interrupts the story with a whoop of inappropriate laughter.

> *Bakshi* (laughing): They took the gold watch your father left you? (Uncontrollable laughter). I'm sorry, it's utterly fantastic. What a wonderful thing for everyone to do. Take everything including your father's watch. It's wonderful, wonderful. I tell you, tonight is one big round of laughter. All fun and laughter.
> *Clutterbuck* (turning, annoyed, to Bakshi): The congressman was just telling us about the time he was robbed.

Bakshi, his smile frozen, continues to cackle embarrassedly before slinking away. Clutterbuck can only shake his head in disbelief.

Meanwhile, the bullying Divot arrives at the party with his newest conquest, Michele (Longet), a shy French actress who catches Bakshi's attention (Divot fails to recognize Bakshi). But not for long. Bakshi first becomes embroiled in a nonstop string of misadventures that would have made Clouseau green with envy.

Heading to the game room, Bakshi meets his idol, moronic cowboy actor "Wyoming" Bill Kelso. Kelso is trying to teach an Italian starlet how to shoot pool and just wants to be left alone with the "signorina here" so he can make his move. But Bakshi's persistent questions irritate Kelso until Bakshi asks to shake the actor's hand.

"What a wonderful strong grip you've got," Baskshi gasps through gritted teeth. "I would have been disappointed if you hadn't crushed my hand!"

Next it's over to the bird cage, where Bakshi attempts to feed "Birdie Num Num," the Clutterbuck parrot, before spilling birdseed all over the floor. The Clutterbucks' elaborate intercom–electrical system is next on Bakshi's list, nd he creates havoc within minutes. First he brings the party to a standstill by coughing and babbling into the intercom, unaware he can be heard throughout the entire house. Then, with the innocent flick of a few buttons, he ignites the fireplace into a roaring inferno, sprays a guest by adjusting the water output from a urinating statue, and destroys the entire bar.

And there's more.

After having his hand crushed a second time by "Wyoming" Bill, Bakshi plunges his sore fist into a bucket of iced caviar. Unable to get into the bathroom to wash his hands—he walks in on Divot rearranging his toupee—Bakshi sets off an odoriferous chain reaction when he shakes hands with Divot, who in turn shakes hands with Clutterbuck.

Sellers was impeccable in these scenes, resurrecting his pinpoint comedic timing and perfectly painting Bakshi's beatific "little man" persona. And if Bakshi was a variation on Clouseau, at least he was equally funny. Sellers, whose admiration for Indian culture dated back to his wartime experiences, appeared to be enjoying himself immensely.

The Party reaches its fail-safe point in an extended dinner sequence showcasing Steve Franken, a talented character actor-comedian. As Levinson, the butler with an insatiable appetite for booze, Franken kept pace with Sellers throughout the first half of the film, silently wringing laughs from improbable alcohol-induced situations. With his lean physique and rubbery clown's mask, Franken cleverly embellished his stereotypical role, turning Levinson into an original work of art.

Levinson grows progressively tipsier as *The Party* progresses, wading nobly through the Clutterbuck's indoor pool several times, and faces his moment of truth when called upon to serve the dinner guests. Edwards shot this scene in the classic two-reeler silent-comedy style, with Levinson wreaking havoc while the dinner guests, including Bakshi, remain oblivious to everything but their private conversations. The overlapping dialogue, reminiscent of Robert Altman's technique, is kept to a minimum here. Our attention is focused more on Levinson's drunken acrobatics. Whether weaving unsteadily while dishing out salad with his bare hands, choking on a cork (slammed down his throat by a swinging kitchen door), or retrieving Bakshi's errant piece of chicken from a guest's headpiece, Levinson was hilarious.

Typically, though, Edwards indulged in visual overkill, and his clever sight gags—along with *The Party*'s plot—quickly vaporize after the dinner scene, leaving Sellers and company in the lurch. The blossoming romance between Bakshi and Michele is contrived and silly. Edwards and the Waldmans, backed into a corner with nowhere to go, throw a troupe of Russian dancers and a painted elephant into *The Party*'s mixture, and the film ends in a lather of soapsuds while Bakshi and Michele ride off into the sunset.

The Party premiered in April 1968 to an indifferent box-office reception. "I think it was just the wrong time," Edwards said later, explaining the film's box-office failure. "It's hard to say why those things don't happen. A lot of my films happen well after the fact. Suddenly they're discovered."[5]

"Because Peter Sellers is an excellent actor who just happens to have great skill at comedy, rather than a comedian with a continuing, easily recognizable character, he is at a loss in something as flimsy as *The Party*," wrote Vincent Canby in the *New York Times*. "A major problem seems to be that

Bakshi and Michele (Claudine Longet) share a tender moment.

Mr. Sellers' Anglicized Indian fool—a characterization for which he is known and loved in England—is here appealing only in direct ratio to the inventiveness of the predicaments in which he finds himself."[6]

Esquire's Wilfrid Sheed, while more charitable in his assessment of the film, noted that "slapstick, even the best, is the most monotonous of forms, and *The Party* dissolves at last in dismal aquatics.... Peter Sellers does his Indian thing demurely, and for once his self-conscious underplaying is a kindness: it keeps the movie from palling for five minutes longer than nature intended."[7]

29
I Love You, Alice B. Toklas

Cast:
Harold Fine .... Peter Sellers
Nancy .... Leigh Taylor-
Young

Joyce	Joyce Van Patten
Mrs. Fine	Jo Van Fleet
Ben Fine	Salem Ludwig
Murray	Herb Edelman

STUDIO: Warner Brothers/Seven Arts
RELEASE DATE: October 8, 1968
RUNNING TIME: 93 minutes (Technicolor)
DIRECTED BY: Hy Averback
PRODUCED BY: Charles Maguire
WRITTEN BY: Paul Mazursky and Larry Tucker
PHOTOGRAPHY: Philip Lathrop
MUSIC: Elmer Bernstein

The swinging 1960s found Peter Sellers in his haggard forties, twice married and the survivor of a massive heart attack that left the once-plump comedian alarmingly gaunt and perpetually worried. But Sellers had enormous reserves of energy, and the same relentless appetite with which he attacked his radio work, film roles, and personal life pushed him into tasting the forbidden fruits of the 1960s counterculture.

Sellers and the "Goon Show" had, after all, been unwitting progenitors of that culture. The Beatles's outspoken leader, John Lennon, often cited the "Goon Show" as one of his biggest influences (his first book, *In His Own Write,* was a collection of goonish writings and illustrations), as did members of the "Beyond the Fringe" and "Monty Python" comedy troupes. (Sellers, incidentally, was a Beatles fan and reciprocated Lennon's admiration by recording "A Hard Day's Night" and "She Loves You" in the voices of Laurence Olivier and Dr. Strangelove, respectively, for a comedy album.)

Sellers had been smoking marijuana since mid-1963 while filming *The World of Henry Orient* in New York,[1] and began using amyl nitrate to prolong his lovemaking with Britt Ekland, seventeen years his junior. So it was with some firsthand experience that he tackled his role in *I Love You, Alice B. Toklas* as Harold Fine, an asthmatic Jewish lawyer turned on to the "groovy" Los Angeles hippie scene by a flower child and her hash brownies.

With his black Lincoln Continental and comfortable bachelor apartment, Harold, 35, leads a drab, routine existence: work all day in the office, then a few hours in the sack at home with his insecure girlfriend, Joyce, horrified at the thought of being single at the ripe old age of 33 and constantly nagging Harold about marriage. After all, doesn't she sleep with him like his "concubine" and serve as his faithful secretary at the office?

So what's a poor schlepper to do? Harold, continuing the tradition of the beaten-down man, finally gives in to Joyce and unenthusiastically proposes. A few days later, Mr. Foley — the family butcher who, legend has it, once saved Harold's life by "breathing life" into his body—dies, and Harold has to drive out to Venice to retrieve his hippie brother Herbie for the funeral.

Herbie, wearing the "traditional burial outfit of the Hopi Indians" (complete with makeup and a feather headdress) takes a philosophical approach to Mr. Foley's death. "In death there is always rebirth," he tells Harold in perfect hippie-speak. But while Harold is disgusted by Herbie's appearance, he is attracted to Herbie's free-spirited friend Nancy (Leigh Taylor-Young), who accompanies the Fine brothers to Mr. Foley's funeral.

Chaos ensues after the funeral when the striking hearse drivers refuse to take Mr. Foley's coffin to the cemetery. Harold volunteers for the job but loses the funeral procession at a red light. Having no idea where the cemetery is, Harold, Joyce, Herbie, and Nancy drive around until nightfall before discovering the burial site.

After dropping off Joyce, Harold is driving back to his apartment when he spots Nancy hitching a ride. Alert to the dangers posed by "sex maniacs and perverts," Harold picks Nancy up and takes her back to his apartment, offering her his couch for the night and promising "no funny stuff." While he nervously inhales his asthma medicine, Nancy fires up a marijuana joint and settles in to watch television.

When Harold leaves for work the next morning, Nancy decides to make some brownies for her hospitable host. But these aren't just regular brownies. They're "Alice B. Toklas" brownies, liberally laced with hashish from a recipe concocted by Gertrude Stein's longtime lover.

Later that evening, Harold returns home with Joyce and his parents to discuss seating arrangements for the wedding. While in the kitchen getting some ice water for his father, Harold finds a note from Nancy explaining that she made some "groovy brownies" for him. Harold, his parents, and Joyce find out just how groovy the brownies are when they dig in for a chocolate treat.

Cut to Mr. and Mrs. Fine, cackling hysterically about nothing in particular while Harold sits on the floor in a stoned stupor, oblivious to Joyce's animallike seduction as she loosens his tie and unbuttons his shirt (growling, "Take me, Harold"). The stoned quartet decide to play miniature golf, and while Joyce, Ben, and his mother concentrate on their game, Harold wanders off to the "mod" boutique where Nancy works to thank her for the brownies.

As if getting stoned for the first time weren't enough for Harold, imagine his surprise when a pipe-smoking man walks into the boutique in search of a woman's dress—for himself! In the film's funniest scene, Harold, giggling uncontrollably, tries to maintain his composure while the man earnestly models his dress for Nancy, suggesting possible alterations to the hemline.

Afterward, Harold and Nancy return to Harold's apartment and engage in some "free love" that cracks Harold's conservative mold and liberates the buttoned-down lawyer. When it comes time for his big wedding day, Harold gets as far as the altar, tells Joyce how nice she looks, then turns around and bolts out of the catering hall, tuxedo and all, and into Nancy's arms, ready to experience the groovin' 1960s.

Within a matter of hours, Nancy transforms Harold into a hippie, and soon they move out of Harold's apartment and into his car. In a series of quick vignettes, we see Harold's immersion in the flower-power movement: his once-coiffed hair now shoulder length, he and Nancy commune on the beach, stark naked. Harold walks the beach with his guru, trying to comprehend the meaning of the universe. Hassled by cops in the back of Harold's car, Harold tells the policemen he "loves" them for doing their job.

But Harold's hippie days are numbered, especially when Nancy invites a bunch of friends over to Harold's apartment. Finding Nancy tattooing another man, Harold creates a "bad scene" by showing his possessiveness, then awakens the next morning and suddenly realizes the madness with which he's lived his life the past few months. Soon it's back to the forgiving Joyce and his square lifestyle—and, of course, the unfinished wedding vows.

But the hippie spirit hasn't completely died within Harold's soul. If anything, Nancy has taught him what it's like to live a life uncomplicated by social routines, including a wife and family. So once again poor Joyce is left standing at the altar as Harold runs away from his responsibilities, seeking a higher truth in the cosmos.

Sellers began filming director Hy Averback's satire almost immediately after wrapping *The Party* for Blake Edwards. Having never cared much for America, especially Hollywood, Sellers was in a surly mood during the film's production, feeding his reputation as an on-set troublemaker. He was stuck in a hostile environment, engaged in cross-country battles with Ekland (who was in New York filming *The Night They Raided Minsky's*), and still haunted by Peg's death.

Joyce Haber, writing in the *Los Angeles Times,* noted that "Peter Sellers is behaving like a brat. He has threatened to walk off his new movie, *I Love You, Alice B. Toklas* unless the entire crew is changed. He contends there's a spy on the set—and indeed all his latest little sorties behind the camera have been reported with unaccustomed rancor by a certain Hollywood columnist...."[2]

On the surface, casting Sellers as an American Jewish lawyer—"pastrami on crumpet," observed one wag[3]—seems downright peculiar. But as he did in *Heavens Above,* Sellers drew from a vast reservoir of personal experience, most notably his half–Jewish background embodied in his love-hate relationship with Peg. It is no coincidence that the one aspect of Harold

Harold and Joyce (Joyce Van Patten) sample the Alice B. Toklas brownies.

Fine's life that rings truest is the scenes in which he appears with his smothering mother, limned campily by *East of Eden* Oscar winner Jo Van Fleet (who, at 46, was only three years older than Sellers). Mrs. Fine, in all her Jewish-mother glory, scolds, cajoles, and nags Harold, yet still takes time out to buy her oldest son a jar of coffee ("they had a sale on instant at the Safeway") and straighten up his apartment. And much like Bill Sellers, Ben Fine (Salem Ludwig) defers to his dominating wife, content to remain in the background.

Performing within this familiar context wasn't much of a stretch for Sellers; had these relationships been more deeply explored, they might have added depth to the film's shallow structure. But Harold's parental relationships were only a subtext of the *I Love You, Alice B. Toklas* plot. Sellers was asked to do much more than interact with his "parents," and the film degenerates into a one-joke premise that was badly dated by the time of its October 1968 release.

Sellers seems strangely subdued throughout in a part screaming for the outrageousness of a Dr. Fritz Fassebender. He played the straitlaced Harold with a melancholia suited to the lawyer's conservative, henpecked existence. But when Harold "drops out" of society, Sellers falters noticeably, self-consciously spouting Harold's pseudohippie jargon with little conviction or enthusiasm.

Harold "turns on and tunes out" with flower child Nancy (Leigh Taylor-Young).

More persuasive and true to the film's spirit was Leigh Taylor-Young, totally believable as an empty-headed flower child symbolic of the period's confused youth.

In addition to its questionable timing, the film suffers badly from Averback's weak direction. A television veteran known primarily for the long-running "F Troop" comedy series, Averback shot his film in a sitcom style. One can almost hear the canned laughtrack behind the pregnant pauses, exaggerated expressions, static movement, and jerky editing style.

Mazursky and Tucker's script—a harbinger of the social commentary they perfected a year later in *Bob and Carol and Ted and Alice*—would have been better suited for a weekly television series than a feature-length film. (Ironically, an attempt to adapt *Bob and Carol* to the small screen failed.)

Mazursky, the film's original director, was reportedly unhappy with Averback's unimaginative direction. But Averback was only partly to blame. The Mazursky-Tucker script is irritatingly smug in its convictions and remarkably one-dimensional in its aspirations.

Although it's virtually impossible to miss the film's redundant sledgehammer symbolism, the Harold Fine character rings false on various fronts. If Harold, the epitome of a 1960s square, *really* surrenders everything at the drop of a hat, why doesn't he give up his apartment? Harold and Nancy live in Harold's car, but somehow Harold, unemployed, manages to pay the rent on his fancy digs, even after renouncing his former materialism.

The film's supporting cast abounds in stereotypes, particularly the eleven-member Mexican Rodriguez family driving around in their broken-down truck with a load of chickens. This gratuitous subplot seems to exist solely for the purpose of minority bashing.

Not surprisingly, *I Love You, Alice B. Toklas* opened to generally negative reviews and didn't fare well at the box office. Sellers was for the most part spared the critics' wrath (which focused on the film's screenplay and direction), but this was of little consolation to an actor desperate for a hit.

"Along the journey to nowhere, Sellers displays a few glimmers of the comic genius that once made him seem like a chip off the old Chaplin," *Time* opinéd. "But most of the time, the movie reduces him to elephantine gestures and TV-sized jokes."[4]

"*I Love You, Alice B. Toklas* . . . is a picture that merely looks experimental, dealing as it does with the world of psychedelics, drop-outs, and kooks," wrote *Saturday Review*'s Arthur Knight. "Actually, both in theme and treatment it bespeaks an utterly safe, conformist kind of experimentalism."[5]

"No one can completely prevent Sellers from being funny, so there are some laughs, skimpy ones," Stanley Kauffman wrote in the *New Republic*. "The picture's chief negative accomplishment is that it makes hippies seem more stale, dull, and conventional (by their own conventions) than anyone in the square world."[6]

Sellers was furious at Warner Brothers. He alleged that the company "hacked the picture around with nail scissors," and proceeded to bribe a night watchman into letting him use the editing room to splice back into the film interviews with Allen Ginsberg and Timothy Leary. Warner, however, insisted no one would know who Leary and Ginsberg were, and the scenes remained cut from the finished film.[7]

"During the making of *I Love You, Alice B. Toklas* in 1968, there were two cuts, ours and the studios, and theirs was the final cut," Sellers told *Rolling Stone*'s Mitchell Glazer. "I wish you'd seen the original one with the interviews with Allen Ginsberg and Tim Leary. [Screenwriters] Paul Mazursky and Larry Tucker and myself, we even got in the lab at night and *we* cut the film. Can you believe it? We bribed the guard, we spent all night with an editor, and when the schmucks came in the following day, we were there bright and early as though we'd just arrived, and we said, 'Listen, we don't like the finished film. We think you should see our attempts.'"[8]

It was a despondent Sellers who returned to Britain in the spring of 1968, divorced Ekland, and set his sights on his next project, an adaptation of Terry Southern's satiric novel *The Magic Christian*.

30
The Magic Christian

Cast:
Sir Guy Grand   ......   Peter Sellers
Youngman Grand   ....   Ringo Starr

STUDIO: Commonwealth United
RELEASE DATE: February 12, 1970
RUNNING TIME: 95 minutes (Technicolor)
DIRECTED BY: Joe McGrath
PRODUCED BY: Dennis O'Dell
WRITTEN BY: Terry Southern, Joe McGrath, and Peter Sellers (from the novel by Terry Southern)
PHOTOGRAPHY: Geoffrey Unsworth
MUSIC: Ken Thorne

By the end of 1969, Sellers's waning popularity was most evident in his shrinking salary structure. During the apex of his career in the mid-1960s, Sellers was commanding roughly $1 million per picture. But after his string of box-office disasters that figure had been cut to about $400,000.[1]

Sellers had failed to capture the younger generation's fancy with *I Love You, Alice B. Toklas* but hoped to strike a countercultural nerve with his next film, *The Magic Christian,* an adaptation of Terry Southern's 1960 novel about the exploits of billionaire Sir Guy Grand, who proves through outlandish pranks that every person has his price.

"It has many imperfections but it's designed primarily for the young," Sellers told *Esquire.* "The message is corruption by money and power. We wanted to show that the Establishment is absolutely destructible. Rules are made to be broken. And they are, by God. You're told, 'Do this. Don't do that. No. Don't. Don't.' And the young are now answering, 'Who says? Why?' It's a film for heads."[2]

For the first time in his career, Sellers took a screenwriting credit and enlisted the aid of Southern and Joe McGrath in helping script *The Magic Christian* narrative. (Future "Monty Python" members John Cleese and Graham Chapman, both of whom had cameos in the film, also were credited with "additional material.") Southern had lent his sexually satiric edge to *Dr. Strangelove* and was an underground legend. McGrath, whose previous working relationship with Sellers ended in a fistfight on the *Casino Royale* set, was also tapped to direct the picture.

In a further attempt to capture a youthful audience, Sellers cast Beatle Ringo Starr as Sir Guy's son and solicited Paul McCartney to pen the film's signature pop tune, "Come and Get It" and its telling chorus: "Did I hear you say that there must be a catch? Will you walk away from a fool and his money?" Sung by Beatles protégés Badfinger, "Come and Get It" was the film's most memorable achievement.

Sellers procured financing from Commonwealth United, a new company overseen by financier Bernie Cornfeld but once again ignored the ominous warning signs. The Boultings told Sellers *The Magic Christian* script spelled "disaster," while McGrath was amazed at how little Commonwealth United questioned Sellers's motives:

> Peter and I met with the Commonwealth United people. They said to me, "How do you see this? What kind of character is this Guy Grand fellow?" I looked at Peter. He said to me, "Go on, Joe, show them." *Me* show them! I was only going to direct the picture; he was going to play the role, if we ever got it set up. Anyhow I did the first thing that came into my head, which was an imitation of Peter doing Inspector Clouseau, while he sat there with a straight face. When I'd finished, the Commonwealth United people said, "Great!" and shelled out fifteen million dollars.[3]

After much soul-searching, Sellers finally decided to play Sir Guy as a "boozed" version of British Prime Minister Harold Macmillan, complete wtih graying wavy hair and fashionable moustache, after a process of elimination that included the "Goon Show's" Major Bloodnok, W. C. Fields, and George Bernard Shaw with red hair, beard, and plus fours.[4]

Out for a brisk morning walk one fine day, Guy encounters a scraggly long-haired young man (Starr) feeding bread to the ducks. Guy decides to join this young man in his trivial pursuit, using a crisp pound note for his "bread" and inviting the man back to his palatial London estate where he adopts his "son," heretofore known as "Youngman" Grand.

As Youngman quickly learns, "Dad" is generous with his wealth—provided it's used to showcase society's greed and exploit man's basic lust for money and power. Not only does Guy bribe people into performing outrageously ridiculous acts, but he delights in perpetuating chaos among the privileged classes, the bane of society. "Sometimes it's not enough to teach," he admonishes Youngman. "One has to punish as well."

So it's off to the theater in Guy's private helicopter—piloted, of course, by Pontius—where a grand scheme lies in wait for the upper crusties watching Laurence Harvey portray Hamlet. Snaking his way down the castle stairs, Harvey suddenly gyrates his hips, begins unbuttoning his shirt, and turns Hamlet's famous soliloquy into a bawdy striptease act. He ends the speech with a flourish, removing his last stitch of clothing to the audience's horrified gasps before being carried Christlike up the stairs.

This scene sets *The Magic Christian*'s surrealistic, frenetic tone and opens the floodgates for Guy's progressively bizarre pranks as he tests mankind's mettle and spears several sacred cows along his road to redemption.

Dining in a fancy restaurant and covered in a plastic wrap, Guy smears Beluga caviar all over his face in full view of the horrified patrons. In a heavyweight boxing match fixed by Guy, the American and British champs clinch, then kiss passionately at the opening bell. An Oxford crew coached by Richard Attenborough and helmed by Chapman is bribed by Guy into destroying the annual race with Cambridge. Policeman Spike Milligan ravenously eats a parking ticket to Guy's tune of £500 ("I'm here every Thursday," he reminds Guy). A Sotheby's manager (Cleese) is talked into selling Guy an "unauthenticated Rembrandt" for three times its value, then watches in horror as Guy attacks the painting with scissors.

But Guy saves his biggest prank for the voyage of the *Magic Christian*, a luxurious ocean liner departing London for New York, its passenger list open only to society's crème de la crème. Of course, the *Christian* really isn't sailing anywhere; it's actually a giant scale model ensconced in a warehouse. But for Guy, the *Christian* is his grandest invention, his chance to unleash his contempt for the power-hungry ruling class and have a giggle at the same time.

During the liner's short voyage, Guy preys on the passengers' fears and prejudices. A snobbish passenger sniffing at blacks is suddenly engaged in a seductive dance by a black bodybuilder. Captain Wilfrid Hyde-White pretends to be taken hostage by a gang of hijackers, throwing the passengers into a frenzy. Yul Brynner, dressed as a woman, sings "Mad About the Boy" to a leering passenger before ripping off his wig. There's Christopher Lee, dressed as Dracula, preying on the female passengers. And with whip in hand, scantily clad Raquel Welch in the ship's engine room, slave-driving a gaggle of naked galley slaves.

For his encore, Guy, wearing a gas mask, pours animal manure and urine into a huge vat, promising "free money" to anyone brave enough to wade into the putrid mixture (which, of course, they do).

Sellers wanted to shoot this scene at the Statue of Liberty in New York, where it took place in Southern's novel. But Commonwealth United refused to grant permission, forcing Sellers to substitute St. Paul's Cathedral.[5]

The Magic Christian aspired to scale the heights of social satire and succeeded on many fronts. Its mixture of psychedelia and black humor hammered its point—perhaps to excess—that every man has his price, and Sellers seemed totally at ease in the guise of Guy Grand, delivering a relaxed, funny performance in a role that didn't tax his talents in any way.

The film's quirky quick-cut editing was at times infuriating and tended to destroy whatever pacing McGrath had instilled into the narrative. But while some complained that McGrath did little but film a succession of vaudeville-type blackout sketches, he succeeded remarkably well in delivering Southern's message to the masses.

When it was released in February 1970, however, *The Magic Christian* fared poorly at the box office and disappeared quickly from view. Perhaps, like *I Love You, Alice B. Toklas,* it was a victim of bad timing. More realistically, its star was no longer a major force in the industry, having lost his loyal audience in his post–*Pussycat* shuffle of bad films.

"The film ... purports to give upper-middle-class shibboleths a jolly beating. Instead, it is just another flagging satire, with ludicrous overtones of homosexual lubricity," *Time* sniffed in its review. "Peter Sellers continues his comic decline...."[6]

"Unfunny camp is contemptible," wrote the *New Yorker.* "*The Magic Christian,* Terry Southern's novel, relocated in England and directed by Joseph McGrath, has been made into such an inert collection of bad jokes that even the mean-spiritedness of the original fails to come through."[7]

Sellers and *The Magic Christian* received a ringing endorsement, however, from the usually staid *New York Times.*

> In filming *The Magic Christian* ... he [McGrath] has filtered some unusually brutal satire through his own compassionate vision [wrote Roger Greenspun]. *The Magic Christian* is funny, uncomfortable and without an ounce of benevolence.... Ringo is fine, and Sellers is finer—in a performance that vastly enriches and normalizes the archly enthusiastic Porky Pig of Terry Southern's imagination.[8]

Sellers undoubtedly took little solace in the fact that upon *The Magic Christian*'s completion he sold his Elstead home to Ringo Starr. And though the film would eventually become something of an underground classic, Sellers's film career had all but ended with a soft thud.

31
Hoffman

Cast:
Benjamin Hoffman ... Peter Sellers
Janet Smith .... Sinead Cusack
Tom .... Jeremy Bulloch

STUDIO: ABP/Longstone
RELEASE DATE: July 16, 1970
RUNNING TIME: 113 minutes (Technicolor)
DIRECTED BY: Alvin Rakoff

PRODUCED BY: Ben Arbeid
WRITTEN BY: Ernest Gebler (from his novel
    and play)
PHOTOGRAPHY: Gerry Turpin
MUSIC: Ron Grainer

It was no coincidence that the bane of Peter Sellers's film career, besides poor judgment, was the roles in which he was forced to play "himself" without the benefit of vocal or physical embellishment. The lifeless performances he delivered in segments of *The Mouse That Roared* and *Casino Royale* would continue on a much larger scale in *Hoffman*, in which Sellers played his character in his own voice and melancholic face. Sellers was a chameleon who needed the comfort of his on-screen personae to escape his confused personal life. *Hoffman* struck an exposed Sellers nerve, causing the actor considerable mental agony.

Director Bryan Forbes had been named production chief at EMI's Elstree film studios and called upon Sellers to star in an adaptation of Ernest Gebler's novel and stage play. After *The Magic Christian* disaster, Sellers's bankability had hit an all-time low. He was no longer being deluged by film offers, and *Hoffman* would at least offer him the refuge of work.

In 1969 the British public had been shocked at the portrayal of Sellers as a depressed, lonely man in *Will the Real Peter Sellers...?*, a BBC documentary filmed by the *Observer*'s Tony Palmer, who shot Sellers's daily routine for nine months. So dismal was Sellers's outlook that the BBC reluctantly broadcast the film. (Spike Milligan had warned Palmer not to proceed with the project. "You can't film despair, so why bother?" Milligan told him.)[1]

Sellers, always concerned about his public image, shrugged off Palmer's documentary and labeled it misleading fiction:

> That film gave a completely distorted, absolutely incorrect picture of me. I got lots of letters from people who saw it and wanted either to mother me or marry me. It was ridiculous, because I'm not at all like that. I'm definitely not miserable or dissatisfied or depressed. Oh, I do have moments of solitude and quietude when I think about life and its meaning—like most people. But on the whole I'm a very happy fellow. Is anyone ever completely happy?[2]

To those who knew Sellers privately or professionally, his remarks could also be construed as fiction. It was apparent that Sellers was sinking into a morass of self-pity, and *Hoffman* was the perfect vehicle to feed the comedian's masochistic feelings of desperation.

Sellers played Benjamin Hoffman, a lonely, friendless fortyish Londoner who blackmails lissome young secretary Janet Smith (Sinead Cusack) into spending a week at his comfortable flat.

Hoffman, echoing Sellers's oft-repeated sentiments, sees himself as one of life's anonymous victims, cursed with a "plain, sad face" that renders his existence utterly forgettable. The victim of an alcoholic wife and messy divorce, Hoffman detests women. They're "fallopian tubes with teeth" who prey on men and destroy their lives.

Hoffman's misogynism, however, takes form in wild sexual fantasies. He bitterly regards women as pure sex objects without minds, yet dreams of "a naked, pale, fair girl found in my bed one summer morning" and projects this fantasy to Janet, who works in the steno pool at Hoffman's office. Hoffman has worshiped the curvaceous Janet from afar for over a year but hasn't forgotten her cruel snub of his one romantic advance—a note asking her out for a date, which she never answered yet shared with the rest of the office.

But Hoffman finally gets his chance to snare his prey and "put her to good use" when he spies Janet's fiancé, Tom (Jeremy Bulloch), selling company information to a gang of crooks. Hoffman threatens to blow the whistle on Tom unless Janet agrees to live with him for a week.

Under the guise of visiting her sick grandmother in Scarborough, Janet travels to Hoffman's apartment where the seemingly lecherous bachelor waits to implement his scheme. Hoffman, however, hides his desires under a cloak of veiled hatred, mentally torturing Janet by referring to her only as Miss Smith, as though she were a nonperson, and refusing to pander to her feminine wiles. "You must never become a person, Miss Smith," he casually informs the confused secretary. "That would be unendurable."

Janet, of course, is horrified at her predicament. "Who would have suspected?" she asks herself. "No one hardly noticed him. I never did." After trying unsuccessfully to escape Hoffman's clutches several times and being warned what will happen should she leave, Janet settles in for what promises to be a long trying week with a most peculiar man.

But there's a method to Hoffman's madness. Although he repeatedly belittles Janet and makes no romantic overtures in their first days together, he really does want her to like him. He takes her to an elegant restaurant (she gets heartburn), and for a splendid walk in the country (she skins her heel), and tucks her in at night (she gets a stiff neck). Before long, Janet begins to take a shine to her strange host's sophisticated manners.

On their fourth day together, Hoffman's suppressed emotions finally overtake him. He kisses Janet for the first time (much to her relief), then takes her to see the new flat he's having renovated. By the time they return to Hoffman's apartment, the couple is a picture of domesticity, she sewing in an overstuffed easy chair while he plays the piano.

But their bliss is cut short by three days when Janet phones Tom and learns he's planning to travel to Scarborough for a visit. She has to leave the next morning, and Hoffman, desperate to retain his newfound happiness,

Lonely London bachelor Benjamin Hoffman plots his next move on Miss Smith (Sinead Cusack). (Courtesy National Films Archive, London.)

phones Tom and lures him to the apartment, where he finds Janet lying in Hoffman's bed, eating breakfast and reading the morning newspaper.

After a hurried explanation, Janet returns with Tom to the flat he shares with his mother while Hoffman sits alone in the dark, taking pity on himself and his lost opportunity. But Janet, realizing he's treated her better than Tom ever could, decides to return to Hoffman as his live-in lover.

Its aspirations as an understated sex comedy notwithstanding, *Hoffman* was a complete disaster in every facet of conception and delivery. The problems started at the top with Alvin Rakoff's dull direction. Rakoff shot his scenes at interminable length with little camera or character movement— like a bad situation comedy—creating a stifling atmosphere that snuffed out any semblance of wit or character development. Gebler's pointless narrative plodded along aimlessly, leaving both Sellers and Cusack to twist in the wind.

Sellers, playing a variation of his real-life persona, was unconvincing and withdrawn, portraying Hoffman as a pathetic soul who could never have undertaken such a devious scheme. He delivered his lines in a soft whisper, perhaps because he was forced to mouth some incredibly embarrassing dialogue ("Please make yourself look as if you want to be fertilized" or "I want to eat you, consume you, lick your knees"). In what was intended as a light comedy, the gravity of Sellers's black, depressing bearing weighed down the entire film.

On the other hand, Cusack delivered a funny, touching performance in a thankless role. Janet's schoolgirl charm, tempered by the limitations of life in the steno pool, was *Hoffman*'s only bright spot.

"Sellers, both as the apparent lecher and the lonely romantic middle age would-be lover, gives a farily glum rendering of the role and at times is listless to the point of tedium," wrote *Variety*. "However, a bonus is Miss Cusack.... She's a distinct find, with only a couple of credits behind her. She has a neat figure, an appealing face, a most intriguingly wary pair of eyes, mouth and voice and with better roles looks to be a young thesp to watch."[3]

"Mr. Sellers is ridiculously sinister most of the time, in a role so solemnly written it allows him no room for wit or whimsy," Janet Maslin wrote in the *New York Times*. "When Alvin Rakoff, the director, finally brings the action out of Hoffman's apartment and into a restaurant, Mr. Sellers positively blossoms, just from the change of pace...."[4]

By the time *Hoffman* premiered, Sellers had already begged Forbes to destroy the picture and when that failed, publicly bad-mouthed the film.[5] Once again, his judgment had failed him.

32
There's a Girl in My Soup

Cast:

Robert Danvers	Peter Sellers
Marian	Goldie Hawn
Jimmy	Nicky Henson
Andrew Hunter	Tony Britton
John	John Comer

STUDIO: Columbia
RELEASE DATE: December 23, 1971 (Eastmancolor)
RUNNING TIME: 96 minutes
DIRECTED BY: Roy Boulting
PRODUCED BY: John Boulting
WRITTEN BY: Terence Frisby (from his stage play)
PHOTOGRAPHY: Harry Waxman
MUSIC: Mike D'Abo

For a fleeting moment in 1970, Peter Sellers reemerged into the cinematic mainstream. It took the persuasive talents of Sellers's old friends John and Roy Boulting to coax Columbia Pictures into bankrolling another Sellers vehicle. The studio hadn't forgotten the *Casino Royale* debacle nor its unofficial Sellers blacklisting, but the Boultings, staking their reputation, promised to keep Sellers in check during the filming of their newest comedy, *There's a Girl in My Soup*.

The film, adapted from Terence Frisby's successful stage play (starring Gig Young and Barbara Ferris on Broadway), promised the spendthrift Sellers not only a $350,000 fee plus a net share of the profits[1] but the chance to work with rising young American comedienne Goldie Hawn. The blond saucer-eyed Hawn, fresh from her Oscar-winning performance in *Cactus Flower* and successful stint on television's *Laugh In*, was being hailed as the next Judy Holliday.

After his angst-ridden portrayal of Benjamin Hoffman, sans makeup or "other" voice, Sellers jumped at the opportunity to transform himself once again into an on-screen alter ego. This time it would be Robert Danvers, a suave womanizer whose persona Sellers based on the dashing Patrick Lichfield, a cousin of the queen.

"He asked us how he should play the part. He didn't always take such advice, but it helped clarify his mind," said John Boulting, the film's producer. "My brother Roy said, 'I think we can take you to meet someone like the character.' In this, I must admit, there was an element of mischief. Roy and I set up a luncheon, so that Peter could study the man at close quarters. It helped that he was a top photographer, as well as a man with a reputation for enjoying life. 'Peter,' we said as he came in, 'we'd like you to meet Patrick Lichfield.'"[2]

Sellers once again was "taken over" by the role and continued to play Robert Danvers once the cameras stopped rolling. *Esquire*'s Helen Lawrenson, who had interviewed Sellers before he embarked on the film, noticed a marked personality change when she visited Sellers on the set of *There's a Girl in My Soup*:

> I realized there was something different about him. His expression, his gestures, the way he walked, his tone of voice—light, flippant, urbane, superficially charming. He certainly wasn't being the same person to whom I had talked in his flat. I couldn't figure it until I watched the next scene being shot.... Obviously he was being elegant, charming and sophisticated off camera as well, a blasé gay-dog type instead of the forthright, serious, rather oldfangled fellow I had first met.[3]

The film's production got off to a rocky start when on the first day of shooting Sellers was convinced a script girl was giving him the evil eye and demanded she be removed from the picture. Director Roy Boulting was

Danvers tries to seduce the unenthusiastic Marian (Goldie Hawn).

able to allay Sellers's fears by telling him the girl had asked to work on the picture because of her "intense admiration" for Sellers.[4]

There's a Girl in My Soup examines two weeks in the life of narcissistic wine connoisseur Robert Danvers, a middle-aged lothario whose aphrodisiac for the nameless women he beds nightly in his swinging bachelor pad is his popular television show, "Robert Danvers' Good Taste." Like Sellers, Danvers is gadget crazy. His plush lair is the ultimate in remote-control seduction, complete with wall-to-wall stereo sound and an automated bed. Unlike Sellers, however, Danvers is an insufferable romantic unable to love anyone but himself.

Enter Marian (Goldie Hawn), a forthright 19-year-old blond American who invites herself back to Danvers's apartment after a fight with Jimmy (Nicky Henson), her long-haired British boyfriend. Danvers quickly learns that Marian is quite unlike any of his past conquests. For starters, she is unimpressed with Danvers and doesn't even know who he is. And she also sees right through Danvers's smooth-talking veneer, refusing to be seduced by his wiles. "You ought to watch that little laugh," she tells him. "It's a dead giveaway."

While he is initially repelled by Marian's sassy attitude, Danvers soon grows enamored of her perky personality, and after she moves into Danvers's apartment—a first for any woman—he invites her to a wine-tasting festival in France. Their mutual admiration soon blossoms into something close to love, and the couple head to the French Riviera where they pretend to be married. Cavorting on the beach by day and dancing their nights away in the swinging French discos, Robert and Marian are the picture-perfect couple.

But Marian knows that Robert could never make a lifelong commitment and decides to return to the self-centered Jimmy upon the couple's return to London. Robert, suddenly finding himself in love for the first time, proposes to Marian in a last-ditch attempt to keep her for himself. She turns him down, but as a compromise promises to continue seeing him even while living with Jimmy.

Although *There's a Girl in My Soup* was nothing more than an extended situation comedy, it presented Sellers with his meatiest role in years and gave him the chance to subtly shade a recognizable character with his sense of the absurd. And he didn't disappoint. If the public wanted to view Robert Danvers as an extension of Sellers's jet-setting private life, then Sellers hit his mark with precision accuracy. He painted Danvers as a vain egocentric with none of the inner humility of a Juan Bautista or Hrundi Bakshi.

The film's critical reception was mixed. "Sellers' sly and weary predator is understated just enough to set off Miss Hawn's toughly insouciant and dopey-wise waif," wrote Alex Keneas in *Newsweek*. "At their best they create two people who are sexual adversaries."[5] "The Boultings seem to have a way of combining contemporary mores with genuine decency.... Miss Hawn's performance is credible and restrained, ditto Sellers, who has his best role since *I Love You, Alice B. Toklas*," *Variety* gushed enthusiastically.[6] *Saturday's Review*'s Arthur Knight, however, scolded Sellers as "an actor who will accept direction from no one. Cast as a television personality with an insatiable letch, he primps, smirks, and rolls his heavy-lidded eyes seductively in shot after shot after shot, as if convinced that his own delight in being Sellers were something that the entire world would automatically share."[7]

Surprisingly, the age difference between Sellers (45) and Hawn (25)— the key element in Frisby's narrative—sparked a believable on-screen chemistry, as did the disparities between Sellers's British playboy and Hawn's American teenager.

"Working with Peter Sellers was one of the high points of my career," Hawn said later. "He didn't criticize or treat me like a novice as some people said he would. He was an extraordinary man and a great talent, and someone I found very complicated, very inspiring and very, very funny. He had a marvelous sense of humor on the set. There were times we were laughing so hard that we'd have to break for lunch. There was no way we could do the scene."[8]

Hawn delivered a bubbly performance in a role tailored for her equally

Danvers meets his match in Jimmy (Nicky Henson), Marian's shaggy boyfriend.

bubbly persona and won a victory of sorts over the "dumb blond" stereotype. Marian was portrayed as an intelligent, sensitive young woman, a far cry from what people expected from the giggly Hawn.

But to Sellers intimates, the upbeat Danvers was a far cry from the mercurial comedian's depressive mind-set, which wouldn't be helped by the upcoming roles he would choose.

33
Where Does It Hurt?

Cast:

Albert Hopfnagel	Peter Sellers
Alice Gilligan	Jo Ann Pflug
Lester Hammond	Rick Lenz
Dr. Zerny	Harold Gould
Nurse La Marr	Eve Druce
Leffingwell	J. Edward McKinley

STUDIO: Josef Shaftel Productions
RELEASE DATE: August 11, 1972
RUNNING TIME: 88 minutes (color)
DIRECTED BY: Rod Amateau
PRODUCED BY: Rod Amateau and William Schwarz
WRITTEN BY: Rod Amateau and Budd Robinson (from their novel *The Operator*)
PHOTOGRAPHY: Brick Marquard
MUSIC: Keith Allison

Whatever momentum *There's a Girl in My Soup* might have given his career couldn't be sustained, and Sellers sank back into the B-movie ranks shortly thereafter.

He followed his starring role alongside Goldie Hawn with a turn as a homosexual in *A Day at the Beach,* written by his pal Roman Polanski and filmed in Denmark by Polanski protégé Simon Hesera. Unreleased to the general public (the first of three unreleased films in which Sellers would appear over the next three years), *A Day at the Beach* revolved around a drunken roustabout (Mark Burns) and the crippled little girl (Beatrice Edney) with whom he spends his rainy day.

"Peter Sellers gives a short (non-credited) lecture in acting as a homosexual kiosk-keeper on the beach," *Variety* wrote in its review of the film, shown as a noncompetitor at the 1970 Cannes Film Festival. "Everything else about the film winds up looking as though it had been left out in the rain, too long."[1]

Sellers refused to discuss his *A Day at the Beach* experience in subsequent interviews. Next, he embarked on a 20th Century–Fox adaptation of *Alice's Adventures in Wonderland,* in which he had a minor role as the March Hare opposite the likes of Dudley Moore, Spike Milligan, Dennis Price, and Ralph Richardson. (Sellers had played the King of Hearts in Jonathan Millers's 1966 British television production.)

Where Does It Hurt?, his next film, found Sellers in his detested milieu,

Sellers (far left) as the March Hare in *Alice's Adventures in Wonderland*. (Courtesy National Film Archives, London.)

Hollywood, playing a corrupt hospital administrator. The film passed itself off as a hip black comedy, which it most definitely wasn't, wildly missing its intended targets and settling for sophomoric smutty humor penned by Rod Amateau, adapting his novel (cowritten by Budd Robinson) *The Operator.*

Yet *Where Does It Hurt?* did achieve this distinction: It ranks as the most technically atrocious fiasco ever associated with Sellers's film career. The careless, unprofessional, lazy production values of the film were unbelievable and had to be seen to be believed: boom microphones (and the hirsute arms working them) visible in almost every scene; visible microphone wires taped to the actors' clothing; and scenes in which the studio ceiling (and klieg lights) could be seen over the tops of the all-too-obvious prop walls and doors. It almost defied explanation.

How this could have escaped the notice of Coproducers Amateau and William Schwarz or Cinematographer Brick Marquard is beyond comprehension—unless, of course, they really didn't care. After all, the film was obviously shot on a minuscule budget under the auspices of something called Josef Shaftel Productions, and a "name" talent like Peter Sellers—desperate now for any kind of work—had been dragged into this sea of celluloid sewage.

Adopting an American accent and variety of fancy suits, Sellers played Albert T. Hopfnagel, chief administrator for Vista Vue, a fraudulent Los Angeles hospital where nurses, doctors, and lab technicians get a "piece of the action"—a percentage of every patient's total hospital bill, inflated beyond belief by unnecessary tests, operations, and long hospital stays.

Hopfnagel, full of annoying catchphrases ("ten–four") and unscrupulously sleazy, communicates covertly with hospital personnel through the hallway Pepsi machine doubling as a secret entrance to his office. But he's also despised by Vista Vue's staff, most of whom he's blackmailing to keep from reporting him to Leffingwell (*The Party*'s J. Edward McKinley), the city's hospital commissioner out to nab the shyster administrator.

Busy romancing secretary Alice Gilligan (Jo Ann Pflug) and busty Nurse La Marr (Eve Druce), Hopfnagel is too preoccupied to notice Vista Vue's next victim, an unemployed laborer named Hammond (Rick Lenz), who shows up for a simple chest X-ray in order to collect some insurance money.

The fact that there's nothing physically wrong with Hammond—quickly mistaken for someone named Epstein—doesn't faze Vista Vue's cracked medical staff. More importantly, Hammond owns a house—he'll be able to afford a heftier medical bill. Before he can blink an eye, Hammond-Epstein is admitted for a battery of expensive tests, then consigned to a hospital room where he'll stay until featherbrained Dr. Zerny (Harold Gould) can conjure up an excuse to operate.

Zerny, it seems, isn't pulling his weight around Vista Vue. His aversion to surgery is costing the staff valuable dollars in operative and postoperative costs. It's up to lab technician Nishimoto (Pat Morita), threatened by Hopfnagel, to tinker with Hammond's white-blood-cell count, thereby justifying an expensive appendix operation. Hammond, knocked out against his will, is brought to the operating room where it's decided to mutilate his otherwise healthy appendix should Leffingwell decide to examine the case more closely.

The plan goes awry, however, when Hammond wakes up to find his appendix scar and angrily decides to expose Vista Vue's chicanery and sue for malpractice. Hopfnagel, smooth as ever, woos Hammond with an expensive hospital suite and the promise of a high-paying job. But Hammond reports Hopfnagel to Leffingwell, and Hopfnagel himself ends up under Zerny's shaky scalpel through a series of pseudowacky misadventures, including a wild Mexican fiesta, a surreptitiously filmed sexual escapade, and a woman willing to pay for her hysterectomy with Green Stamps.

Not only was *Where Does It Hurt?* a moronic exercise in comedic futility—referring to Hammond-Epstein as "that matzo ball" was one such witticism—but its insulting meanspiritedness dropped the film several notches

Unscrupulous Hospital Administrator Alfred Hopfnagel debates whether to accept Green Stamps in lieu of cash for a hysterectomy.

below its subpar standing ("Never a pretty girl, your wife has matured into a quick-tempered, tightly-corseted bitch that exemplifies every negative quality in American women," for example).

The film's cast was left to mug unsuccessfully for eighty-eight minutes while Sellers virtually sleepwalked through his role, intermittently pumping life into a lifeless character. (Hopfnagel's British pronunciation of "in hospital" instead of "in the hospital" was only one of many inconsistencies littered throughout the feeble Amateau-Robinson screenplay.) The film lived a fleeting box-office life and mercifully faded into oblivion.

"Peter Sellers and a staff of assorted comics doggedly try to make a laughing matter out of bloated hospital costs and medical monkeyshines.... But most of the time they manage to be only frenetic, rather than funny," wrote the *New York Times*'s A. H. Weiler. "Rod Amateau ... proceeded on the theory that speed, gags, explicit cracks and sex were sufficient to make life at 'Vista Vue Hospital' hilarious.... But despite all the activity, Sellers gives the bland impression of simply walking through a pedestrian role."[2]

Where Does It Hurt? might be "exploited as an English-type comedy," *Variety* thought, while somehow overlooking the film's back-alley production efforts. "Sellers is his usual capable self although frequently part is overdrawn and Jo Ann Pflug as the admitting nurse on the make for the administrator . . . is properly sexy," the magazine opined. "Lenz does well enough by his straight role."[3]

34
The Blockhouse

Cast:

Rouquet	Peter Sellers
Visconti	Charles Aznavour
Grabinski	Jeremy Kemp
Lund	Per Oscarsson
Aufret	Peter Vaughan
Kramer	Nicholas Jones
Khozek	Leon Lissek

STUDIO: Galactacus Productions/Audley Associates
RELEASE DATE: Unreleased
RUNNING TIME: 88 minutes (Eastmancolor)
DIRECTED BY: Clive Rees
PRODUCED BY: Anthony Isaacs and Edgar Bronfman, Jr.
WRITTEN BY: John Gould and Clive Rees (based on the novel by Jean-Paul Clebert)
PHOTOGRAPHY: Keith Goddard
MUSIC: Stanley Myers

The Blockhouse, which he undertook in mid–1972, would follow in the path of *A Day at the Beach* to become the second of Sellers's three unreleased films.

Shot on a shoestring budget in Guernsey by director Clive Rees, *The Blockhouse* is notable only in that it marked Sellers's second, and final, strictly dramatic role. Sadly, this eventful effort was underscored by poor direction, dismal cinematography, and a horrendously butchered soundtrack that obliterated most of the film's dialogue.

Rees based his film on the true story of eight prisoners of war trapped underground in a German blockhouse during 1944's Normandy invasion. The men, seeking refuge from the strafing of Allied planes, hide in the blockhouse only to be entombed when an exploding mortar seals off their only exit.

Their only hope for escape an impenetrable granite wall, the men descend thirty meters to the bowels of the blockhouse where they discover the Nazis' inexhaustible cache of wine, cheese, and candles. The candles are used to light their prison; the wine, besides its obvious function, to wash.

The Blockhouse presented Rees with a fascinating narrative and promised a complex psychological study of eight distinctive personalities faced with the nightmare of being buried alive. Besides Sellers, the film's cast included popular French singer Charles Aznavour and the respected Per Oscarsson.

But this was all terribly wasted. For starters, Rees opted for "realistic" lighting in the blockhouse. "It's a film about human beings," he said. "Too many directors are able to hide behind fight scenes, glamour and explosions. *The Blockhouse* did not offer us anything like that."[1]

Nor did the film offer any technically impressive qualities. Notwithstanding its opening scene, filmed outdoors in the Guernsey sunlight, cinematographer Keith Goddard shot the blockhouse interior in near candlelight, turning the characters into an indistinguishable array of shadows and extinguishing any semblance of individuality. The film's soundtrack, irritatingly low in volume and hopelessly garbled, only added to the confusion.

Thus, through no fault of their own, it was difficult to judge the cast's performances. Sellers, complete with scruffy beard, soft French accent, and granny glasses, played Rouquet, a former schoolteacher who tries to retain his sanity by scrawling poetry on the blockhouse walls and devising games for his fellow inmates. One of the film's producers, Anthony Isaacs, labeled Sellers' performance "the best thing he's ever done ... his Macbeth,"[2] but Rouquet was only one more interchangeable shadow of little substance.

And Rees's stultifying direction added to *The Blockhouse*'s suffocating atmosphere. Not only did he find it necessary to film entire scenes in total darkness, but he never initiated any action. The plot moves at a snail's pace once the men realize their predicament. Only their beards and hair lengths are indicative of any scene exposition, and their subsequent deaths are glossed over without any emotion or explanation. And though two of the men survived the six-year ordeal, living in total darkness for at least four years, Rees ends his film on an ambiguous note. The few nuggets of narrative substance—a hint of homosexual activity and the creeping madness that slowly envelops the men—are quickly brushed aside by Rees in favor of stagnant scenes portraying the men in drunken stupors.

The Blockhouse did absolutely nothing for Sellers's career and was quickly shelved after being previewed in June 1973 at the Berlin Film Festival, where it was reviewed by *Variety*.

Sellers followed his dramatic role in the unreleased *The Blockhouse* with a multiple-role stint in *Soft Beds, Hard Battles*, which opened in 1974 to negative reviews. (Courtesy National Film Archive, London.)

Director Clive Rees, a recruit from television and his co-scripter John Gould have opted to play their material 'straight,' eschewing the invented hokum and dramatic fireworks of similar pix about trapped humans (in subs, mines, etc.). On an absolute level, a commendable decision which certainly adds to the realistic approach adhered to. But it conversely concedes nothing—or almost nothing—to audience needs. Nor, for similar reasons, are the actors allowed much individual range, most being held to muted, underplayed performances.... It may perhaps be unfair to say so, but as we know little or nothing about the men, and learn not much more, we care less and less about what befalls them.[3]

An apt description of the way Sellers himself was now held by his once-adoring public. Neither a *Dr. Strangelove* attempt at multiple role-playing in his next effort—the Boulting Brothers' miserable comedy *Soft Beds, Hard Battles* (released as *Undercovers Hero* in the United States)—nor a whirlwind, short-lived romance with Liza Minnelli boosted Sellers's cause as he sank further into his personal and professional torpor.

35
The Optimists of Nine Elms

Cast:

Sam .... Peter Sellers
Liz .... Donna Mullane
Mark .... John Chaffey
Bob Ellis .... David Daker
Chrissie Ellis .... Marjorie Yates

STUDIO: Chettah/Sagittarius
RELEASE DATE: April 25, 1974
RUNNING TIME: 110 minutes (Eastmancolor)
DIRECTED BY: Anthony Simmons
PRODUCED BY: Adrian Gaye and Victor Lyndon
WRITTEN BY: Anthony Simmons (from his novel)
PHOTOGRAPHY: Larry Pizer
MUSIC: George Martin

It was no secret that Peg Sellers was the dominating influence in her son's life. Peter Sellers was spoiled by his actress mother from the moment he arrived on earth, and the strong Oedipal bond existing between the two grew uncomfortably strong as Sellers forged ahead in life, fed by his mother's constant adoration and her own failed show-business aspirations.

In 1961, when Sellers, then 36, moved his entire family from his Chipperfield estate to the Carlton Tower Hotel in an effort to save his failing marriage, Peg was asked for her reaction. "I'm sure it can't be right," she told the London *Daily Mail*. "Peter rings me up nearly every night for a mother-and-son heart-to-heart. And he hasn't mentioned anything to me about moving."[1]

Lost in the shuffle, of course, was Bill Sellers, a retiring, gentle man who faded quietly into the background of his son's life while Peg took center stage. A Protestant-born Yorkshireman, Bill was a talented musician who once served as assistant organist at Bradford Cathedral and, according to legend, taught British folk humorist George Formby to play the banjo. Bill met Peg in 1921 while she was appearing in a show called *More Splashes* at the King's Theater in Portsmouth.[2] The couple were married in 1923, and Peter Richard Henry Sellers arrived two years later.

When Bill Sellers died of a heart attack in 1962 at the age of 62, his son felt a sudden remorse about the man he had largely shunned his entire adult life. Twelve years later, his career in a nosedive and growing exceedingly nostalgic for the past, Sellers had a chance to repay his paternal debt when he agreed to star in *The Optimists of Nine Elms* as an old-time vaudevillian busker.

The role of Sam reminded Sellers of his father, and during breaks in filming—unrecognizable in Sam's guise—he entertained sidewalk throngs with an impromptu musical act.[3] Coming as it did at this career nadir, *The Optimists* offered Sellers a ray of hope not only for his easily identifiable role but for the talents of *Oliver* lyricist Lionel Bart, who provided Sam's delightful sidewalk ditties.

Ironically, despite his love-hate relationship with his own three children, Sellers meshed well in his grandfatherly *Optimists* role opposite child actors Donna Mullane and John Chaffey. They played Liz and Mark Ellis, a precocious sister-brother combination bumming around London to escape their bickering parents, stuck with an infant and the additional burden of making ends meet on a steelworker's salary. While their parents chase their elusive dream of moving out of their grimy cramped apartment into "the flats," a more fashionable section of town, Liz and Mark invent their own make-believe world free from drudgery, crying babies, and rent payments.

Out for a walk one winter's day, the children chance upon Sam's dilapidated, garbage-strewn residence, located behind a landfill next to a junkyard. At first hurling childish insults at the curmudgeonly pointy-nosed busker, who chases them away with a broomstick, the kids decide to follow Sam the next day as he makes his appointed street rounds, entertaining anyone who'll listen to his hoary songs ("No Matter How Long Your Stockings Are, the Tops Are Always Nearest to the Bottom") and pitch a penny or two to Bella, his cute little ragamuffin dog begging for money on her hind legs.

After helping him do a brisk business outside a rugby match—Liz volunteering for the old blindfold trick and Mark soliciting donations—the children follow Sam home and quickly ingratiate themselves with the lonely busker, who spends most of his time in his sparsely decorated apartment drinking, talking to Bella, and ruminating on the past and his dead wife

Sam and Bella return home after another long day.

("you can forget all about humans—may just as well take poison—but a dog will always be your friend"). Soon Liz and Mark find themselves drawn to Sam's doorstep daily as he lectures them on death ("having a good funeral's like having a good life ... something to look forward to") and takes them to Hyde Park to see a pet cemetery in which he hopes Bella will one day be buried.

Noticing the children's attachment to Bella, Sam suggests they get their own dog and takes them to the Battersea city pound where he poses as their grandfather while they choose a white terrier they name, appropriately enough, Battersea. But Sam can't afford the £3.50 fee and offers his young friends ten pence each per hour to watch Bella—now taken ill—while he goes out to perform. Fearing their father's reaction to feeding another mouth, Mark and Liz resort to stealing before Sam gives them the rest of the money to liberate Battersea from the pound.

But the kids are victims of bad timing, confronting their angry father with Battersea just as he's announcing their long-awaited move to the flats—where animals are not permitted. When Bella dies, they offer to share Battersea with the heartbroken Sam, who gets drunk and leaves angrily from his apartment. In his absence, the kids take Bella to the Hyde Park cemetery where they bury her remains and decide to spend the night, not having told their parents where they were going.

A worried Bob Ellis, searching for his kids, learns from the locals about Sam's friendship with Liz and Mark, and confronts the drunken busker in a local pub. Sam leads him to the cemetery where a search for Liz and Mark turns up empty when the kids hide from the police. Threatening to harm Sam should his children be in any danger, Bob leaves the park (and Sam, who sleeps on a bench near the cemetery with Battersea) but returns the next morning to find Liz and Mark and bring them home. Sam, finding Bella's grave and grateful for the kids' sensitivity, decides to keep Battersea and begin his sidewalk act anew.

Although somewhat muted in tone, *The Optimists of Nine Elms* was a warm little tale that thankfully avoided sliding into a morass of sentimentality while making its point about life and death. With Sellers's wistful approach to Sam—whose past life as a music hall entertainer was heard in intermittent voiceover snippets—and the uncompromising performances of Mullane and Chaffey, *The Optimists* (as it was called in America) was an enjoyable little parable awash in fun and good feeling.

"Peter Sellers, with a wardrobe of old music hall clothes, a talented but aged dog named Bella and a pram he pushes around London, plays the lonely, idiosyncratic old busker. And commendably, he submerges himself sufficiently in the part to allow old Sam to have a life of his own," wrote the *New York Times*. "On the level of story, *The Optimists*, with songs and music by Lionel Bart, is the sort of old-fashioned excursion into sentiment that

Sam performs his sidewalk routine.

ought to warm the hearts of parents in search of that elusive piece of merchandise that goes under the name of good family entertainment."[4]

PTA Magazine took a grimmer view of the film: "The death and burial of Bella, and the bitter frustration of the children's dreams of having a dog of their own, are depressing. The surfeit of detail about life on the wrong side of the Thames detracts from the film's entertainment potential."[5]

Variety warmly praised Sellers's performance, calling it "better than he's been for several years, with a minimal amount of ostentatious shtick interfering with a sympathetic characterization."[6]

But while Sellers delivered a credible performance and received generally favorable reviews, the film did little to revive his career and even less business at the box office where it sank quickly and quietly, another in the long list of Sellers disappointments.

36
Ghost in the Noonday Sun

Cast:
Dick Scratcher .... Peter Sellers
Pierre Rodriguez ..... Anthony Franciosa
Billy Bombay .... Spike Milligan
Jeremiah .... Richard Willis
Abdullah .... Thomas Baptiste

STUDIO: Calvacade/World Film Services
RELEASE DATE: Unreleased
DIRECTED BY: Peter Medak
PRODUCED BY: Thomas Clyde and Ben Kadish
WRITTEN BY: Evan Jones
PHOTOGRAPHY: Michael Reed

Dick Scratcher. That name in itself describes the inane depths to which Sellers sank during *Ghost in the Noonday Sun,* a 1973 pseudo–Goonish *Treasure Island* parody that was never completed or released to the general public.

With two unreleased films already behind him and *The Optimists* failing miserably at the box office, Sellers beat a nostalgic retreat to the safe confines of his past. Spike Milligan, who contributed "additional material" and inexplicably served as the film's "technical advisor," was slated to costar in *Ghost,* and Sellers called David Lodge and invited him to join the "enormous bloody giggle"[1] promised by Evan Jones's narrative.

No one was laughing, however, when Sellers's disruptive behavior once again reared its ugly head. In the midst of divorcing third wife Miranda Quarry, whom he married in 1970, and already forging an intense dislike for costar Anthony Franciosa, who cut Sellers's eye in a mock sword battle causing Sellers to fly immediately to England to consult his ophthalmologist, Sellers was in a sour mood when filming began on location in sweltering Cyprus. It was a feeling shared by the cast and crew, as Lodge said:

We had this horrible old pirate ship. They'd equipped it with a huge mast which caused it to tilt sickeningly with every little movement of the sea. We had to have it moved round to suit the sun. We were *always* in the sun. There were rotten fish in the galley and no loo. Anyone who needed the loo had to jump into a dinghy and be rowed to the loo boat. Meanwhile Peter would loll aboard his private yacht, in the shade, drinking iced champagne, and calling crossly to Peter Medak who was directing, "Are you ready yet? Are you *sure* you're ready for the shot? Because I'm not coming aboard till you are bloody ready." Most days we were all rowed ashore looking green and red respectively from seasickness and sunburn.[2]

Sellers's close connections to the royal family also disrupted the film's shooting schedule; in the middle of production he jetted off to attend Princess Anne's wedding in London. He returned to Cyprus with Titi Wachtmesiter (daughter of the Swedish envoy to the United States), with whom he was having an intermittent affair. Her presence — and the couple's ensuing arguments — only added to the tension-filled atmosphere.

Sellers, perhaps unhappy with his own performance and sensing another disaster, directed his anger toward Medak and Producers Thomas Clyde and Ben Kadish. He banished Clyde and Kadish from Cyprus and in the middle of production reportedly fired Medak, incurring the wrath of Columbia Pictures and invoking memories of the *Casino Royale* mess. Spike Milligan hastily grabbed the directoral reins. Said Lodge:

It was a case of the wrong people in charge of the right people. It was left to everyone to pull comedy out of chaos. Peter stepped in to protect himself as much as salvage the production — and got no thanks at all. Anthony Franciosa and he didn't get on at all well together. Franciosa was playing another swashbuckler, but no one had told him he was supposed to be burlesquing Douglas Fairbanks, Sr. On my first day we were all being made up on the waterfront, a bunch of ugly mugs being rendered even uglier, when a car screeches to a halt. Out jumps Franciosa, white with rage, and screams at us, "Where's that fucking Sellers? He's truncated my fucking part!" What an opening line! We all looked at each other blankly. Some of us, like me, had just arrived and didn't know what was going on — and some of us didn't even know what Franciosa was talking about. "What's truncated mean?" asked one of the co-stars. I began to get the idea that Peter was up to his old tricks.[3]

During *There's a Girl in My Soup* Columbia had gambled on Sellers's mercurial temperament and won, but the studio was taking no chances this time around. When a terrific tropical storm swept through Cyprus and delayed production for a week, the studio decided to pull *Ghost*'s plug and shelve the film altogether. Production was never resumed, and the film gathered dust until it was revived a decade later for an appearance on Canadian cable television in June of 1984.

Hindsight, as the saying goes, is 20/20, but Columbia really did Sellers and his career a favor by never releasing *Ghost in the Noonday Sun*. Sellers would soon stage his triumphant *Pink Panther* comeback, and the *Ghost* fiasco, had it been seen by industry executives, might have completely scratched that effort.

The film begins on a promising note. Shot in silent-movie style complete with black-and-white photography and title cards, *Ghost*'s opening montage introduces Dick Scratcher (Sellers), cowardly Irish cook on a marauding pirate ship. Tired of being bullied by the crew, Scratcher kills Captain Ras Mohammed (an unrecognizable Peter Boyle) and steals the map upon which is marked the location of Mohammed's hidden treasure. Before Mohammed dies, he warns Scratcher his ghost will haunt the cook for eternity. This is the film's basic premise from which Medak (and Milligan) alight on a confused, humorless course.

The bumbling Scratcher, ignoring Mohammed's threat and the disdainful crew, assumes the ship's helm, only to discover that Mohammed's map is drawn with invisible ink. Searching for the treasure, Scratcher mistakenly navigates the ship to Ireland, where the men indulge in food and drink and befriend young Jeremiah (Richard Willis), whom Scratcher is convinced can spot "ghosties" and lead the men to the dead captain's treasure. Jeremiah is kidnapped and taken aboard the ship.

The ship eventually sails into Algiers, where the king (Clive Revill) tells roguish pirate Pierre Rodriguez (Franciosa) to find Mohammed's treasure and kill Scratcher. But "ghostie spotter" and con man Billy Bombay (Milligan), along with his gaggle of look-alike brothers, is also hot on the treasure's trail. Scratcher discovers what he believes to be Mohammed's treasure, only to find it's Bombay's silver cannonballs. In the end, Jeremiah, Pierre, and ship's mate Abdullah (Thomas Baptiste) discover the real treasure while Scratcher, buried in the ground up to his head, and Bombay, tied to a tree, are left to die.

The *Ghost* narrative is as disjointed as it sounds, making absolutely no sense. This is probably due in part to the fact that *Ghost* was largely unedited until its Canadian television debut. Milligan's influence can be felt throughout, both in snippets of Goonish dialogue ("It's bean stew." "Never mind what it's been, what is it now?") and silly sound effects, but it wasn't nearly enough to save this horrendous, embarrassing monstrosity.

Sellers, with a scruffy beard, Dr. Pratt–type makeup, and familiar Irish brogue, added nothing original to his interpretation of Scratcher. By now he was repeating his physical and vocal tics in film after film, and Scratcher was yet another in a long line of uninspired, dull performances.

Variety called the film "an unpretentious comedy of modest merits.... The original script by Evan Jones appears to be quite thin on tension and one imagines both Sellers and Spike Milligan (credited with additional dialogue), as a rival bumbling pirate chief, camping and padding their antics during filming. Their efforts produce lengthy and tedious slapstick tracts. . . . Acting is largely uninspired and frantic with the story finally running out of steam rather than reaching a satisfying conclusion."[4]

For all intents and purposes, it appeared that Sellers's career had reached its own unsatisfying conclusion.

Part IV:
A Sellers Market
(1975–1980)

37
The Return of the Pink Panther

Cast:

Inspector Clouseau ...	Peter Sellers
Chief Inspector Drey-	
fus	Herbert Lom
Lady Litton	Catherine Schell
Sir Charles Litton	Christopher Plummer
Cato	Burt Kwouk
Pepe	Graham Stark

STUDIO: United Artists
RELEASE DATE: May 22, 1975
RUNNING TIME: 113 minutes (De Luxe)
DIRECTED BY: Blake Edwards
PRODUCED BY: Blake Edwards
WRITTEN BY: Frank Waldman and Blake Edwards
PHOTOGRAPHY: Geoffrey Unsworth
MUSIC: Henry Mancini

By 1975, the careers of both Sellers and Director Blake Edwards had reached their nadir. Although both men often vowed to sever their fruitful professional relationship, the grim reality of their sagging stock caused them to reconsider their personal differences when producer Lew Grade showed interest in Edwards's proposal to revive the *Pink Panther* series. Both men certainly had nothing to lose: Sellers was fresh from a cameo appearance as Queen Victoria in Spike Milligan's *The Great McGonagall*, and Edwards, having left Hollywood for Europe in 1972, had already directed one unsuccessful film (*The Tamarind Seed*) for Grade.

The Pink Panther and its sequel, *A Shot in the Dark*, had been huge financial and artistic successes for Sellers and Edwards. Had it not been for the dreaded "artistic differences," Sellers would have starred in the third *Panther* installment, Bud Yorkin's *Inspector Clouseau* (1968). But Sellers and the film's producers were on different creative planes, and the role was given to Alan Arkin. Sellers, feeling cheated by the Mirisch Company, bore an intense grudge. Said Edwards:

> In all the years I knew Peter, in spite of all the times he swore he was never going to do another *Panther*, he never stopped complaining about the fact that the Mirisch Company had chosen Arkin. Peter was a collector of grievances. But he seemed to bear more of a grudge concerning the Arkin thing than just about anything else. For the sake of my own sanity, I have long since stopped trying to figure it out, but it is interesting to note that the Arkin role was first offered to Peter, and he refused it. Also, it was the only unsuccessful *Panther*, yet Peter seemed to take little consolation in that.[1]

But in 1974, with his exposure in America largely limited to a series of television commercials for Trans World Airlines, Sellers jumped at the opportunity to revive Clouseau. Even if it meant working with Edwards. "I'd been trying to resurrect the Panther for years, but it was a Mirisch Company–United Artists property, and the studio had to be talked into doing it—they weren't interested," Edwards said. "So I approached Lew Grade with the idea, and he wanted to do it as a television series."

Grade wanted to produce *The Return of the Pink Panther* as a twenty-six-part television series directed by Edwards and starring Sellers, said Edwards.

> That was all right with me, and Peter also agreed, probably because his career was at an ebb again. Being essentially a film person, as soon as I started writing the first script, I started trying to talk Lew into doing it as a movie. At first he absolutely and totally refused, but then he finally got around to saying, "Well, how much is it going to cost me?" I've always been a gambler and I'd always put my money where my mouth was, so I said, "Lew, I won't take a nickel, and I've talked to Peter and he won't take a nickel. All we each want is expenses and ten percent of the gross from the first dollar on."[2]

It was apparent from the film's enthusiastic reception that Sellers's public hadn't forgotten what he could accomplish within the right comedic framework. And Sellers was older now. *The Return of the Pink Panther* played to a new generation of filmgoers sampling Clouseau for the first time. The inspector's cartoonish demeanor certainly appealed to less highbrow cinematic tastes.

Sellers and Edwards, aware of the series past success, wisely adhered to the *Panther*'s proven formula. Not only did the Pink Panther himself grace the film's opening animated sequence—accompanied by Henry Mancini's familiar *Panther* theme—but series regulars Herbert Lom, Burt Kwouk, David Lodge, and Graham Stark returned to the *Panther* fold.

Before embarking on *The Return of the Pink Panther,* Sellers made a cameo appearance as Queen Victoria in Spike Milligan's *The Great McGonagall* (1975). (Courtesy National Film Archive, London.)

Unlike the studio-bound *A Shot in the Dark, Return* featured on-location shooting in London and Gstaad.

Clouseau begins the adventure as a beat cop, hassling a blind man and his monkey while a bank robbery takes place right under his nose (he even retrieves a dropped money bag for the crooks before they speed off in their getaway car and clubs the bank manager when he pulls a gun in pursuit). But there are more pressing matters at hand: The Pink Panther diamond is stolen from its berth in a Lugash museum, and Chief Inspector Dreyfus (Lom), under orders from above, reluctantly promotes Clouseau to inspector and assigns him to the case.

Since the thief left his calling card—a white glove embossed with a fancy *P*—Clouseau immediately suspects his old nemesis, "the Phantom," alias Sir Charles Litton (Christopher Plummer subbing for David Niven). Although Litton retired from the crime world some years before, Clouseau is convinced he's made his grand reappearance. Disguised as a telephone repairman, Clouseau visits Litton's country estate and eavesdrops on a staged conversation between Lady Litton (Catherine Schell) and her butler (Lodge) in which they detail their Gstaad travel plans.

Demoted to a beat cop, Clouseau hassles a "blind" beggar and his "minkey."

Thinking he's hot on the Phantom's trail, Clouseau journeys to Gstaad. Meanwhile, in Edwards's homage to *The Maltese Falcon* and *Casablanca*, Sir Charles travels to Lugash, where he meets with a sniveling Peter Lorreish character named Pepe (Stark) who works for "the Fat Man." (When Pepe and Charles first meet, "A Kiss Is Just a Kiss" is playing in the background.) While Charles tries to clear his name and catch the "other" Phantom, Clouseau's attempts to follow Lady Litton degenerate into a series of silly blackout sketches.

In one scene Clouseau, disguised as a German domestic, sneaks into Lady Litton's hotel room. Switching on a powerful vacuum cleaner, he manages to suck a parrot out of its cage and destroy an oil painting. Fussing with a light bulb that repeatedly pops out of its socket, Clouseau nearly electrocutes himself and is sent hurtling into an adjacent wall. When Lady Litton returns to her room, Clouseau and a bellboy hide in the sauna, which she fires up before a powerfully built female masseuse arrives. Trying to sneak out of the room, Clouseau is spied by the masseuse. Panicking, he turns on the vacuum cleaner, which, much to her horror, gets stuck on the masseuse's burly chest before Clouseau makes a hasty exit, muttering in broken German.

Next, disguised as loudly dressed playboy "Guy Gadoir," Clouseau attempts a clumsy seduction of Lady Litton in a swinging Gstaad night-club. After running through a series of corny clichés ("Here's looking at you, kid"), Clouseau gets himself invited back to her hotel room where he's rendered unconscious by a Mickey Finn she's dropped into his drink.

As we soon learn, it's Lady Litton who's stolen the Pink Panther, and she reveals her little crime to Sir Charles, who suspected as much. Somehow, Clouseau bumbles his way into making an arrest but is cornered by the Lugash police chief, who wants the Panther for himself and is about to murder Clouseau and the Littons.

Their lives are saved, however, by Clouseau's worst enemy—Dreyfus. Driven insane by Clouseau's antics, Dreyfus picks up where he left off in *A Shot in the Dark* and continues his bad luck and bad aim. Gunning for Clouseau in the Littons' hotel room, he accidentally murders the police chief. When last seen, a straitjacketed Dreyfus—found not guilty by reason of insanity—is in a mental asylum, painting *Kill Clouseau* on the walls with his feet (and setting the stage for *The Pink Panther Strikes Again*).

On the surface, *The Return of the Pink Panther* looked very much like its predecessors. But obvious differences soon emerged in the way Sellers and Edwards approached Clouseau and the film's entire narrative. Sellers had proven his slapstick virtuosity in Clouseau's two previous adventures. With *Return*'s farcical plot escalating to dizzying heights, Edwards broadened Clouseau's physical range to encompass a variety of outlandish situations. As the film's plot grew thinner around the edges, Edwards stretched the limits of his inventiveness. It wasn't enough for Clouseau to battle Cato or his own uncooperative body. Now he was wrestling a vacuum cleaner, driving two trucks into a swimming pool, gluing himself to a chair, or getting stuck underneath Litton's desk and destroying his study.

The film's humor also grew exceedingly violent and sophomoric. Clouseau nearly castrates himself with a mechanical steel clamp. Dreyfus, limned with loony glee by Herbert Lom, shoots off his nose, shoots his assistant in the arm, and strangles his own psychiatrist while fantasizing how he'd kill Clouseau. And Litton repeatedly breaks Pepe's fingers.

Sellers also adopted a twisted French accent far removed from Clouseau's previous diction. In Clouseau's lingo, "monkey" now became "minkey," and "room" became "rim." It was a humorous exaggeration that eventually grew laborious and highlighted the film's cartoonish dimensions.

Still, Sellers retained Clouseau's haughty dignity in the face of adversity, adding subtle touches here and there to complement his performance: Inspecting the Lugash crime scene, Clouseau watches helplessly as his entire bag of fingerprint powder spills before he slips and pretends to be tasting the floor wax for clues. At his Gstaad hotel, Clouseau surrenders his hat, coat, and gloves to a complete stranger, thinking him to be a bellboy,

Clouseau, alias "Guy Gadoir" and missing half his mustache, entertains Lady Litton (Catherine Schell).

then watches calmly as the man drives off. Posing as "Guy Gadoir," Clouseau tries his suave moves on Lady Litton, unaware that half of his fake mustache has fallen off. Clouseau cooly grapples with a revolving door while trying to retrieve an errant suitcase. And so on.

"From the moment Sellers makes his entrance, tipping his nightstick into his own eye, we are in the hands of a master comic," wrote *Newsweek*'s Paul Zimmerman. "Everything Clouseau touches gives way beneath him, leaving him pratfallen. But the best belly laughs don't lie in the belly flops. The comic heart of the movie lies in the absolute aplomb and imperturbable self-confidence with which Sellers, as Clouseau, confronts the catastrophes of his own making."[3]

For the first time since the early 1960s and his arrival in America, Sellers once again was a media darling, hailed by the press for his comic invention. "Peter Sellers does some beautiful things in this matured portrait of Clouseau. . . . This Clouseau—following from the earlier ones, and from the Indian in *The Party*, the Italian in *After the Fox*, and the Los Angeles lawyer in *I Love You, Alice B. Toklas*—is the funniest, most sober, and most tenderly observed man Sellers has created since his famous

Bombay Indian on a gramophone record of long ago," wrote the *New Yorker* in a three-page review, labeling Sellers's performance "one of the most delicately cataclysmic studies in accident-proneness since the silents."[4]

Edwards, too, was praised for his collaborative efforts. "Edwards has directed some smart Hollywood entertainments (the underrated *Darling Lili,* for example) and two of the three previous Clouseau excursions," wrote *Time*'s Jay Cocks. "This one is the most raucous of the lot, and possibly the best. It may not be as wild or inventive as Woody Allen or Mel Brooks or the Monty Python team. But *The Return of the Pink Panther* is fully as funny, in its own brassy, uncomplicated way, and that is probably what counts."[5]

Produced on a relatively modest $3 million budget, *The Return of the Pink Panther* went on to gross nearly $30 million. But more than the wealth accrued by its financially strapped star, Clouseau's return hastened Sellers's remarkable career resurrection, casting him into a spotlight that had all but faded from view.

38

Murder by Death

Cast:

Sidney Wang .... Peter Sellers
Sam Diamond .... Peter Falk
Dick Charleston ..... David Niven
Dora Charleston ..... Maggie Smith
Milo Perrier .... James Coco
Jessica Marbles ...... Elsa Lanchester
Nurse .... Estelle Winwood
Lionel Twain .... Truman Capote

STUDIO: Columbia
RELEASE DATE: June 24, 1976
RUNNING TIME: 94 minutes (Metro Color)
DIRECTED BY: Robert Moore
PRODUCED BY: Ray Stark
WRITTEN BY: Neil Simon
PHOTOGRAPHY: David M. Walsh
MUSIC: David Grusin

Peter Sellers always hated Hollywood's inherent phoniness.

"There are dozens of hangers-on, of 'schleppers' as they say in Jewish," he once said. "They are like the tides of the ocean. If you make a hit film, they come in and almost drown you. If you make a flop, they recede into the distance."[1]

Now that his career was on the upswing—*The Return of the Pink Panther* earning millions at the box office—Sellers once again found himself at the center of Hollywood's hypocrisy, inundated with film offers from people who a year earlier had written him off for good. Even Columbia, the studio bearing the heaviest brunt of Sellers's past shenanigans, agreed to finance his next picture, Neil Simon's *Murder by Death*.

A delightful parody-homage to the B-movie detective, featuring an all-star cast, *Murder by Death* ironically linked Sellers to his checkered career. He was reunited with idol Alec Guinness, who tutored the fresh-faced "Goon Show" star in the intricacies of big-screen comedy while filming *The Ladykillers* in 1955; with David Niven, from whom Sellers stole *The Pink Panther* in 1964 and with whom he later shared in the *Casino Royale* debacle; and with Neil Simon, who wrote the unfortunate *After the Fox* in 1966.

But Simon, like Sellers, was now a hot property, and his *Murder by Death* script was frantic, clever, and replete with witty one-liners ("I smell crime in the air." "I'm not surprised, you just ran over a small animal"). The cast, Sellers included, seemed to enjoy themselves immensely, and their delight translated into a breezy, spirited picture featuring fine ensemble acting.

Sellers, with droopy Fu-Manchu mustache and stringy beard, played Chinese detective Sidney Wang, he of the hoary aphorisms and missing prepositions. Wang, with his "number-three adopted son" Willie, is invited to the secluded baroque mansion of bizarre millionaire Lionel Twain (Truman Capote), where he's joined by four of the world's greatest detectives: natty Dick Charleston (Niven) and wife Dora (Maggie Smith); rotund Belgian chocoholic Milo Perrier (James Coco); tough-talking gumshoe Sam Diamond (Peter Falk) and sultry mistress Tess Skeffington (Eileen Brennan); and Jessica Marbles (Elsa Lanchester), who arrives caring for her ancient nurse (Estelle Winwood).

And of course there's the blind butler, Jamesir Bensonmum (Guinness), who not only ushers the guests to their rooms but parks their cars. He's joined by Yetta (Nancy Walker), the deaf-mute cook hired to prepare dinner.

The elfin lisping Twain makes a grand entrance during dinner and offers $1 million to the detective who can solve a murder to be committed at midnight. It won't be easy. Not only is Twain an electronics genius who's rigged his mansion with disappearing rooms and a host of illusory objects,

Sidney Wang confers with Sam Diamond (Peter Falk).

but he's planted a bunch of red herrings designed to confuse the detectives as they try to thwart the murder.

The first victim is Bensonmum, who's found in the kitchen. His body disappears, however, and soon thereafter Yetta is discovered in a packing case. She's not dead, nor was she ever alive. She was one of Twain's ingenious gadgets, left as a warning of sorts for the detectives. But when Twain turns up with a knife in his back, the detectives begin to suspect each other as they settle into bed for the night.

Jessica Marbles (Elsa Lanchester), Wang, and Milo Perrier (James Coco) investigate the murder of blind butler Jamesir Bensonmum (Alec Guinness).

Sure enough, each detective's room is rigged with some sort of deadly device. Wang is saved from death when he shoots a huge snake. Jessica avoids force-fed gas asphyxiation when her helpless nurse inhales all the fumes. The chivalrous Dick eludes poisoning by allowing Dora to be stung by a scorpion. And Perrier's companion—"the strongest man on earth"— manages to hold up a collapsible ceiling designed to crush the French detective.

Of course the snake, gas, scorpion, and ceiling are Twain's fakeries, but is Twain a phony himself? He reappears as Bensonmum, the perfectly sighted butler who claims to be Twain himself. But is he really Irving Goldman, Twain's attorney who killed the millionaire five years earlier? Or Marvin Metzner, Twain's murderous accountant? Or how about Miss Irene ("I prefer to be called Rita") Twain, Lionel's hirsute vengeful daughter?

And what about the detectives, each of whom has a motive for murder? Didn't Lionel pick Sam up in a gay bar? ("I was working!" Sam explains defensively. "Every night for six months?" asks Tess). And there's Wang, who turns out to be Lionel's adopted son. He still holds a grudge for being kicked out of the Twain household when Dad noticed, after sixteen years, that he was oriental. And the well-bred Charleston, for all his pretensions, is in debt to Twain for millions of dollars after losing his wife's fortune in the stock market. Even Perrier has a motive—his beloved French poodle, killed in cold blood when run over by Twain's car.

But it doesn't really matter because no murder ever really occurred. Nor is Twain's true identity ever truly revealed. After the detectives drive off into the sunset, "Twain" rips off his mask, revealing none other than Yetta, who lets her red hair down and laughs heartily in Twain's voice.

Working with Simon's razor-sharp dialogue and Robert Moore's lively direction, the *Murder by Death* cast turned in excellent performances. Peter Falk, in particular, notched a brilliant Humphrey Bogart send-up, chewing up Simon's tough-guy dialogue with gusto.

Sellers, accustomed to grabbing the spotlight, restrained himself in the ensemble atmosphere and contributed his sharply drawn, humorous portrait of Wang in a quiet manner. He obviously enjoyed escaping the confines of Clouseau for a brief moment and used his Charlie Chan parody to milk some genuinely funny moments, never pandering to the audience by turning Wang into a laughable caricature. Instead, he concentrated on studying Wang's behavior down to the smallest detail and produced his finest turn since *There's a Girl in My Soup.*

"All of the performances are good, and if some seem better than others, it may simply be the material," Vincent Canby wrote in the *New York Times.* "James Coco is very, very funny as the somewhat prissy take-off on Hercule Poirot, his toupee and his eating habits. David Niven and Maggie Smith are marvelous as Dick and Dora Charleston, though they haven't enough to do, and Eileen Brennan is an inspired hybrid of Joan Blondell and Lauren Bacall as Sam Diamond's secretary-mistress. If Peter Sellers is not quite as funny as we expect, it may be because we've seen him do his Oriental bit before. It no longer surprises."[2]

"The cast list reveals the adroit mating of performer to send-up prototype, plus Alec Guinness as Capote's butler, Nancy Walker as mute maid," wrote *Variety.* "The multi-purpose ending isn't the greatest, but this isn't the kind of project which demands a socko fadeout; one almost is content to have observed the fine work of a group which, to a person, possesses an extraordinary talent to amuse."[3] "In the end, *Murder by Death* is a mildly amusing diversion, packing more chuckles than guffaws, but generally pleasant and elegant," wrote the *Christian Science Monitor's* David Sterritt.[4]

But Sellers, as usual, found fault with his performance and the film itself. To Producer Ray Stark, he complained that the film was "the epitome of 8 mm home moviemaking" and was so disgusted, he sold his percentage for about $1.3 million.[5] Naturally, *Murder by Death* did a fairly brisk box-office business, depriving the spendthrift Sellers of some hefty profits. Once again, his questionable judgment had failed him miserably.

39
The Pink Panther Strikes Again

Cast:
Chief Inspector Clou-
  seau .... Peter Sellers
Dreyfus .... Herbert Lom
Cato .... Burt Kwouk
François .... Andre Maranne

STUDIO: United Artists
RELEASE DATE: December 16, 1976
RUNNING TIME: 103 minutes (Panavision/De
  Luxe)
DIRECTED BY: Blake Edwards
PRODUCED BY: Blake Edwards
WRITTEN BY: Frank Waldman and Blake
  Edwards
PHOTOGRAPHY: Harry Waxman
MUSIC: Henry Mancini

Revitalized by his resurrected career and new romance with actress Lynne Frederick (soon to become his fourth wife), Sellers directed his energies to the fourth installment in the *Panther* series, *The Pink Panther Strikes Again*.

Producer-writer-director Blake Edwards once again assembled the familiar *Panther* crew—Herbert Lom, Burt Kwouk, Graham Stark, and Andre Maranne—and collaborated on the screenplay with Frank Waldman. It was, for Edwards and Sellers, a reunion guaranteeing a handsome monetary return on their minimal artistic investment.

Unlike the other *Panthers*, *The Pink Panther Strikes Again* picked up where its predecessor left off, three years after Clouseau's maddening misadventures drove Chief Inspector Dreyfus into an asylum for the criminally insane.

Daily psychiatric therapy with a kindly doctor and cathartic Clouseau rag doll seem to have healed Dreyfus's ravaged mind and nervous tic. No longer does the mention of Clouseau's name send him into paroxysms of rage, and the former chief inspector is considered healthy enough to be freed from the institution upon an appearance before the insanity review board.

But Dreyfus's newfound happiness is tested severely when Clouseau, now Chief Inspector Clouseau, appears at the asylum on behalf of his former boss and immediately wreaks havoc while sauntering through the grounds. Not only does he hit Dreyfus in the head with a croquet ball, knocking him into an adjacent pond, but his bumbling rescue attempts immediately throw Dreyfus into a state of psychiatric regression. His tic suddenly reappearing, Dreyfus, maniacal glint in eye, involuntarily wrings Clouseau's neck before being dragged away.

But no sooner has Clouseau returned to his Paris apartment—where Cato lies in wait for his master—than he's informed of Dreyfus's escape from the asylum. Actually, Dreyfus is directly underneath Clouseau's apartment, trying desperately—and failing miserably—to destroy his arch enemy.

Convinced that the only way to destroy Clouseau is to assemble the world's greatest criminal masterminds, Dreyfus arranges the escape of Turnier, a notorious French villain, and kidnaps Professor Fassbender (Richard Vernon) and his daughter. Fassbender has invented a machine that can erase people or objects, and Dreyfus threatens to erase the United Nations Building in New York with his self-styled "Doomsday Machine" (a nod to *Dr. Strangelove* and the laser beam used by *Goldfinger*'s Gert Frobe). Eager to aid the madman, twelve countries dispatch assassins to eradicate Clouseau at the Munich Oktoberfest.

Clouseau, meanwhile, is at the scene of the crime, interrogating the Fassbender household staff and single-handedly destroying valuable pieces of furniture. As if leaping from the parallel bars in the gym and falling down the stairs weren't enough, Clouseau gets his hand stuck in a medieval mace, knocking the Fassbender beekeeper unconscious, destroying a priceless Steinway piano, and burning his hand when the mace dangles too close to the fireplace.

Clouseau tails Jarvis, the butler, to a gay bar where he doubles as a female impersonator. When Jarvis is killed, Clouseau travels to the Oktoberfest to search for the murderers. Through perfectly Clouseauean logic, he manages to elude his assassins and climb into bed with a comely Russian secret agent (Lesley-Anne Down).

From his Munich sojourn Clouseau goes to the Alps, where, disguised as a dentist, he infiltrates Dreyfus's castle. In one of the film's funnier scenes, Dreyfus begs the disguised Clouseau to extract his aching tooth. Clouseau, high on laughing gas, pulls the wrong tooth before his facial disguise literally melts away and he's recognized by Dreyfus. Chased throughout the castle, Clouseau somehow manages to land on the Doomsday Machine (which has already zapped the United Nations), which points itself at Dreyfus and

Dreyfus's (Herbert Lom) nervous tic returns upon a visit from Clouseau at the mental hospital.

erases the lunatic from the face of the earth (until *The Revenge of the Pink Panther*).

Although Edwards and Waldman once again dreamed up outlandish situations into which Clouseau would stumble, Sellers was beginning to rely more and more on stuntmen—a sign of his weakening physical condition. "With each film, Sellers cooperated less and got stranger and madder," Edwards explained. "And the sicker he got—and his illness had a lot to do with it—the less he was able to function. I mean, Sellers was a pretty strange gentleman to begin with, but that awful heart he had apparently affected his memory. If you gave him any kind of intricate physical moves in scenes in which he also had lines, he became literally incapable of doing both."[1]

But the public loved Clouseau, double or no double, and *The Return of the Pink Panther*, opening to generally favorable reviews (the *New Yorker*'s description of Sellers's "fish-eyed deadpan" as "joyless" a minority exception[2]) grossed about $15 million more than its predecessor.

"Ineptitude again triumphs—gloriously. Bungling is rewarded, and Clouseau goes blithely on demonstrating that what he doesn't know, which is everything, can't possibly do him permanent damage," Vincent Canby wrote in the *New York Times*. "I'm not sure why Mr. Sellers and Mr. Lom

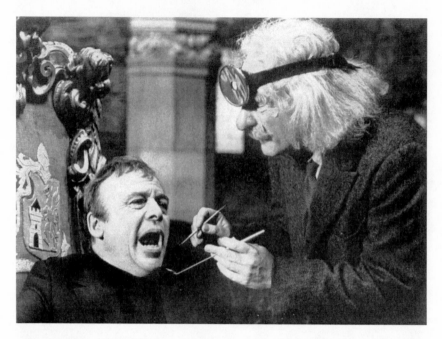

Disguised as a dentist, Clouseau pulls the wrong tooth from Dreyfus's (Herbert Lom) mouth.

are such a hilarious team, though it may be because each is a fine comic actor with a special talent for portraying the sort of all-consuming, epic self-absorption that makes slapstick farce initially acceptable—instead of alarming—and finally so funny."[3]

"The current installment is a bit funnier than its predecessor, but the success of the *Panther* series has never depended solely on laughs," wrote Janet Maslin. "Blake Edwards' slick, seamless direction makes even the flimsiest routines seem stylish; in addition to its comic virtues, this is one of the best-looking movies of its kind in recent memory."[4]

40
The Revenge of the Pink Panther

Cast:
Jacques Clouseau   ....   Peter Sellers

Dreyfus .... Herbert Lom
Cato .... Burt Kwouk
Simone .... Dyan Cannon
Douvier .... Robert Webber
Auguste Balls .... Graham Stark
François .... Andre Maranne

STUDIO: United Artists
RELEASE DATE: July 13, 1978
RUNNING TIME: 100 minutes (Technicolor)
DIRECTED BY: Blake Edwards
PRODUCED BY: Blake Edwards
WRITTEN BY: Frank Waldman, Ron Clark
and Blake Edwards
MUSIC: Henry Mancini

"Years before he had this heart attack he always worried about it, was always searching for the bloody thing, as if it were a letter that he knew had been posted and hadn't arrived.... He had about 40 heart attacks before the real thing turned up."[1]

That was how his old friend Spike Milligan once described Sellers's obsessive concern with his weak heart. After knocking on death's door in 1964, Sellers's health remained generally stable. His career, meanwhile, took a dramatic nosedive. Ironically, his remarkable professional resurrection in the mid-1970s, spurred by the return of the *Panther* series, was dampened by recurring heart problems.

Preparing for *The Revenge of the Pink Panther,* Sellers suffered another in a series of heart-related attacks while flying from Nice to London in March 1977. While doctors initially thought he had suffered a moderate coronary, Sellers's minuscule pulse rate and fainting spell were eventually attributed to heart-medication side effects. But his 51-year-old heart had weakened to an alarming level, and doctors considered Sellers's condition serious enough to warrant the implantation of a pacemaker to regulate his heartbeat.[2]

While his pacemaker kept Sellers's heart beating at a normal clip, it only underscored his deteriorating physical condition and sank Sellers into a deep depression. Privately, he referred to himself as a "cardiac cripple" while publicly—concerned as always with his image—it was business as usual. And that meant more work, the most pressing business at hand *The Revenge of the Pink Panther,* once again cowritten, produced, and directed by Blake Edwards.

The *Panther* films had become the highest-grossing comedy series in cinematic history, and United Artists was willing to gamble on Sellers's health in light of the films' box-office clout. Although Edwards thought he was finished with the series after *The Pink Panther Strikes Again,* "sheer greed" prompted his involvement in *Revenge,* he said. "I understood it was going to be the last one, no matter what happened, and the deal UA offered me to do the third film was so much beyond the two others that I thought, one more, and I'll be able to put enough away so that I'll never have to work again. I wasn't wrong about that, either."[3]

Even the twitching Dreyfus (Herbert Lom), last seen erasing himself out of existence with a laser beam in *The Pink Panther Strikes Again,* was resurrected for *Revenge,* as were the rest of the *Panther* crew: Burt Kwouk, Graham Stark, and Andre Maranne. Edwards once again cowrote the screenplay with Frank Waldman and new team member Ron Clark, while Henry Mancini provided the musical accompaniment.

To no one's surprise, *Revenge*'s plot bore no relation to its diamond namesake, and silly bang-em-up gags abounded—that's what the *Panther* series had come to represent. But *The Revenge of the Pink Panther* also provided a surprisingly strong showcase for Sellers to make his last stand as Sûreté Chief Inspector Jacques Clouseau, now the assassination target of a French crime syndicate, led by Douvier (Robert Webber), trying to negotiate the "French Connection" forty-kilo heroine sale with New York mobster Scallini (Paul Stewart).

Douvier decides the only way to complete the transaction is to impress Scallini, and the only way to impress Scallini is to murder the indestructible Clouseau, who's already survived countless attempts on his life and grown into a national hero.

But it won't be easy.

Not only does Clouseau survive a Douvier-planted bomb blast while donning a Toulouse-Lautrec disguise in the shop of Auguste Balls (Stark), but he overpowers Douvier's hired killer Mr. Chong upon returning to his apartment, mistaking the hulking mass for Cato (Kwouk), his oriental manservant and karate partner.

Douvier thinks he's finally accomplished his task when he assigns transvestite killer Claude Rousseau to eradicate Clouseau. But Rousseau has ideas of his own and hijacks Clouseau's car, forcing the chief inspector to strip while assuming Clouseau's identity. When Rousseau crashes into a tree and Clouseau's car bursts into flames, Douvier and the rest of France assume Clouseau is dead.

Cut to the state psychiatric hospital, where twitch-free former Chief Inspector Charles Dreyfus is rejoicing over Clouseau's assumed death. Now cured of his Clouseau-oriented psychoses, Dreyfus is reinstated to his former position in the wake of Clouseau's "death," with only one provision: that he lead the investigation into Clouseau's murder. Meanwhile Clouseau, dressed in Rousseau's dress and wig, is taken by disbelieving police officers to the same hospital as Dreyfus's where he escapes and hides in a closet, only to be discovered by Dreyfus, who faints dead away. Hoping against hope, Dreyfus nervously agrees with police it was Rousseau, not Clouseau, he saw hiding in the closet.

Clouseau escapes from the hospital by donning a trench coat and impersonating Dreyfus, and is picked up by François (Maranne), who drives "Dreyfus" to Clouseau's apartment to begin his investigation. To his astonishment, Clouseau discovers that Cato, thinking his former boss dead, has turned his apartment into a den of iniquity, an old-fashioned brothel where Cato is the ultimate pimp (turning a hefty profit) and "Inspector Clouseau" serves as the secret password.

After a brief close encounter with bosomy "Tanya the Lotus Eater" ("I warn you, Tanya the Easter Lotus, I am opposed to the women's libs," he stutters), Clouseau gets Cato back in line and decides to conduct his own undercover investigation into his murder ("as I glide through the underworld like a shadow," he explains).

Disguised as a vicar, Clouseau first visits his "funeral" where by a cruel twist of fate none other than Dreyfus—giggling maniacally at his misfortune—is forced to deliver Clouseau's eulogy. Dreyfus's already bad afternoon ends when he spies Clouseau through his disguise and faints headfirst into Clouseau's open grave.

Meanwhile Douvier, bowing to his wife's blackmail threats, dumps his longtime private secretary–mistress, Simone Legree (Dyan Cannon), who vows to get even with her former lover. She gets her chance when she's thrown out of her favorite nightclub and literally lands on Clouseau, clumsily casing the joint with Cato.

Simone invites Clouseau back to her apartment and tells him about Douvier and the French Connection drug ring. They decide to travel to Hong Kong, where Douvier is scheduled to meet with Scallini, and their plan is overheard by Dreyfus, into whose apartment the pair accidentally stumble (he lives in Simone's building). Dreyfus decides to follow them to Hong Kong where he'll crack Douvier's drug ring and kill Clouseau once and for all.

Of course, that never happens. Clouseau, disguised as his interpretation of Scallini (a 1920s-style pin-striped Chicago gangster suit with white hat, tie, and cotton stuffed into his cheeks), accompanies Douvier to the "Lee Kee" shipyards, where all the gangsters—and Dreyfus—somehow end up in a shooting spree at a fireworks factory. Dreyfus, striking a match to cast Clouseau in a better deadly light, accidentally ignites the fireworks, causing a huge colorful explosion. *Revenge* ends with Clouseau not only getting the girl (Simone) but another government decoration for cracking Douvier's drug ring.

The Revenge of the Pink Panther opened to generally favorable reviews and became the tenth-highest-grossing film of 1978. Audiences still loved Clouseau, no matter how predictable he and the *Panther* films had become, yet they were unaware how difficult it had become for Sellers to perform in the role.

To illustrate this point, Edwards later described the scene in which Clouseau and Cato meet Simone when she's thrown out of the nightclub. In the version released to the public, Clouseau and Cato, in disguise, bumble around outside the nightclub until Cato, climbing on Clouseau's shoulders, falls backward through the window of a neighboring bakery shop. But Edwards, Clark, and Waldman originally scripted a different scene, said Edwards.

> Clouseau and his Oriental manservant, Cato, were to go into a black nightclub dressed according to their own concept of what a couple of sharp black dudes should look like—we gave them Afros and the most outrageous outfits you've ever seen. Peter was then supposed to come out with a lot of what Clouseau thought was very hip black street lingo and, of course, screw it all up. Peter absolutely couldn't get it. That made him very angry and resulted in a very unpleasant day on the set. About two o'clock in the morning, though, Peter telephoned me, as was his wont, to say, "Don't worry about tomorrow. I know how to do it...."
>
> The next morning, he came in and wanted to do the scene immediately. We still had some work to do with the cameras, but Peter said, "Leave things as they are and just roll it." I said OK, and Peter made his entrance at the top of some stairs—and it was perfectly obvious that he didn't have *anything* planned. He just believed that by some miracle he'd do something brilliant, but what he did was awful.... We had to cut the entire sequence and replace it with a new one, which was a physical sequence in which we used a double. It was very sad.[4]

Regardless of Sellers's physical condition, *Revenge* ranks as the most solid of the mid-1970s *Panther* sequels. Lacking the physical violence of its predecessors (Clouseau and Cato do not fight) and featuring a mellower Clouseau who ends the film involved with a warm, interested woman (and the possibility of a lasting relationship), *Revenge* was a refreshing variation on the tired *Panther* themes.

For the first time in the series, Burt Kwouk's role was expanded, allowing Cato to emerge as a flesh-and-blood character different from the bug-eyed Bruce Lee parody he had become. The *Revenge* plot, while confusing, also gave Kwouk the chance to show his nimble comedic abilities in a different environment when Cato travels incognito to Hong Kong with Clouseau and Simone. Disguised with too-thick glasses and homburg, Cato stumbles around the hotel unintentionally wreaking havoc a la Clouseau. Cato, it seems, has learned more than the art of karate from his boss.

"Sellers has achieved a rich comic creation, down to the last quiver of the haughty Clouseau nostril. The ripeness of his accent in this new film almost defies phonetic reproduction," wrote *Saturday Review*'s Arthur

Upon returning to his apartment—turned into a brothel by Cato—a flustered Clouseau encounters Tanya the Lotus Eater (Valerie Leon), ("I warn you, Tanya the Easter Lotus, I am opposed to the women's libs!")

Schlesinger, Jr. "One's only fear is that this brilliant actor, who was so extraordinary in such movies as *Lolita* and *Dr. Strangelove*, may be imprisoned for too long in what must eventually become a routine role."[5]

"The wispy narrative (Inspector Clouseau foiling a French drug ring) is merely an excuse to develop the Mack Sennett gags and allow Sellers free

Clouseau returns, this time as a Swedish herring merchant.

rein on his inspired Inspector," *Maclean's* critic, John Lownsbrough, thought. "If the style and romance of the original *Pink Panther* are but a memory, at least the current entry is a more judicious blending of the old formulas than its immediate predecessor."[6]

The Revenge of the Pink Panther, released in July 1978, was to be Sellers's last hurrah as Clouseau. "Blake and I know Clouseau so well, all the facets of the character and the stories that accompany it, I don't know how we managed to do it all," he said upon the film's release. "I've honestly had enough of Clouseau, myself. I've got nothing more to give."[7]

But it was his death—rather than an unwillingness to reprise the role—that stopped Sellers from incarnating the chief inspector for a sixth time. At the time of his death, Sellers had already completed a script for *The Romance of the Pink Panther,* cowritten with Jim Moloney (who also cowrote *The Fiendish Plot of Dr. Fu Manchu*).

The Romance of the Pink Panther was to be directed by Clive Donner (United Artists bought out Edwards from the film) and produced by Danny Rissner, to whom Sellers vowed he would never again speak after Rissner made some notations on Sellers's *Romance* script. In the film, Clouseau would fall in love with a beautiful French agent called "the Frog," who, unbeknownst to Clouseau, is the criminal he is trying to track down.[8]

(Two years after Sellers's death there appeared another *Panther* "sequel," in name only: *Trail of the Pink Panther*, in which Edwards used Sellers outtakes from previous *Panther* films and called in Burt Kwouk, Graham Stark, and Herbert Lom, among others, to string together a story about Clouseau's disappearance at sea. It was a ghoulish moneymaking ploy that justifiably failed miserably at the box office as did 1983's *Curse of the Pink Panther*, a further attempt to prolong the series, this time with Ted Wass in the lead role.)

41
The Prisoner of Zenda

Cast:

Syd Frewin/Prince Rudolph	Peter Sellers
Michael	Jeremy Kemp
Princess Flavia	Lynne Frederick
General Sapt	Lionel Jefferies
The Count	Gregory Sierra
Natalie	Elke Sommer

STUDIO: Universal/Mirisch Corp.
RELEASE DATE: May 23, 1979
RUNNING TIME: 108 minutes (Technicolor)
DIRECTED BY: Richard Quine
PRODUCED BY: Walter Mirisch
WRITTEN BY: Dick Clement and Ian La Frenais (based on the novel by Anthony Hope)
PHOTOGRAPHY: Arthur Ibbetson
MUSIC: Henry Mancini

During her ill-fated marriage to Sellers, Britt Ekland had starred with her famous husband in *After the Fox* and *The Bobo,* disasters that helped seal the end of their stormy four-year relationship.

A decade later, it looked as if Sellers's romantic history might be repeating itself. In 1977 he married Lynne Frederick, a British childhood television star who became the fourth Mrs. Sellers. Soon thereafter, following the release of *The Revenge of the Pink Panther*, Frederick prepared to star opposite her new husband in the fourth big-screen version of Anthony Hope's classic novel *The Prisoner of Zenda.*

The tremendous success of the *Panther*—at that point the highest-grossing comedy series in cinematic history—opened new doors for Sellers. *The Prisoner of Zenda* was to be the first of three pictures financed by Producer Walter Mirisch, and *The Romance of the Pink Panther* was in the planning stages. More importantly, the project for which Sellers had lobbied nearly a decade—an adaptation of Jerzy Kosinski's novella *Being There*—was almost a reality.

As always, the strain of beginning a new film and trying to "find" his character took its toll on Sellers's psyche, and he was having problems with the *Zenda* script, which he disliked intensely. Before shooting began, Sellers threatened to quit the film altogether and forfeit his $425,000 fee, a portion of which he had already been paid. Threatened with a possible $9-million lawsuit, he finally caved in. In July 1978, Sellers and Frederick flew to Vienna to begin work on *The Prisoner of Zenda.* [1]

Frederick, working with her husband for the first time, might have been surprised at the on-set friction that quickly developed between Sellers and Director Richard Quine. But for several members of the *Zenda* cast, it was an all-too-familiar routine. Lionel Jefferies, the old comedy warhorse accused by Sellers of "going over the top" in *Two-Way Stretch,* played loyal General Sapt, and *A Shot in the Dark* costar Elke Sommer reprised her sex-kitten role, this time as Natalie, Prince Rudolph's curvaceous lover. Fellow *Blockhouse* inhabitant Jeremy Kemp limned Rudolph's evil half brother Michael.

It would have been hard for anyone to improve on David O. Selznick's 1937 *Zenda* original, starring Ronald Colman and Douglas Fairbanks, Jr., and Sellers was justified in his inherent distrust of Dick Clement and Ian La Frenais's unoriginal, unfunny script, which added absolutely nothing to the *Zenda* mystique.

The film opens with the untimely death of King Rudolph of Ruritania (Sellers), killed when he pops a champagne cork and punctures the hot-air balloon he's piloting to celebrate his eightieth birthday. Naturally the crown is passed to Rudolph's eldest son, Rudolph, Jr., a wimpy, lisping skirt chaser living in self-imposed exile in London. Rudolph's half brother Michael desperately wants the crown for his own and plots to assassinate Rudolph as he leaves his beloved casino.

Enter cockney cabbie Syd Frewin, who foils the assassination plot and saves Rudolph's life. Frewin, who bears an uncanny resemblance to Rudolph, is offered a job as the future king's driver—at least that's what he's told by General Sapt, Rudolph's chief of staff. But Frewin is really being used to decoy Michael's henchmen while Rudolph, taking an alternate route, is driven back to Ruritania for his coronation.

Frewin, mistaken for the king, manages to stave off Michael's attack en route to Ruritania and arrives safely just behind Rudolph. The two men, meeting face-to-face for the first time, learn they share more in common than their identical looks. Frewin's mother was a music-hall actress, the same actress impregnated by Rudolph's philandering father with an illegitimate son.

But the half brothers' drunken reunion is cut short when Rudolph is kidnapped from under Frewin's nose and thrown into the Zenda prison. Frewin grudgingly takes Rudolph's place at the coronation and fools everybody—except Michael and the beautiful Princess Flavia (Frederick), the young woman promised to Rudolph years before in an arranged marriage. While Michael fails time and again to kill Frewin, Flavia agrees to go along with the charade. She gradually falls in love with Frewin, who would much rather give up this king business and return to his cabbie route in London.

But Michael stands in his way, and after trying to sneak out of the castle at nightfall, only to end up in Natalie's room being seduced by her unwitting husband, the count (Gregory Sierra), Frewin is approached by Antoinette (Catherine Schell), Michael's mistress. Worried that Michael will assume the Ruritanian throne and marry Flavia, Antoinette schemes to help Frewin free Rudolph.

At the same time, she's instructed by Michael to invite Frewin for a clandestine meeting at a windmill, where Michael will be lying in wait. But General Sapt, smelling a trap, accompanies Frewin to the meeting and clashes with Michael. During their ensuing battle, Frewin disguises himself as a coachman but is unmasked by Michael and later thrown into a cell next to Rudolph. The undynamic duo, about to be sadistically tortured, are saved at the last minute by Antoinette, who, gun in hand, materializes in the Zenda prison and sets them free.

Thus, all is well in the kingdom of Ruritania. After all, what the people of Ruritania don't know can't hurt them. And they can't possibly know that Frewin and Rudolph have actually traded places, with Frewin assuming the throne—this time for real—and marrying Flavia while Rudolph retreats back to London and his gaming tables.

If only Sellers's life could have imitated his art. But it was never that easy, not for Sellers or those with whom he associated professionally. With his unhappiness over the *Zenda* script and directional difficulties now behind him, Sellers set his sights on the finished *Zenda* product, which, he well knew, was a clunker. Always hating his own work, Sellers was particularly aghast when the film was screened at Universal Studios for himself, Frederick, Mirisch, Quine, and his agent, Marty Baum.

"Peter kept muttering to himself all through the film. He was never good at seeing himself in a new film for the first time, but this was worse than anything," Frederick said. "Sometimes I'd even hear him swear. When the lights went up, we all sat in total silence for a second or two. Then

The lisping Prince Rudolph at the London gaming tables, joined by his main squeeze, Natalie (Elke Sommer). (Courtesy Academy of Motion Picture Arts and Sciences.)

Peter got up stoney-faced. He walked to the door, turned around, and said to Walter Mirisch, 'I have only one comment to make. My lawyers will be in touch with you.'"[2]

Hugely disappointed with *Zenda*, especially now that his career was finally back on track, Sellers complained to the press about the film and warned the public to stay away. "I don't know how I held myself in check that evening," he said about the film's Universal preview. "The version I saw was so bad. It could have been a really lovely adventure story in the classic tradition—with a new twist. And it still could: the material is all there. But Mirisch has tried to turn it into a sort of poor man's *Pink Panther* and shot extra scenes using doubles which I knew absolutely nothing about. The result is a disaster."[3]

Mirisch reportedly said he never again wanted anything to do with Sellers, and their three-picture deal was terminated. If *The Prisoner of Zenda* wasn't quite a "disaster," neither was it an enjoyable, imaginative work, by any stretch. It was a boring, meandering effort with little life of its own save for its beautiful Austrian scenery and Henry Mancini's lush musical score.

Sellers, now 53 and noticeably frail, turned in a sluggish performance and was miscast in a role calling for a much younger man. Although he had some fun with Rudolph's mangled speech pattern—a cross between Gilda Radner's "Baba Wawa" from television's "Saturday Night Live" and Elmer Fudd—and Frewin's cockney working-class accent, Sellers couldn't overcome the film's sophomoric humor. The rest of the talented supporting cast was left to mug helplessly for the cameras, and Frederick's big-screen career, like Ekland's, was helped little by her turn opposite Sellers.

"The script by Dick Clement and Ian La Frenais strains for wackiness without producing many results and Richard Quine, making his first pic in five years, directs in rather subdued fashion. Some of the comic set-pieces seem strangely over-cut and awkwardly matched, resulting in muted impact," *Variety* wrote upon the film's release. "More than anything, pic resembles some of Danny Kaye's comic romps of decades past, such as *The Court Jester*, but with a lot fewer laughs. What yocks do arise come mostly from inventiveness of the players. Sellers is in good form, especially as the English imposter who falls for the Princess Flavia, appealing played by the lovely Lynne Frederick."[4]

"As the foppish King Rudolph of Ruritania (or Wudolph of Wuwitania), Sellers is the consummate aristocratic twit, a ridiculous roue from whose overbred lips the English language emerges like bubbles from a guppy," *Newsweek*'s David Ansen wrote in his review. "The secondary pleasure of the movie is watching Sellers play straight man to himself.... As Sydney Frewin, London cabbie, Sellers does a deadpan Cockney accent that sounds like a perfect-pitch imitation of Michael Caine. Lest this sound too enticing it should be quickly added that *The Prisoner of Zenda* has precious little to offer aside from its star's verbal acrobatics."[5]

But Sellers had more important things to worry about. With his weak heart continuing to deteriorate—he suffered an attack of tachycardia and possible coronary in December 1978—he prepared to film the role for which he had been preparing a lifetime.

42
Being There

Cast:
Chance .... Peter Sellers
Benjamin Rand ...... Melvyn Douglas
Eve Rand .... Shirley MacLaine

President Bobby ..... Jack Warden
Dr. Allenby .... Richard Dysart

STUDIO: Lorimar
RELEASE DATE: December 19, 1979
RUNNING TIME: 130 minutes (Technicolor)
DIRECTED BY: Hal Ashby
PRODUCED BY: Andrew Braunsberg
WRITTEN BY: Jerzy Kosinski (based on his
novel)
PHOTOGRAPHY: Caleb Deschanel
MUSIC: John Mandel

Ironically, Sellers's quest to launch an adaptation of Polish novelist Jerzy Kosinski's *Being There* began eight years earlier, when the comedian's career had reached its lowest ebb.

Being There was first published in 1971, and Sellers, reading the book for the first time, immediately identified with its hero, a naive simple-minded gardener named Chance whose worldview is shaped completely by television. Sellers saw in Chance a side of himself—the immature man-child cast adrift in the outside world—that struck an immediate inner chord, and he became obsessed with bringing Chance to life on the big screen. He immediately began deluging Kosinski with cards and letters signed, simply, "Chance."

"I remember after years of telling me he could play Chance ... once in Malibu he proved it," Kosinski said. "We were walking in a garden at a friend's house and he saw a small tree that was drying out, dying. He bent, stiffly, picked up the hose and began watering the little tree. Very quietly. Complete contentment on his face. He *was* Chance."[1]

Yet as much as he wanted to bring *Being There* to fruition, Sellers faced two major hurdles—financing and credibility. By 1972, his career had reached rock bottom and wouldn't be resuscitated until *The Return of the Pink Panther* premiered three years later. Yet Sellers worked relentlessly to set up a film deal and had already pegged Director Hal Ashby for the project.

"When I read *Being There* I was crazy about it," Sellers said. "I had just seen *Harold and Maude,* which I thought was sensational, so I rushed a copy of the book to Ashby. Then I tried to get a hold of Jerzy, who is a very private person. At that time he hadn't heard of Ashby, and I think he thought I was a member of the 'Goon Show.'"[2]

Sellers had in fact taken a personal interest in Ashby's *Harold and Maude,* a black comedy about a death-obsessed young man (Bud Cort) who has an affair with an 80-year-old woman (Ruth Gordon). The film attracted an underground audience, and Sellers, who saw the film at a "tiny"

London theater, launched a one-man campaign to bring Ashby's effort into the cinematic mainstream. He tried, to no avail, to get the film distributed on a larger scale and even offered to fly Cort and Gordon to London to "launch the film properly." They declined.[3]

But the Sellers-Ashby friendship was now cemented, and both men agreed that whoever got "hot" first would try to turn *Being There* into a reality. By January 1979, *Being There* finally reached fruition. Not only was Sellers once again a top box-office draw, but Ashby had reeled off a string of hits with *The Last Detail, Shampoo,* and *Coming Home.*

Lorimar Pictures agreed to finance the $7 million film and pay Sellers $750,000 plus 10 percent of the gross domestic (and Canadian) receipts in excess of $10 million, plus 10 percent of the gross foreign receipts in excess of $3 million.[4]

Filming was set for George W. Vanderbilt's 10,000-acre estate in Asheville, North Carolina, Washington, D.C., and Los Angeles. Shirley MacLaine, Sellers's *Woman Times Seven* costar, signed on to the film, as did venerable Hollywood legend Melvyn Douglas. Douglas had first met Sellers nearly thirty-five years earlier in Calcutta during World War II and had treated the young "Gang Show" entertainer and his future agent Dennis Selinger to dinner after a boxing match.[5]

But Sellers, who had worked so hard to realize his dream and even gained a considerable amount of weight for the role, now panicked when he couldn't "get" Chance's voice as filming was about to begin. Although he later said, "I hadn't practiced the accent too much, because I knew I could get that eventually,"[6] wife Lynne Frederick told a different story.

> We spent a chaotic weekend feverishly putting Chance together. If Peter found the voice, he felt all else would follow, so we tried imagining how Chance sounded. Peter tried out a whole continent of American accents, which I taped and played back. Chance had to have an American intonation, but because the character seems to come from nowhere — even the FBI, the CIA and the KGB can't trace his background when they try — he couldn't have an accent tied to a particular locality. One of Peter's voices would be too New Yorkerish, another too West Coast, a third too Deep South.... To listen to Peter's repeated efforts was a little like watching a man unpacking a travel bag for something he fears he hasn't packed.[7]

Sellers always traveled with a poster-size autographed picture of comedian Stan Laurel, one of his idols, and finally decided to base Chance's neutral tones on Laurel's soft British accent (with a noticeably American twist, of course). Shooting could now get under way.

Kosinski, afraid of how others might convolute his beloved novel, decided to write the *Being There* screenplay himself. He adhered closely to the novel's allegorical tone, a mood captured splendidly by Ashby and Sellers, and its chronological pacing.

The film opens with Chance being awakened one morning by his "alarm clock"—the click of his color television set. Television, in fact, plays the only role in Chance's everyday existence. Employed since childhood by a rich old man and cared for by Louise, the elderly black maid, Chance has been kept a virtual prisoner in the house. He's never been allowed outside, and his retarded view of reality is shaped and molded by television, which he watches constantly. There's even a TV in the greenhouse where, as the old man's gardener, Chance spends his time working with Mother Nature.

But the roof over Chance's sheltered existence is blown off when the old man dies. Chance, of course, understands death only in terms of plant life. He can't relate to anyone or anything on human terms, and the old man's death leaves him emotionless. He can only sit near the cold corpse and click on the television set, oblivious to death's shattering reality.

Left alone in the house after Louise retires, Chance is visited by Thomas Franklin and Miss Hayes, lawyers representing the old man's estate. They're interested in whether Chance will file a claim to collect some of the old man's money and are somewhat suspicious of the simpleton who greets them at the front door wearing an ill-fitting 1930s-style suit.

"The garden is a healthy one, Thomas, I have no claim," Chance states blankly, oblivious to the estate's legal intricacies.

The lawyers tell Chance there's no record of his employment in the old man's house; in fact, there's no record of his existence. But that doesn't bother Chance, who takes them on a tour of the house, proudly showing them his immaculate bedroom ("I like to sleep with my head facing east," he explains) and, of course, his beloved garden. Assured that he won't file a claim, Franklin tells Chance he's to vacate the premises by noon the next day.

So, with homburg on head and suitcase in hand, Chance ventures out of the house for the first time and onto the streets of Washington, D.C., in search of a garden in which to work. Surprisingly, the house sits in the middle of a decaying neighborhood, and Chance stares wide-eyed at the bums and riff-raff littering the nearby streets, doffing his cap like the Stepin Fetchit character he's seen on TV. But television hasn't prepared him for the harsh reality surrounding him. Threatened at knifepoint by a gang of young hoodlums, Chance can only take out his trusty remote control and try to change reality's channel. Hungry after a long day of walking, he stops a black woman in the busy street and, equating her color with Louise, asks her to make him lunch. She stares at the strange man in disbelief.

But Chance's seemingly doomed existence takes an unbelievably lucky turn later that night when he stops in front of a store window to watch himself on television. Transfixed by his own image—and testing his remote control—Chance backs onto the street between two parked cars, one of them a long black limousine that suddenly backs up, pinning Chance's leg.

After the death of the old man, Louise (Ruth Attaway) tells Chance she's leaving.

He cries out in pain, raps the limousine with his fist, and is offered profuse apologies by its occupant, Eve Rand (MacLaine), the youngish wife of elderly wealthy industrialist and presidential adviser Benjamin Rand.

Eve persuades Chance to have his leg examined by the physician treating her sick husband, and they settle into the limousine for the ride back to the Rand estate. "This is just like television but you can see much further," Chance says to Eve, who offers him a stiff drink. "Yes, please, I'm very thirsty," Chance answers innocently, never having had alcohol in his life. While he is coughing up his drink, Eve asks Chance his name, and he croaks out, "Chance, the gardener," which Eve mistakes for "Chauncey Gardiner." Chance neglects to correct her.

> *Eve:* Chauncey Gardiner. Mr. Chauncey Gardiner. Are you related to Basil and Perdita Gardiner?
> *Chance:* No, I'm not related to Basil and Perdita.
> *Eve:* Well, they're such a wonderful couple. My husband and I are good friends of theirs and we often visit their island.

During the ensuing ride, Chance of course watches the limousine's small television set while Eve tries to make small talk with "Chauncey" and tries to figure this strange man who would rather watch cartoons than engage in conversation.

Back at the opulent Rand mansion, Chance is treated by Dr. Allenby (Richard Dysart) and advised to stay for a couple of days to rest his bruised leg. Not only is Chance an immediate hit in the Rand household—the staff, and Dr. Allenby, mistake his childlike questions and answers as a sign of sarcastic humor—but he impresses the bedridden Benjamin Rand (Douglas), who's suffering from a terminal blood disease.

Rand, a powerful businessman, joins Chance, Eve, and Dr. Allenby at dinner and reads into Chance's reserved manner and pat answers the mark of a sage man.

> *Rand:* Do you need a secretary?
> *Chance:* No, thank you. My house was shut down.
> *Rand:* You mean your business was shut down?
> *Chance:* Yes, shut down and closed by the attorneys.
> *Rand:* What'd I tell you? That's exactly what I mean. The businessman today is at the mercy of kid lawyers from the SEC!

And when Chance tells Rand, "I would like to work in your garden," Rand of course reads this as a deep philosophical statement.

> *Rand:* Isn't that what any businessman is, a gardener? He works on flinty soil to make it productive with the labor of his own hands. He waters it with the sweat of his own brow. Makes a thing of value for his family and the community. Yes indeed, Chauncey, a productive businessman is a laborer in the vineyard.
> *Chance:* I know exactly what you mean, Ben. The garden that I left was such a place. I don't have that anymore. All I have left is the room upstairs.
> *Rand:* Now wait a minute, Chauncey. You've got your health. You can't let those bastards get you down, you gotta fight! I don't want to hear any more from you about that "room upstairs." That's where I'm going, too damn soon.
> *Chance:* It's a very pleasant room, Ben.

Ben is so impressed with Chance and his "gardening" philosophy that he invites the simpleminded gardener to his audience with the president (Jack Warden), who in turn misconstrues Chance's description of seasonal change in the garden as a metaphor for the nation's economic growth.

The president uses the gardening metaphor—and Chance's name—in a nationally televised speech, embellishing Chance's words and transforming him into an overnight national celebrity whose insight into world economic affairs is sought by the *New York Times*. Chance, who has never before spoken on a telephone, is called by a *Times* editor, who describes him as "laconic and to the point" when Chance hangs up on him. Invited to appear on a "Tonight Show"–style television talk show, Chance brings down the house when, asked by the host what he thinks of the president's economic viewpoint, he responds, "Which view?"

The CIA and FBI, assigned by the president to produce an in-depth dossier on Chance's background, are having no luck, and soon the press and political insiders are talking about a Watergate-style security cover-up and cloak-and-dagger operation.

Chance, meanwhile, continues to glide easily through the upper crust, purveying misunderstandings every step of the way. Accompanying Eve to a Washington dinner, he charms the Russian ambassador (Richard Basehart), who mistakes Chance's simple sentences as "Krylovian" in manner and proceeds to talk to Chance in Russian. By the evening's end, Chance has been approached by a publishing agent about writing a book ("I don't write," he tells the agent. "Of course you don't; who does nowadays?" the agent responds) and by a seedy homosexual, who tries to seduce him ("Have you ever had sex with a man?" "No, I don't think so"). Adding to the "Gardiner" myth is the circulating rumor that Chance speaks eight foreign languages and holds degrees in both medicine and law.

As Ben's health continues to deteriorate, the flirtatious Eve begins to respond more strongly to Chance, dropping none-too-subtle sexual hints and caressing Chance as he sits in bed, robotically eating his breakfast and watching television. A few nights later, Eve goes for broke, entering Chance's bedroom with seduction on her mind. Chance, confused by her behavior, can only say, "I like to watch," which Eve mistakes for kinky voyeurism. She proceeds to masturbate while Chance, uninterested, watches television.

Chance's stature is elevated to an even higher plane when Ben dies, telling his cronies just before his death that he would like Chance to be the next presidential candidate. *Being There* ends as the Washington powers that be, carrying Ben's coffin to its final resting place, decide on Chance as their man. Chance, meanwhile, wanders off to a lake on the mansion grounds. Stooping to help a dying plant, he gazes out over the lake, then proceeds to walk on the water, a Christlike figure purified by his tunnel-vision existence. (This final touch was not included in Kosinski's novella and was seen by some as a gratuitous gesture that weakened the film's symbolic message.)

Although *Being There*'s foundation was built upon a one-joke premise, Sellers pulled it off impressively, turning in his best performance in fifteen years and silencing his harshest critics, who were wondering if Jacques Clouseau would be Sellers's cinematic epitaph.

Sellers, as Kosinski said, *was* Chance, and his determination in bringing the character to life paid handsome dividends on-screen. The role demanded that Sellers be very limited in his range and dialogue yet convey a powerful presence. He transformed Chance into a touching, sympathetic person and one of the screen's most enduring, recognizable characters. For his efforts, Sellers was showered with his most indulgent press notices since *Dr. Strangelove.*

"Peter Sellers keeps an expression of dreamy contentment on his face, interrupted only by the slightest flickerings of unease when some threat approaches; acting out of the half-formed impulses of a retardate, he does a stylized, graceful version of physical clumpishness," Critic David Denby wrote in *New York* magazine. "It's a beautiful performance, yet we might feel more if Chance struggled a bit or suffered or occasionally failed."[8]

"There are several excellent gags en route, but I must confess to cordially loathing the unreal contrivance of it all," wrote the *New Statesman*'s John Coleman. "Chance's lines have to be improbably set up, pauses unnaturally prolonged, to lend a semblance of satire. It is built around nothing."[9]

"For the gag to work repeatedly, the audience must believe that Chance is so completely blank that he could indeed seem to be all things to all people he meets," wrote *Time.* "Peter Sellers' meticulously controlled performance brings off this seemingly impossible task; as he proved in *Lolita*, he is a master at adapting the surreal characters of modern fiction to the naturalistic demands of movies.... Sellers' gestures are so specific and consistent that Chance never becomes clownish or arch. He is convincing enough to make the film's fantastic premise credible; yet he manages to get every laugh."[10]

Sellers's efforts resulted in his second Oscar nomination as best actor, while costar Melvyn Douglas was nominated for best supporting actor. But his joy at being nominated was tempered by his fears over Ashby's insistence on including outtakes during the final credits.

Sellers felt, correctly, that the outtakes, showing him giggling repeatedly in the scene where Chance meets Ben for the first time in the Rand infirmary, destroyed the film's mood and threatened to wreck his chances of winning the elusive Oscar. It had been fifteen years since *Dr. Strangelove,* and Sellers hoped the Hollywood community had forgiven him for his outrageous behavior and outspokenness. Winning an Oscar for his most important role would be the crowning achievement of Sellers's career.

On March 18, 1980, Sellers sent Ashby an angry telex riddled with anxiety over the outtakes. "I must reiterate once again, the outtakes you have placed over the credits do a grave injustice to the picture for the sake of a few cheap laughs. It breaks the spell, do you understand? Do you understand, it breaks the spell! Do you hear me, it breaks the spell! I'm telling you how it breaks the spell and as I said in my previous telegram there's not much point in the film going to Europe as I saw it last night.... For goodness sake, don't ruin what opportunities we have left."[11]

Sellers knew from whence he spoke. He lost the Oscar to Dustin Hoffman for his performance in *Kramer vs. Kramer,* and his hopes were dashed further when the film—the outtakes now replaced by television "snow"— failed to claim a major prize at Cannes later that year.

"My ambition in the cinema, since I came across it, was to play Chance the gardener in *Being There*," Sellers said shortly after the film's release. "I have realized that ambition, and so I have no more. The older I get, the less I like the film industry and the people in it. In fact, I'm at a stage where I almost loathe them. If all films were like *Strangelove* and *I'm All Right, Jack* and *Being There,* it would be a different thing."[12]

Sinking to new depths of depression, Sellers entrenched himself for his final film performance.

43

The Fiendish Plot of Dr. Fu Manchu

Cast:

Nayland Smith/Dr. Fu Manchu	Peter Sellers
Alice Rage	Helen Mirren
Sir Roger Avery	David Tomlinson
Joe Capone	Sid Caesar
Peter Williams	Steve Franken
Robert Townsend	Simon Williams
Perkins	John Le Mesurier

STUDIO: Orion Pictures
RELEASE DATE: August 13, 1980
RUNNING TIME: 104 minutes (Technicolor)
DIRECTED BY: Piers Haggard
PRODUCED BY: Zev Braun and Leland Nolan
WRITTEN BY: Jim Moloney and Rudy Dochtermann (based on characters created by Sax Rohmer)
PHOTOGRAPHY: Jean Tournier
MUSIC: Mark Wilkinson

It would have been fitting—and truly touching in light of his Lazarus-like professional resurgence—for Sellers's film career to end in a final blaze of glory.

Sellers had poured his heart and soul into *Being There,* and to those around him seemed almost to surrender life's grasp after the film's completion. "He had turned into an old man," said Sue Evans, Sellers's personal secretary. "Previously he had been an attractive, fairly active man in his early fifties. Now he appeared smaller because he had contracted a stoop. He had become very forgetful. Halfway through conversation, you'd become aware of his 'absence'—it was as if his concentration was going."[1]

Sellers poured what little energy he had left into his next venture, Orion Pictures's *The Fiendish Plot of Dr. Fu Manchu,* for which he would be paid $1 million plus a percentage of the gross receipts. His agent, Marty Baum, already had negotiated a $3 million fee for *The Romance of the Pink Panther* (which Sellers was cowriting with *Fu Manchu* screenwriter Jim Moloney) and a $2 million fee for a remake of the 1948 Preston Sturges classic, *Unfaithfully Yours.*[2] (Dudley Moore inherited the *Unfaithfully Yours* role after Sellers's death. The 1983 version, directed by Howard Zieff, costarred Nastassia Kinski and Armand Assante. It opened to a lukewarm critical reception.)

But this solid financial security and the promise of a busy schedule— always his best therapy in the past—now did little for Sellers's state of mind. Obsessed with his failing heart and convinced his death was close at hand, Sellers found no solace in tackling the dual roles of Dr. Fu Manchu and his nemesis, retired Scotland Yard detective Nayland Smith.

Inevitably, problems arose once production began in September 1979. Sellers found fault with director Piers Haggard—chosen after *The Prisoner of Zenda*'s Richard Quine and John Avildsen were dropped from the project because of creative differences—and was unhappy with his one-dimensional performances.

Based on characters created by Sax Rohmer, *Fu Manchu* reunited Sellers with frequent costar John Le Mesurier, David Tomlinson (*Up the Creek*), Steve Franken (*The Party*), and Burt Kwouk, and wife Lynne Frederick checked in as production executive.

The casting of legendary American television comedian Sid Caesar— whose rise to stardom in the 1950s paralleled Sellers's "Goon Show" success—promised an interesting stylistic mix of transatlantic improvisation. But even had Caesar or Sellers been at the top of his form, which wasn't the case, there was little they could have done to salvage Moloney and Rudy Dochtermann's weak script.

Fu Manchu opens in 1933 on the 168th birthday of the fiendish Chinese doctor, kept perpetually ageless by an elixir vitae that extends his life in six-month increments. But before Fu can sip the wondrous elixir, a clumsy attendant (Kwouk) ruins the party by accidentally spilling the liquid while trying to douse his flaming shirtsleeve. Forced to obtain the elixir's priceless diamond ingredients within six months, Fu immediately masterminds a series of daring robberies, stealing not only England's crown jewels but the famed Star of Leningrad diamond from Washington, D.C.

Scotland Yard, stumped by the robberies, calls on the deductive reasoning powers of retired detective Nayland Smith, Fu's lifelong foil who immediately suspects his old archenemy. A pipe-smoking eccentric with a strange emotional attachment to his lawn mower—and a side collector of "Fu memorabilia"—Smith agrees to work with the Yard and FBI (in the person of Caesar and Franken as bumbling agents) to stop the insidious Fu and recover the stolen gems.

Although Fu has the gems, he still needs one final elixir ingredient: England's George V diamond, guarded by a couple of hoary beefeaters and Townsend (Simon Williams), the king's corpulent key bearer who has a weakness for Chinese food. Fu plans to kidnap the king and queen as ransom bait for the diamond. But Smith, always one step ahead, quashes the plan by "auditioning" star-struck Constable Alice Rage (Helen Mirren) to play the queen's double, thereby hoping to lure Fu with this royal bait.

Fu strikes during the "queen's" tour of a gardening show, using a noxious gas to knock out Smith and his police entourage while he unwittingly kidnaps Constable Rage. She soon falls under Fu's spell—calling him "Fred," his nickname when he ran the laundry service at Eton—and schemes with Fu to trick Townsend into surrendering the keys to the safeguarded George V diamond.

One of Fu's henchmen, disguised as a doctor, tells the obese Townsend that he must go on a diet, exercise by walking on stilts, and forgo Chinese food forever if he wants to remain alive much longer. Townsend, frightened, follows the "doctor's" advice and alights on a rigorous stilt-walking regimen, only to chance upon a mouth-watering buffet of succulent Chinese food while out on the trails the next day. Fu, striking at the stomach of the matter, makes a deal with Townsend: He'll let him go hog-wild on the Chinese food if he surrenders the keys to the diamond. Townsend, knowing full well the consequences but in desperate need of a Chinese food fix, agrees.

But Smith once again has second-guessed his adversary and procured the diamond himself, hiding it in his tobacco pouch. The diamond Fu steals is a worthless fake, diluting the elixir and pushing Fu one step closer to death. Using the crown jewels as a bargaining chip, a desperate Fu forces Smith, who's finally tracked the doctor down, to trade the real George V diamond for the crown jewels and a Star of Leningrad facsimile.

The film's final scene, in which Fu drinks the elixir and reappears as a modern-day Elvis Presley–type rock star complete with white rhinestone studded jumpsuit and backup band, illustrated the depths to which Sellers and company sank in search of laughs.

But Sellers's Fu provided precious few laughs throughout *The Fiendish*

Dr. Fu Manchu.

Plot of Dr. Fu Manchu. An exhausted Sellers, pale and wan after having shed his *Being There* plumpness, resorted to painting Fu Manchu with broad, unoriginal brush strokes, relying more on Fu's heavy makeup and stereotypical accent than any studied personality quirks for his ordinary portrayal. Fu's need to receive electric jolts to stimulate his heart in lieu of the elixir was tasteless in light of Sellers's recurring heart problems, and these scenes would take on an air of eeriness when Sellers's heart stopped shortly after the film's wrap.

It was Sellers's sentimental portrayal of Smith that harkened back to his salad days of playing "little men" on the screen with resounding success. Moloney and Dochtermann seemed to take a little more care in scripting Smith's character, or perhaps it was Sellers who brought the role to life. Whatever the case, Smith came across as a lovable eccentric in a film peopled by unfunny cardboard cutouts.

Part of the film's overall flatness could be attributed to production problems that stemmed from Sellers's physical problems and emotional temperament. In November, two months after shooting got under way, he

Retired Scotland Yard detective Nayland Smith is visited by FBI agents Joe Capone (Sid Caesar) and Peter Williams (Steve Franken) while Sir Roger (David Tomlinson) and Robert (Simon Williams) look on.

jetted to his Gstaad retreat for the weekend, where he suffered another tachycardia attack and was forced to take a few months' sick leave. When filming finally resumed in the early spring of 1980, Sellers fired Haggard and assumed the directorial reins himself, adding to the stress and strain on his heart and emaciated body.

It was an unhappy time for all involved in the production, and the final results were telling. Sellers, fearful of the reception the film would receive, directed his hostilities at Orion executives in a series of angry telegrams. "I very much regret your lack of enthusiasm for the film because, while I realize it is not of the *Animal House* genre, nevertheless it's an amusing film which will not be embarrassing or a total loss to you," he wrote in one telegram. "Please heed my words and leave the film as it is."[3]

But Sellers's words apparently fell on deaf ears. Orion cut the picture by ten minutes, and Sellers cabled the company shortly thereafter with these words:

> If you allow the King George V telephone scene to be cut, you will without any doubt drive the final nail into the casket of yet another Orion film. The movie, already doomed, will sink without a trace.... *Fu Manchu* could just have scraped by but now there is no hope whatsoever. I would

advise you to endeavor to sustain the loss, however difficult, and retain the dignity still remaining for a once great company. Yours sadly and sincerely, Peter Sellers.[4]

The Fiendish Plot of Dr. Fu Manchu premiered in the United States on August 13, 1980, about three weeks after Sellers's death. It was a sad epitaph for a man who had brought laughter to so many for so long.

"Sadly, Peter Sellers's last film is a misfire from beginning to end. Feature has no reason to exist except for the star to try on some new accents and makeup," *Variety* wrote in its review. "Sellers's many fans will certainly choose to regard *Being There* as his final testament and this should accordingly slip from sight before long."[5]

"Sellers, as always, makes elegant play with the character's improbable Orientalisms . . . but his best moments are as the brilliant but senile detective Smith, a tweedy British soul whose pacifier, which he carts wherever he goes, is a lawn mower," *Newsweek*'s David Ansen wrote. "*The Fiendish Plot of Dr. Fu Manchu* may have the worst ending of any movie this year—a silly rock production number which suggests that the filmmakers, faced with an intransigent plot, simply threw up their hands and gave up. It's hardly the finale one would have wished for Sellers, but even at such a ludicrous moment, it's a pleasure to notice how he holds his mike, his pinky raised like a Vegas crooner—Fu Manchu crossed with Wayne Newton."[6]

44
Epilogue

Having completed *The Fiendish Plot of Dr. Fu Manchu* and finalized plans for *The Romance of the Pink Panther*, a sickly Sellers, scheduled to visit Los Angeles to investigate open-heart surgery possibilities, turned his immediate attention to a London reunion with Spike Milligan and Harry Secombe.

The threesome had remained good friends through the years, reprising the "Goon Show" to commemorate the BBC's fiftieth anniversary in 1972 and establishing an elaborate network of "inter-Goonal" correspondence, a portion of which was published in *The Book of the Goons* (1974). Sellers always looked forward to these reunions; it was a chance to reminisce about the good times, to relive, as he once said, "the happiest time in my life, professionally."

But this time there would be no laughter.

Shortly after 2:00 P.M. on July 22, 1980, complaining of faintness and shortness of breath, Sellers collapsed into an armchair in his Dorchester Hotel suite, the victim of a massive heart attack. Two hotel nurses appeared immediately, one administering mouth-to-mouth resuscitation while the other massaged Sellers's chest, trying to restart his dead heart. About two minutes later, a weak pulse registered, and wrapped in foil to retain his body heat,[1] an unconscious Sellers was rushed to Middlesex Hospital where he lingered, comatose, on life-support systems for two days before succumbing to "natural causes" on July 24. He was fifty-four.

Sellers once said he wished to be remembered as a Goon more than anything else, and he got his final wish. After a celebrity-packed funeral on July 26, attended by three of his four wives, Sellers was cremated to the bizarre musical accompaniment of Glenn Miller's "In the Mood," the outgrowth of some "Goon Show" banter between himself and Milligan ("Any special hymn you'd like to have played when you go?" "Yes, 'In the Mood.'" "Is that in *Hymns Ancient and Modern?*" "No, it's in Glenn Miller").

On September 8 — Sellers's fifty-fifth birthday — in the Royal Parish Church of St. Martin-in-the-Fields, Trafalgar Square, Michael Bentine led "A Service of Thanksgiving for Peter Sellers" with David Niven delivering an uncompromising eulogy.

For the press and his public, often (justifiably) harsh toward him in his post–*Strangelove* period, Sellers's death meant a time to reflect on his checkered career, to praise his elusive genius, and, more often than not, to forgive his character defects. "Although he got into a few traffic snarls with movie companies, Sellers managed to emerge unscathed. It was in private life that he never learned to apply the brakes," wrote *Time*'s Stefan Kanfer. "Three of his four marriages failed; he suffered his first heart attack at 38 and refused to cut down his schedule; when the world closed in, he sought refuge variously in women, yoga, vegetarianism and overwork.

"It is that workaholism that has secured Sellers's reputation. In 52 features, he demonstrated a knack for stealing the soul of his characters and the scenes of his films. In every Peter Sellers's performance there are constant elements: meticulous detail and trenchant wit. Imitations alone could not make him the prime *farceur* of his age. Audiences did not pay to watch the mask; they came to see the man."[2]

Part V:
Interview with
Blake Edwards

By the time Peter Sellers and *The Pink Panther* knocked at his door, Blake Edwards had compiled an impressive Hollywood résumé. The son of Jack McEdward, an assistant director at 20th Century–Fox, and grandson of J. Gordon Edwards, who directed Theda Bara in *Cleopatra* (1917), Edwards was born in Tulsa, Oklahoma, in 1922. He made his first screen appearance as a bit player in *Ten Gentlemen from West Point* (1942) and after Fox signed him to a $150-a-week contract, appeared in a slew of forgettable films before serving in the coast guard during World War II.

Always more interested in writing than acting, Edwards coauthored, produced, and acted in *Panhandle* (1947) before creating the "Richard Diamond: Private Detective" radio series in 1949 for actor William Powell. While writing and directing a good portion of the "Richard Diamond" series, Edwards also wrote for the "Yours Truly, Johnny Dollar" and "The Lineup" radio series.

Edwards segued from radio to film in 1952, cowriting the comedy *Sound Off* for Columbia Pictures and star Mickey Rooney. After writing several more pictures (and collaborating frequently with director Richard Quine), Edwards made his directing debut with *Bring Your Smile Along* (1955), which he also wrote. He spent the next three years writing and directing comedies like *Mister Cory* (1957), *This Happy Feeling* (1958), and *The Perfect Furlough* (1958) before creating the "Peter Gunn" and "Mr. Lucky" television series in 1958 and 1959, respectively.

Edwards's Hollywood stock rose dramatically after directing Cary Grant in *Operation Petticoat* (1959), and he joined the rarefied ranks of big-time talent with *Breakfast at Tiffany's* (1961), which garnered an Oscar nomination for Audrey Hepburn, and *Days of Wine and Roses* (1963), which did the same for Jack Lemmon and Lee Remick.

But much like Sellers, Edwards experienced a horrendous string of flops following 1964's *The Pink Panther* and *A Shot in the Dark*, both of

Blake Edwards.

which he cowrote and directed. *The Great Race* (1965), *What Did You Do in the War, Daddy?* (1966), *Gunn* (1967), and *The Party* (1968) all were box-office failures, as was the enormously expensive *Darling Lili* (1970). Along with wife Julie Andrews, whom he'd married in 1969 and herself in a drought following *Mary Poppins* and *The Sound of Music,* Edwards left Hollywood for Europe in 1972 after production conflicts on *The Carey Treatment.*

After directing Andrews and Omar Sharif in *The Tamarind Seed* (1974), Edwards's comeback received an enormous boost when he reteamed with Sellers for *The Return of the Pink Panther* (1975), a huge box-office success that spawned two more popular sequels—*The Pink Panther Strikes Again* (1976) and *Revenge of the Pink Panther* (1978). His triumphant return to Hollywood was marked by *10* (1979), followed by his scathing industry diatribe *S.O.B.* (1981) and *Victor/Victoria* (1982), for which Andrews, Robert Preston, and Lesley Ann Warren received Oscar nominations.

Following Sellers's death, Edwards tried, and failed, to revive the *Panther* series with *Trail of the Pink Panther* (1982) and *Curse of the Pink Panther* (1983). His more recent works have included *Micki & Maude* (1984), *Blind Date* (1987), and *Switch* (1991).

I understand Peter Ustinov was originally supppposed to play the role of Clouseau in The Pink Panther. *How did Sellers get involved in the project? Had you been an admirer of his previous work?*

Edwards: No, I really wasn't aware of his previous work at that time. I think I had seen *I'm All Right, Jack,* but only to that extent was I aware of his work. It was through his agent—there are a number of agents who take credit for it, and they all belonged to the same agency. This began with the American agents, who were at the time Freddy Fields, Dick Shepherd—those guys. I don't remember which one suggested it; I'm sure it was a community effort, and I don't know where it originated. But Ustinov bowed out [from *The Pink Panther*] at the last minute.

I've heard it was because he was disappointed Ava Gardner wasn't cast in the picture.

Edwards: That was his reason. He really didn't have any right to take that action, but what are you going to do if an actor takes a walk—sue him and say "Get back to work"? It's really not that good, and he was never legally qualified to take that kind of position, but he did. So he was gone, and the thing I found out later that was quite interesting was I believe he went into *Topkapi,* and Sellers had just made an exit from that movie.

Somebody just said, "What are we going to do? We have to start tomorrow, practically, and here we don't have anybody," so they suggested Sellers. There was a lot going on between the producers—the Mirisch Company—and myself, talking transcontinental about Sellers. It was agreed that we had spent so much money, and to shut down and sue Ustinov for damages wasn't very constructive. We had other good people cast in the film, like David Niven and Claudia Cardinale and people like that. We were told there was a window for Sellers—I think it was four weeks or something like that—and if we could condense the role into those four weeks, we could get him.

He was scheduled to do Dr. Strangelove *next.*

Edwards: Something like that. So we agreed to do it. And the first time that I met Sellers was at the Rome airport. I went out to meet him, and we rode back to his hotel and we talked.

About the character of Clouseau?

Edwards: No, we talked about that, but more, we just talked, feeling each other out, trying to find out, I think, where we were coming from. And we quickly found out that we were both coming from practically the same place, in terms of comedy. We were both great fans of Laurel and Hardy, and we began to giggle a lot, and we suddenly realized that at least in that respect, we were soul mates.

I know Sellers always kept a picture of Stan Laurel in his dressing room....

Edwards: Well, he didn't always. You may have heard that rumor. I've been in his dressing room a lot, and I don't recall Stan Laurel being there too many times. I mean, perhaps he was on one or two occasions but not as part of the furnishings.

Had you heard anything about Sellers's on-set behavior before you met him?

Edwards: I heard nothing at that point. I don't think there *was* that much behavior on the set; I don't think he'd done that many films at that point. I only saw a couple of moments where he exhibited at least the potential for problems.

How did the character of Clouseau initially develop?

Edwards: We both agreed that we could take what was essentially there in the character and embellish it, make him much more accident-prone and really invent those kinds of things on the set. And we began to do that. And we had a wonderful time.

Was the part of Clouseau rewritten when Sellers came in?

Edwards: It wasn't rewritten, it was embellished.

Would Ustinov have handled the role the same way?

Edwards: No, absolutely not. The accident-prone, falling-in-the-closet stuff, that whole routine in the bathroom, was all dreamed up there. I would never have done it to that extent with Ustinov.

Was your relationship with Sellers during The Pink Panther *a typical director-actor relationship?*

Edwards: That's all it was at that time. There wasn't much more. We didn't get remarkably close at that point because I had my whole family there. I was ensconced in a house, living a family life, and Sellers was living pretty much of a bachelor existence, having a great time on the town. We didn't get together much outside of the set.

When you began work on The Pink Panther, *did Sellers strike you as someone who would open up immediately, or was he a difficult person to acquaint oneself with?*

Edwards: Well, I felt on that first film that he was very complicated—I sensed that—and that he also had a great spirit of fun. And that's really all I cared about. At that point in my career, I was not particularly interested in making close friends with my actors unless they were pretty ladies maybe [laughs]. But there were no real remarkable highlights or lowlights in that first film.

Was much of The Pink Panther *improvised?*

Edwards: Oh, yes, lots of it, principally with Sellers. The entire bedroom scene, the running around, [Capucine] slipping out of his arms onto the bedsheet, into the bath—all of those things were indicated in the original script, but they were greatly embellished with Sellers, as most of the film was. You know, "We must catch that woman!"—Clouseau puts his hand on the globe and falls down. That was not in the script, obviously.

So at that point it was a harmonious working relationship without any problems?

Edwards: When the picture was finished, I got the first sense of these unpredictable crazy kind of actions when Sellers—after we had this wonderful time and the picture was run—went crazy and sent word to the Mirisches that it was a disaster, which was very typical of him on all the films he would do. I was kind of stunned, and I couldn't believe what had happened. In fact, I sort of disengaged myself from all of it. I didn't wish to get too involved. First of all, I couldn't afford to because I was in the process of finishing it off and scoring it—doing the titles and stuff like that—and I didn't want to have a lot of negative crap coming down on me. But I also didn't listen too hard to the stories I was getting back; I was aware of what was going on because David Niven told me about it, but I didn't give it too much credence. But it stayed there somewhere.

Sellers did this constantly—talk to Ray Stark about it—but that was typical, it was like a manic depressive pattern with him. He was very high on the film and then almost immediately saw it, and it was "This is terrible and I want out, it's an awful movie and you can't release this picture!" I never witnessed it (at the time) with Sellers, I just heard about it and I thought, shit, who wants to get involved with that? I'm never going to see him again so what difference does it make?

Did you feel at that time The Pink Panther *would be as successful as it was?*

Edwards: No. I thought it would be a real good comedy and would be successful, but I didn't think it would break the ground that it did.

Did you decide to do A Shot in the Dark *when* The Pink Panther*'s box-office figures came in?*

Edwards: No, it had nothing to do with that. I was off doing other things. I had made a successful comedy with Peter Sellers, and that was that, and I didn't think about a sequel or working with him again.

He was then scheduled to do *A Shot in the Dark* and came to me with tales of woe—the script was awful, the director [Anatole Litvak] was a problem—all of those things. And he asked me if I would come in and save it, and I said, "I can't do anything like that. You've already got a director and I've got other things to do." And then Harold Mirisch—he'd obviously gotten to Harold Mirisch—came to me and said, "We have a serious situation here. Once again we're getting ready to make a movie, we've got a director signed, and Sellers is threatening to walk. He won't do it. Will you help us out?" I was under contract with the Mirisches at the time and I said, "Well, let me think about it, because I really don't know if I want to get into this, and I really don't know whether I can because I haven't read the piece."

So I familiarized myself with everything they'd done, and I finally said, "Well, if I'm going to take over at this stage, there's only one way I can possibly do it, and that's if the character of the policeman became Clouseau. Because that I'm familiar with, that I know I can do with Sellers—I'm not breaking new ground." And they said yes, go ahead. So I boarded an ocean liner with a writer (William Peter Blatty), and we wrote going over there, and we were, I think, shooting within four weeks of the time that I said okay.

Is this when the problems started between you and Sellers?

Edwards: Yes, that's when it started. It's a little hard to remember precisely what happened. We started off great, having great fun. But about midway he began to act up, act out, complain, not show up on time, do things that I felt I should have knowledge of. I had come along to do this out of deference to him and the Mirisches, and I didn't need what was going on there. All of this trouble that he was beginning to cause, all of the complaints that things weren't going well. There are some things I really don't want to get into at this point because some of those people are still around.

He complained about actors, actresses—just generally starting trouble. And I thought I'd nip this in the bud right away. I couldn't get in touch with him, and I wrote him a note and shoved it under his door and said, "Come on, Peter, act like a professional," which was the biggest mistake in the world because it was like punishing a bad little boy and taking a parental attitude about this whole thing. He pouted and went up and down with his attitudes, and his modus operandi—I mean there were times when he was terrific, but again it was very manic-depressive.

Did you feel he was already growing bored with Clouseau?

Edwards: Yes, that's exactly what was happening. He got bored with parts. You see, there were two things you could count on to possibly keep Sellers afloat. One was if you did it all in a very short time so he couldn't get bored; the other was if he was really broke and in desperate need of a film. That would somehow support him, get him through the whole thing.

Did Graham Stark's presence on the Shot in the Dark *set help Sellers's frame of mind?*

Edwards: I think any of those people helped him to some degree. As long as he could have his kind of stock company around him, it supported him, but it certainly didn't guarantee that he wasn't going to act like a madman, a lunatic, and be very hurtful to those people and to people he didn't know and didn't care about.

Was A Shot in the Dark *improvised much like* The Pink Panther?

Edwards: "Improvised" is not the correct term for what we did. There were two things that used to happen. You would take what was essentially there and perhaps embellish it—which was a kind of improvisation—or there were things that were not there at all, and suddenly one of us would say, "What if he did or I did the following?" and within the context of the scene we would improvise. But improvisation carries with it the connotation that we would say, "Yeah, it's funny, go ahead and do it" and I'd run a camera on it. That never happened, ever, not even in *The Party*, which you could say was mostly improvisation. What would happen was, we would start to improvise, and we would refine it, refine it, and refine it until it might just as well have been written down. By the time we were done, it was set in concrete, and that's what we were doing. It began as a kind of improvisation and ended up being something fixed.

So Sellers's "up and down" behavior led to some friction on the Shot in the Dark *set . . .*

Edwards: Oh yes.

Were you able to communicate your ideas with Sellers when he was in one of his better moods?

Edwards: Yes, pretty much, I could still get to him. It wasn't as much give-and-take; it was more give on my part. I mean it was more directing on my part, and we somehow got through it. There was not a lot of yelling at each other—not real confrontation with each other as much as there was "back door" confrontation with his agents, who would call up in the middle of the night and try to placate me or get things straightened out.

I understand Sellers was famous for late-night phone calls to directors and agents.

Edwards: Oh yes. He didn't do that too much to me, because he knew that after *A Shot in the Dark* he couldn't get away with it.

Based on his reaction to The Pink Panther, *were you waiting for the proverbial bomb to drop after Sellers had seen* A Shot in the Dark *for the first time?*

Edwards: I suppose so; I don't recall it that well. I mean I finished it and was very pleased with what we did. If somebody said to me, "Sellers once again is saying he hates it"—and I kind of recall that he did do that—I just said, "I'm never going to work with the man again," and that's the end of it, it's over with, and I'm glad I got what I got out of it.

From what I understand, that's pretty much what happened on both your parts after A Shot in the Dark—*saying you'd never work with the other again.*

Edwards: That's what I *heard* he said—he never said that to me. I made it very clear to the Mirisches. I don't think I made a public announcement; he was much more public with those kinds of things. I probably said to Harold, "Listen, don't ever get [me teamed] with this guy again." I didn't come out and publicize it.

So at that time, as far as you were concerned, you would never work with Sellers again.

Edwards: Yes, that's right.

So what happened between 1964 and The Party *in 1968 to change that situation?*

Edwards: It's a little hard to figure out, because I had one very good experience on the original *Panther* and one pretty bad experience on *Shot in the Dark* and then a considerable length of time when we had both gone on and done other things.

Roddy McDowall is publishing a book of photographs and people talking about the people in the photographs. My wife talks about me, and I talk about Sellers. And in it, I likened [working with Sellers] to the good times being like a narcotic—that they were so heady, that they were so good, that you couldn't forget them, you were hooked. And I think that's probably a good analogy. It really is true, because seldom did I have as much fun—as the good times I had with Sellers.

Somehow you don't remember the bad as much as you long for the good. Sellers was down—I think he'd had his heart attacks by that time—and his career was not flourishing at all, and mine wasn't doing great at that time.

One thing we had constantly talked about during the good times—because of the improvisational quality of what we did—was wouldn't it be great to take a structure, just that, and mostly improvise a whole film? I had this notion which didn't have anything to do with Sellers to begin with—it was a comedy notion—but the more I developed it along those lines, the more it seemed impossible to do with anybody else. First of all, I knew what a genius he was at improvising, and I knew the good part of me and the good part of him were so closely aligned. And I longed for a fix, I needed to shoot up, that's what it was. I was addicted. And I think conversely he probably was too, in his own way.

Was there a change in Sellers's mood once filming began on The Party*? By this time, he'd suffered his heart attacks and lost a lot of weight. Had he grown even further to reach?*

Edwards: No. It was fascinating, although I was aware he'd had heart attacks and was concerned about them and everything. Once again, here was a guy, this genius talent who was reasonably broke, who needed a hit. He wasn't getting any jobs, and the whole milieu appealed to him so much, the improvisational quality and just getting back to work. We went through *The Party*, for the most part, having a joyous time. We really had fun. It was the best of all of those possible times. We just sat and giggled all the time. That's the best kind of moviemaking; if you can feel that good about what you're doing, you can't beat it.

So The Party *was a harmonious experience?*

Edwards: Yes, tremendously so. Unfortunately, it was not a great roaring success. I don't even know whether at the end of it Peter repeated his usual seeing it and disliking it—I don't think so. I think that film he kind of cherished somewhat.

You didn't feel at that point Sellers was having trouble remembering his lines?

Edwards: Oh, no, absolutely not. He just had trouble getting on the set without laughing. There were a couple of little things but nothing I can even remember.

Let's move on to The Return of the Pink Panther. *By this time, seven years had passed since* The Party.

Edwards: You see, once again, it caught Sellers at a really low ebb, and me at a particularly low ebb. I had said "fuck you" to Hollywood and taken off and gone to Europe. I was finished here as far as I was concerned, so again it was a couple of soul mates getting together.

The original idea was to make The Return of the Pink Panther *a television series, is that correct?*

Edwards: At that time I had a deal with Sir Lew Grade—who is now Lord Lew Grade—and I had made one film for him [*The Tamarind Seed*] that wasn't successful. It's a whole plot. I sold him on the idea of doing the *Pink Panther* as a television series with Sellers, who was agreeable to that. At one point, I conned Lew Grade into making *The Return of the Pink Panther* as a feature—he didn't want anything to do with films—but I convinced him on two levels—that if he made a successful film, it would make the television show that much more important and that Sellers and I would do it for nothing except expenses and a share of the gross. Lew didn't understand about "gross" deals in those days, so all he could see is that he's got one actor and one director willing to do the picture for nothing, except for expenses, which amounted to probably a couple hundred thousand dollars between us.

We made the picture for a little over two million dollars, and it grossed enormously, and Lew made many millions of dollars, and so did we, which then made Lew greedy and got him into the next *Panther* while the television show just went by the boards. Sellers had never planned on doing the television show, and neither had I—it was all a plot to get another film.

Do you feel the Clouseau character developed more in The Return of the Pink Panther?

Edwards: Yes. What had happened was that midway through *Shot in the Dark* Sellers had gone to France. And he came back, and he told me he had run into a French concierge, and then he gave me an example of those Clouseau-isms—the "bimp," the "mith"—all of those things that you saw mostly in the interrogation sequence where Clouseau talks about the closet and receiving a "bimp" on the head, et cetera. So that became a fixture with Clouseau; he did it throughout *Return of the Pink Panther,* and it just became part of the character.

How was Sellers's behavior on this film?

Edwards: Great. He had some problems, but they didn't directly influence me; they had to do with a girl he was going with at the time, and he did a couple of—I was told, I didn't see it so I don't know—terrible kinds of things. She was hit by a glass that broke, and she was cut, but those things never got to the set, I was never bothered by them. Again, it was another wonderful experience and was obviously a huge success. It brought us both back tremendously.

Was Sellers's health a factor here? Was he having problems?

Edwards: No, not on *Return of.* Not that I recall.

Was there a sequel planned at that point?

Edwards: No, it was a decision made afterward. I don't recall that we readily agreed [on a sequel], I don't really remember. It becomes very muddy at that point as far as the next one is concerned, because *Return of* was such a huge success and because the people making those films wanted to continue with the success. We were encouraged in many ways to do another, not the least of which was money and ownership.

The next one [*The Pink Panther Strikes Again*] was, I think, done for the wrong reasons—because we'd had a success, let's have another success. And I was prompted to do another one with an additional factor: I found I could get things done—other projects like *10*—that I wanted to do by agreeing to another *Panther*. So I was—"coercing" isn't the right word—I guess to some extent I would try to coerce Sellers into doing it because I wanted to do other things. And I think he probably was agreeable because he wanted to do other things too. But there was no reason not to, because we'd had a very good time on *Return of.*

It was during *The Pink Panther Strikes Again* when he began to show the effects of the heart attacks and the effects of boredom. He now was successful, had money, and he was doing a lot of things that were damaging his health. He was drinking, he was heavy on valium—I don't know what else—but you can't drink and take valium and not expect it to damage you a lot, to affect your behavior a lot too.

What was the scenario between you and Sellers on The Pink Panther Strikes Again?

Edwards: We began well, but little by little, he was like a bad child who would—it's very hard behavior to describe—but who would....

Needed to be scolded?

Edwards: Well, not needed to be scolded so much, because the more you would scold him, the more entrenched he would become, the more angry he would become. I remember one time saying, "Jesus, Peter, you've gotten things to the point where everybody is really angry with you," and in a rage he said, "Everybody? I drive through that gate in the morning, and that officer salutes me, he's not angry at me!" You know, mad, crazy answers.

He would sulk, he would get into black moods, he would withdraw, and he would punish himself by not being able to do something. If he couldn't get a handle on it—you see, part of it was because he couldn't get a handle on it—it would frustrate the shit out of him, and he would become worse and worse and worse in order to justify the fact that he couldn't do it. He would blame it on somebody else, blame it on conditions, blame it on God— blame it on anybody except Peter Sellers. And he was very cruel to people during those periods. He would threaten, even pretend physical violence, like he would beat somebody up. If it wasn't so sad, it was laughable.

Was it a hostile set on The Pink Panther Strikes Again? *Was there bad blood between Sellers and the crew?*

Edwards: No, it wasn't too bad as far as the rest of the crew was concerned because I have the ability of keeping the set lively and we've got all those other people to have fun with. You can say a fish stinks from the head—and it does—because Sellers's antics and behavior would just permeate. But somehow we would rise above it, and it wouldn't be too bad.

Did Graham Stark's presence here help at all?

Edwards: Not really. Sellers was beginning to really decline, to really go downhill, and you could see it, and it was frustrating and sad.

Do you feel some of Sellers's memory lapses were attributable to his heart medication?

Edwards: Well, I don't know whether it was heart medication or the fact the heart itself just wasn't pumping enough and he wasn't getting enough oxygen to his brain. He even made remarks about it. He said, "I just had one too many heart attacks; I can't walk and chew gum at the same time" or remarks like that. He really believed that perhaps that was what was happening. That was when we were in the good times when he would admit those sorts of things—there weren't enough of those. And of course it was all complicated by his personal life and the women he was getting involved with, and the enormous amounts of drugs he was taking.

Do you know what kinds of drugs specifically?

Edwards: I know valium and vodka specifically. As to what else he was getting into, I didn't know, and I didn't want to know. I didn't want to get into that.

After The Pink Panther Strikes Again *was there thought of doing another* Panther *installment?*

Edwards: No. After *Strikes Again,* I didn't think we'd ever do another one. I thought, "Oh, boy, we're getting into a sick area here, it's dangerous, it's too much grief, it's all of those things." But once again it was that need to go back to that water hole, plus the success factor and the hope that maybe it was one of those times when it would change.

But were you still getting that same charge? It seems it just wasn't there anymore as far as the high of working together and seeing things click.

Edwards: Yes, but you have to remember *Strikes Again* was the first time since *Shot* that it wasn't there anymore. So if you really look at the graph, the first *Pink Panther* was boom! and *Shot in the Dark* was this way and sort of dropped off halfway through—it was a miserable experience. Then *The Party* was a great experience—forget whether it was successful or not—and *Return of* was wow! So *Strikes Again*—although it was bad—was really the first time that it had dropped down since *Shot*, so there was a long period of good times there. Yes it was bad, but I think we could both make compromises in our own minds about the next one. I'm sure Peter said [to himself], maybe the next one I'll be able to function better. And at that time Sellers's lifestyle needed so much money with the women and all—or woman, depending on who he was with—that there it was, every time he did one of those films, he made a lot of money. And with me it was the additional factor of okay, I want to do *10*, I'll do another *Panther* for you.

Was Revenge of the Pink Panther *really Sellers's nadir? How bad was he at that point?*

Edwards: Really bad. Really bad.

You once told Playboy *that the funniest scene ever written for a* Panther *featured Clouseau and Cato disguised as black men who enter a bar speaking jive. That scene never made it into* Revenge of the Pink Panther. *What happened?*

Edwards: Sellers thought it was the funniest thing he'd ever read. He just couldn't do it, he just couldn't cut it. It didn't happen. And you could see he was brooding before he even did it, you could see there was almost an intentional "it's so great that I'm not going to concede to it." It sounds really self-abusing, but it's true. I mean we were stunned by it. That was the situation where he called me in the middle of the night and said, "Don't worry about it, God has showed me how to do this." And I made the serious mistake the next day of letting him do it, and I said to him, "Do me a favor. Tell God to stay out of show business." We were finished then. I had to shoot him in bits and pieces; that scene at the fireplace was a classic example. I just stuck him there and just kept covering and covering. It was getting to be more the rule than the exception at that point. And the worst part about it was that he couldn't coordinate the lines and the physical action anymore.

Did Sellers look like a dying man at this point?

Edwards: Yes. He had bad pallor, wasn't in shape, obviously, and was haggard. He looked like he was on his way out.

Sellers had a script for The Romance of the Pink Panther *and was preparing to shoot the picture when he died. Were there any overtures made to you to come in and direct that?*

Edwards: There was some talk about it originally. But I had made it very clear that I could not make another movie with him. He wanted to do it for whatever his reasons were, so they asked me to consider it. I said no, and they made a deal with me.

It sounds like he was a manic-depressive.

Edwards: I don't think there's any doubt about it. You couldn't get him near an analyst. He tried it once but hated the thought of psychoanalysis or psychotherapy. I think he was a paranoid schizophrenic.

That could have had something to do with his relationship with his mother.

Edwards: Oh, God, yes, as much as I know about him, he couldn't have gone any other way.

Did you ever meet Peg Sellers?

Edwards: Never did.

Did you see that aspect of Sellers's personality? Supposedly he phoned his mother every night, even in the 1960s when he was an international star.

Edwards: I saw the result of that.

A man who resented his mother . . .

Edwards: And adored her at the same time. A lot of love-hate, the whole Oedipal complex. Jesus God, yes! Although he called her every night and talked to her every night too, he carried that shrine around with him and left his life to psychics and believed he was going to exist for a certain number of years.

I know he was very superstitious.

Edwards: Terribly superstitious. My mother-in-law walked on the set one day in a purple coat, and I saw Sellers come through the door, and then he stopped, turned around, and walked off the set, and would not come back on until I got rid of my mother-in-law.

What led to Trail of the Pink Panther? *Was it a moneymaking ploy?*

Edwards: Well, it wasn't just that, it was not a moneymaking thing because I didn't need the money—we all need money, I guess—but I was well off. I referred earlier to the fact I had done the last *Panther* really in order to get other projects done, and I did *Trail* for the same reason.

Were most of the Sellers outtakes used in Trail of the Pink Panther *from one specific* Panther *film or a combination of them?*

Edwards: They were mostly from *Strikes Again.* I had hoped we'd have much more than that.

After Trail of the Pink Panther *there was* Curse of the Pink Panther, *both of which fared poorly at the box office.*

Edwards: They fared a lot better than publicly known. *Curse* particularly didn't fare well because at that point I was in terrible battles once again with MGM—in fact, I had to sue them for it, and I won the lawsuit. They did not do what they were supposed to do with that film. They just buried it.

Do you feel the films would have done better had Sellers been there?

Edwards: Oh, I don't know, it's hard to say. It's possible, but I look at *Curse of the Pink Panther,* and it's a good film and a funny film. It may not have done what the others did, but had it gotten the proper send-off—had MGM done what it was supposed to do—it would've done much better.

Could Sellers's manic states have affected his personality to the extent that they made him a mean person?

Edwards: Not nice because he wasn't in one of his manic states? That's hard to say. You would have to say, "Well, wait a minute, look at his kids and how he behaved about family." You can say he wasn't capable of anything else, but that doesn't take away from the fact in terms of family and how he treated his kids. I mean I had his daughter living with me for quite some time. I really felt sorry for her. It was sad, really bloody sad. But he was basically not a nice man. I would defy anybody to tell me what was nice about him.

In contrast, he surrounded himself with nice people like Graham Stark and David Lodge....

Edwards: They're great, wonderful people who took a lot of punishment from him. Bad-mouthing was what he did all the time. I guess if you had to sum him up, you'd say he couldn't help it, that's just who he was, but he was not nice.

It's ironic, because Sellers was always saying he didn't have a personality of his own.

Edwards: He had a personality of his own. He felt better when he was living in someone else's skin for a while. What would happen was, if it was stretched out too long, there was no real substantial character there, it was "let's pretend." And you can only pretend for a while, and then you suddenly realize there's nothing really solid about the character.

Did you ever witness him staying in character once filming stopped?

Edwards: I never saw that, but I'm sure he was very capable of it. I think it was a show as much as anything else.

Do you feel you really got to know this "man behind the mask"?

Edwards: I think I got to know him as well as anyone could get to know him.

And you would describe him as not being a nice person?

Edwards: No, not a nice guy.

Was he selfish?

Edwards: Very selfish. I mean he was generous—quite often he would give all kinds of gifts—but they were bribes. He was generous in material things, not really generous in his heart because he really didn't know how to do that. When I say "generous," he was generous because he had his chums, he would see to it that they were hired. That was to ingratiate himself and make himself liked, among other things. It also gave him a sense of security, a sense of family, which was important to him. But he was a tortured man, an angry man and a lonely man, terribly lonely. I have great compassion for anybody like that. I would not want to be like that.

I guess you could step back and say, "I feel sorry for this guy."

Edwards: No, I couldn't. I wish I had been more generous. It usually was only after the fact when the heat cooled off a bit and I could say, "Well obviously I feel miserable about this. I'm so pissed off and angry at him, I could kill him, and I don't like that feeling in myself. So I've got to make peace with him in some way, and the way you make peace is to forgive and forget, and the way you forgive and forget is to try to understand why people are like that." I mean, Hitler had problems too. But it's very hard when you take that kind of abuse, and he could really abuse you. It was frustrating because I couldn't really fight back to any great extent because I had to finish a movie, I had to finish that film, so I had to make all kinds of concessions, and he knew it, and he'd take advantage of it.

He certainly had a knack for strange behavior.

Edwards: He must have had a real problem. He must have loved me kind of like I loved him, and hated me to such a degree that it was kind of like his mom, that terrible tearing feeling. I know he had a big emotional investment in me—he couldn't have hated me that much—but he hated the fact that I was so responsible for pulling him back.

Did you love him?

Edwards: Well, you know, I loved things about him. I couldn't love him as a man because he was too mean, and he was not a nice person, so you couldn't love that person. But there were qualities about him that I probably identified with, demons that I identified with. You couldn't help but respect and be in awe of his amazing talent. "Love" is a strange word. I've seen people who have gone through a lifetime of marriage really hating each other but being so stuck together, it becomes a real bond, so you don't know whether it's love, hate, or both. So I was emotionally involved with him tremendously, as he was with me. No doubt about it.

What's your opinion of the Panther *series? Do you look at it as the highlight of your career?*

Edwards: No, but it has a place. *The Return of the Pink Panther* brought me back to Hollywood in good style.

Has your opinion of Sellers as a person changed since his death?

Edwards: I've become more generous in my forgiving and forgetting. I wish he were still here, with all his craziness, and I wish he were well. I'm not sure that I wish to make another film with him, but I wish for those times.

As a director, do you think Sellers had reached the tether of his artistic rope at the time of his death, or do you think he could have continued to grow as an actor?

Edwards: I think he could have gone on, but it's hard to say. I feel that Sellers would also have gone on to become crazier and crazier, whether he'd had the heart attack or not. I think he was so close to being certifiable, and I don't say that facetiously, that at some point in his life he would have either killed himself—and I don't mean put a gun to his head necessarily but kill himself with booze and drugs—or he would have destroyed himself some other way.

How did you feel about Sellers's death? Did it surprise you?

Edwards: No. I probably would've reacted more, but I was stunned he wasn't dead long before. He made a joke about giving up cigarettes—he was really giving up heart attacks, he said. So when he died, I was not at all surprised. There was a loneliness suddenly—like when somebody you respect dies—and even when villains go, your villains are gone, and it leaves a hollow space because who do you rail against, who do you blame?

I'll tell you an interesting story. The last time I saw Sellers was on a Christmas in Gstaad, Switzerland. My family and I were in a local disco, and I saw Sellers and his wife come in. And they wouldn't acknowledge us.

They saw you?

Edwards: Oh, yes. By then, he was not speaking to me. It wasn't that I wasn't speaking to him, he wasn't speaking to me. And I watched from a distance, and I watched him have a fight with his lady and leave. She stayed and was dancing with a wardrobe person who Sellers kind of carried around with him at that point.

About a half hour later my son came in—he was meeting us there—he sat down and said, "Dad, I just saw Peter Sellers." And I said, "Yeah," and he said, "He's standing across the street. I thought it was a statue." And I said, "You're kidding. It's snowing out there!" He said, "Yes, he looks like a snowman, it's the weirdest thing I've ever seen!"

I thought, "Well, it's Christmas, and it's crazy, at least for me, to play the game of not speaking or talking. In spite of the problems, there were good times too." So I excused myself to Julie and said, "I'm going to go over and say something to him."

I walked out, and it was spooky—he had a coat on, but he was just standing there. I mean it was snowing heavily, and he was covered with snow, he hadn't moved, it was like he was catatonic. So I walked across the street to him, and I walked up to him, and he acted at least like he hadn't seen me coming or heard me. And I said, "Peter," and he was just standing there, and he kind of snapped out of it, and he looked, and he saw it was me, and he didn't know quite what to do with it. I said "Peter, go home or get inside. You're going to catch cold." And I kissed him on the cheeks and said, "Merry Christmas" and walked back into the place. And as I walked through the door, I looked back, and he was still standing there. That's the last time I ever saw him.

Notes

Prologue

1. Peter Evans. *Peter Sellers: The Mask Behind the Mask* (Englewood Cliffs, N.J.: Prentice-Hall, 1968), p. 173.

Chapter 1

1. Alexander Walker. *Peter Sellers: The Authorized Biography* (New York: Macmillan, 1981), p. 66.
2. Evans, p. 76.
3. Walker, p. 84.

Chapter 2

1. *The New York Times*, February 21, 1956, p. 37.
2. Walker, p. 88.
3. *Variety*, December 28, 1955, p. 6.

Chapter 3

1. Walker, p. 90.
2. *Variety*, April 17, 1957.
3. "The Girl Was Forgotten," *Newsweek*, November 25, 1957, p. 125.
4. *The New York Times*, November 23, 1957, p. 11.

Chapter 4

1. Walker, p. 166.
2. *Variety*, December 11, 1957.
3. *The New York Times*, July 1, 1958, p. 36.

Chapter 5

1. "The Secret Life of Tom Thumb," *The New York Times*, October 19, 1958, sec. 2, p. 8.
2. *Variety*, December 3, 1958, pp. 6, 20.
3. *Newsweek*, December 29, 1958.

Chapter 6

1. *Variety,* May 21, 1958, p. 16.

Chapter 7

1. Walker, p. 97.
2. Walker, p. 98.
3. Walker, p. 99.
4. *The New York Times,* June 15, 1960.
5. *Variety,* March 18, 1959.

Chapter 8

1. Walker, p. 93.
2. Sylvester, p. 31.
3. "When the U.S. Lost a War," *Life,* November 9, 1959.
4. *The New York Times,* October 27, 1959, p. 40.
5. *Variety,* August 5, 1959, p. 6.
6. *The New Yorker,* November 7, 1959, p. 205.
7. "Mighty Mouse," *The Reporter,* October 29, 1959, p. 38.

Chapter 9

1. Evans, pp. 91–92.
2. Evans, p. 94.
3. Walker, p. 101.
4. "Talk With a Star," *Newsweek,* May 9, 1960, p. 113.
5. *Commonweal,* May 27, 1960, p. 229.
6. *Time,* May 2, 1960, p. 34.

Chapter 10

1. Walker, p. 108.
2. *Newsweek,* May 2, 1960, p. 89.
3. *The New York Times,* April 19, 1960, p. 40.
4. *The Nation,* April 30, 1960, p. 392.

Chapter 11

1. Walker, p. 49.
2. Walker, p. 50.
3. Walker, p. 126.
4. "Rambunctious," *Newsweek,* January 30, 1961, p. 77.
5. Roger Angell, *The New Yorker,* January 28, 1961, p. 71.
6. *Newsweek,* January 30, 1961, p. 77.

Chapter 12

1. "Sellers Straight," *Newsweek*, July 1, 1963, p. 68.
2. Walker, p. 113.
3. Evans, p. 99.

Chapter 13

1. "An Evening with Peter Sellers," an edited version of the BBC TV "Parkinson Show" originally transmitted on November 9, 1974; BBC Records & Tapes.
2. Evans, p. 100.
3. Evans, p. 100.
4. Sylvester, p. 43.
5. Walker, p. 117.
6. Walker, p. 122.
7. *Time*, February 3, 1961, p. 68.
8. *Variety*, October 26, 1960, p. 17.
9. *The New Yorker*, May 26, 1962, p. 133.
10. Walker, p. 124.

Chapter 14

1. Evans, p. 110.
2. Stanley Kauffmann, *The New Republic*, April 6, 1962, p. 26.
3. "Exhibition Game," *Newsweek*, March 12, 1962, p. 102.
4. "Barmy in the Back Stacks," *Time*, April 6, 1962.
5. Walker, p. 126.
6. Walker, pp. 127–28.
7. Peter Harcourt, *Sight and Sound*, Spring 1962, p. 96.
8. "The Exhibition Game," *Newsweek* March 12, 1962, p. 102.
9. Hollis Alpert, *Saturday Review*, February 10, 1962, p. 35.
10. *Commonweal*, April 6, 1962, p. 39.
11. *The Nation*, April 14, 1962, p. 340.

Chapter 15

1. Walker, p. 122.
2. Walker, p. 123.
3. Walker, p. 130.
4. *Time*, August 17, 1962, p. 75.
5. "Waltzing Around Again," *Commonweal*, September 7, 1962, p. 497.
6. "Sellers' Market," *Newsweek*, August 20, 1962, p. 86.

Chapter 16

1. Peter Benzel, *Life*, May 25, 1962, p. 97.
2. Ibid., p. 97.

3. Ibid., p. 97.
4. Marcel Ciment, *Kubrick* (New York: Holt, Rinehart and Winston, 1980), p. 201.
5. *Time*, June 22, 1962, p. 94.
6. Brendan Gill, *The New Yorker*, June 23, 1962, p. 90.
7. James Price, *The London Magazine*, January, 1963, p. 73.
8. Derek Sylvester, *Peter Sellers* (New York: Proteus, 1981), p. 46.
9. Walker, p. 134.
10. "The Strange World of Peter Sellers," *Rolling Stone*, April 17, 1980, p. 46.
11. Walker, p. 135.
12. "The People Inside Peter Sellers," *Esquire*, November, 1970, p. 122.
13. Ciment, p. 92.
14. Price, p. 73.
15. Ciment, p. 61.
16. Price, p. 74.
17. Ciment, p. 92.
18. *Time*, June 22, 1962, p. 94.
19. Dwight McDonald, *Esquire*, September 1962, p. 45.
20. Robert Hatch, *Nation*, June 23, 1962, p. 563.
21. Stanley Kauffmann, *The New Republic*, July 2, 1962, p. 29.
22. *Time*, June 22, 1962, p. 94.
23. *Newsweek*, June 18, 1962, p. 86.

Chapter 17

1. *Variety*, October 3, 1962, p. 7.
2. "Sneaky Pete & Co.," *Time*, March 22, 1963, p. 101.
3. "Vintage Sellers," *Newsweek*, March 18, 1963, p. 103.

Chapter 18

1. Walker, pp. 27–28.
2. Isabel Quigly, "Hell!," *The Spectator*, May 31, 1963, p. 707.
3. *Esquire*, October 1963, p. 44.

Chapter 19

1. Walker, p. 145.
2. "Ustinov Is Sued by Movie Company in Contract Dispute," *The New York Times*, January 10, 1963, p. 5.
3. "Strange World," April 17, 1980, *Rolling Stone*, p. 46.
4. Walker, p. 145.
5. "No Shot in the Dark," *The New York Times*, January 19, 1964, sec. 2, p. 9.
6. "Strange World," *Rolling Stone*, p. 46.
7. Sheridan Morley, *The Other Side of the Moon: A Biography of David Niven* (New York: Harper & Row, 1985), p. 231.
8. *The New York Times*, July 16, 1978, sec. 2, p. 15.
9. Walker, p. 147.
10. "Has Skis, Needs Lift," *Time*, April 17, 1964, p. 130.

11. *Rolling Stone*, p. 46.
12. "Screen: Sellers Chases a Jewel Thief," *The New York Times*, April 24, 1964, p. 25.
13. "Has Skis, Needs Lift," p. 130.
14. "Peter, Peter," *Newsweek*, March 30, 1964, p. 52.
15. *Saturday Review*, February 29, 1964, p. 23.

Chapter 20

1. Evans, p. 109.
2. *Rolling Stone*, April 17, 1980, p. 45.
3. Gelmis, Joseph, *The Film Director as Superstar* (Garden City, N.Y.: Doubleday, 1970), p. 309.
4. Walker, p. 138.
5. *Rolling Stone*, pp. 45–46.
6. Walker, p. 137.
7. *Rolling Stone*, p. 46.
8. "Detonating Comedy," *Time*, January 31, 1964, p. 69.
9. *The London Magazine*, May 1964, p. 70.
10. *The New Statesman*, January 31, 1964, p. 178.

Chapter 21

1. "Teen-Age Tyros' New 'World,'" *The New York Times*, March 29, 1964, p. 7.
2. Walker, pp. 142–43.
3. "Two in One," *The Spectator*, June 19, 1964, p. 824.
4. "Films of Today," *The New York Times*, March 29, 1964, p. 2.
5. *The New Republic*, April 18, 1964, p. 26.
6. Philip T. Hartung, *Commonweal*, April 3, 1964, p. 43.
7. Brendan Gill, *The New Yorker*, March 28, 1964, p. 144.

Chapter 22

1. Jean-François Hauduroy, "Sophisticated Naturalism: Interview with Blake Edwards," *Cahiers du Cinema in English*, no. 3, 1966, p. 26.
2. *Rolling Stone*, April 17, 1980, p. 46.
3. Walker, p. 149.
4. *Playboy*, December, 1982, p. 97.
5. Bosley Crowther, *The New York Times*, June 24, 1964, p. 28.
6. Hollis Alpert, *Saturday Review*, July 11, 1964, p. 22.
7. *The New Yorker*, July 4, 1964, p. 58.
8. "Keystone Cop," *Newsweek*, July 6, 1964, p. 76.

Chapter 23

1. Walker, p. 155.
2. *Life*, July 31, 1964, p. 29.

3. Ibid.
4. Evans, p. 135.
5. Evans, p. 131.
6. Evans, p. 135.
7. Eric Lax, *On Being Funny: Woody Allen & Comedy* (New York: Manor Books, 1977), p. 52.
8. Walker, p. 161.
9. Evans, p. 135.
10. Lax, p. 57.
11. Nicholas Wapshott, *Peter O'Toole* (New York: Beaufort Books, 1983), p. 130.
12. Lax, pp. 61, 64.
13. *Variety*, June 23, 1965.

Chapter 24

1. Walker, p. 164.
2. Walker, pp. 164–65.
3. Walker, p. 165.
4. "Grave Fun," *Time*, August 12, 1966, p. 59.
5. *The Nation*, August 8, 1966, p. 134.
6. "The Funniest Thing," *Newsweek*, August 1, 1966, p. 83.

Chapter 25

1. Walker, p. 163.
2. *Venture*, April 1966, p. 124.
3. Evans, p. 138.
4. Walker, p. 164.
5. Evans, p. 139.
6. Michael Sellers, *P.S. I Love You* (New York: Berkley Books, 1982), p. 109.
7. Arthur Knight, *Saturday Review*, December 31, 1966, p. 36.
8. Bosley Crowther, *The New York Times*, December 24, 1966, p. 11.
9. "Ready for Nothing," *Newsweek*, January 2, 1967, p. 64.

Chapter 26

1. Barbara Leaming, *Orson Welles: A Biography* (New York: Penguin, 1985), p. 570–71.
2. Leaming, p. 573.
3. *Look*, November 15, 1966, p. 54.
4. Leaming, p. 572.
5. Evans, p. 146.
6. Leaming, p. 573.
7. Walker, p. 171.
8. Walker, p. 169.
9. *Look*, November 15, 1966, p. 54.
10. Evans, p. 152.
11. Evans, pp. 156–57.

12. Walker, p. 172.
13. "Keystone Cop-Out," *Time,* May 12, 1967, p. 100.
14. *Esquire,* August 1967, p. 30.
15. Walker, p. 173.

Chapter 27

1. Evans, p. 159.
2. Michael Sellers, p. 110.
3. Evans, p. 159.
4. Evans, p. 160.
5. Evans, pp. 160–61.
6. Evans, p. 162.
7. Walker, p. 176.
8. Evans, p. 176.
9. Bosley Crowther, *The New York Times,* September 29, 1967, p. 53.
10. "Blue Matador," *Newsweek,* October 13, 1967, p. 107.
11. Richard Schickel, "Sellers as a Singing Matador," *Life,* September 15, 1967, p. 12.

Chapter 28

1. *Playboy,* December, 1982, p. 97.
2. Walker, p. 187.
3. Michael Starr, Interview with Blake Edwards.
4. Wilfrid Sheed, *Esquire,* August 1968, p. 22.
5. Blake Edwards Interview.
6. Vincent Canby, *The New York Times,* April 5, 1968, p. 56.
7. Wilfrid Sheed, *Esquire,* August, 1968, p. 22.

Chapter 29

1. Walker, p. 152.
2. *Los Angeles Times,* January 8, 1968.
3. Joel Siegel, *American Film,* May 1984, p. 63.
4. "Journey to Nowhere," *Time,* November 22, 1968, p. 78.
5. Arthur Knight, *Saturday Review* September 21, 1968, p. 47.
6. Stanley Kauffman, *The New Republic,* December 7, 1968, p. 41.
7. Walker, p. 188.
8. "Strange World," *Rolling Stone,* April 17, 1980, p. 44.

Chapter 30

1. Walker, p. 195.
2. "The People Inside Peter Sellers," *Esquire,* November, 1970, p. 225.
3. Walker, p. 194.
4. Walker, pp. 194–95.
5. Walker, p. 195.

6. "Dead End," *Time,* Feburary 23, 1970, p. 74.
7. *The New Yorker,* March 7, 1970, p. 95.
8. *The New York Times,* February 12, 1970.

Chapter 31

1. Walker, pp. 192–93.
2. "People Inside," *Esquire,* November 1970, p. 122.
3. *Variety,* July 22, 1970, p. 20.
4. "Captive for a Week," *The New York Times,* March 12, 1982.
5. Walker, pp. 195–96.

Chapter 32

1. Walker, p. 197.
2. Ibid.
3. "People Inside," *Esquire,* November 1970, p. 123.
4. Walker, p. 197.
5. "Galloping Gourmet," *Newsweek,* December 28, 1970, p. 67.
6. *Variety,* December 16, 1970, p. 17.
7. "Flashes in the Pan," *Saturday Review,* December 19, 1970, p. 38.
8. Peter Haining, *Goldie* (London: W. H. Allen, 1985), p. 79.

Chapter 33

1. *Variety,* May 13, 1970, p. 15.
2. *The New York Times,* October 1, 1972, p. 66.
3. *Variety,* August 16, 1972, p. 14.

Chapter 34

1. Sylvester, p. 91.
2. Ibid.
3. *Variety,* July 4, 1973, p. 30.

Chapter 35

1. Evans, p. 102.
2. Evans, p. 25.
3. Walker, p. 206.
4. *The New York Times,* October 19, 1973, p. 58.
5. *PTA Magazine,* January, 1974, p. 5.
6. *Variety,* October 17, 1973, p. 14.

Chapter 36

1. Walker, p. 210.
2. Walker, p. 211.

3. Ibid.
4. *Variety,* June 27, 1984, p. 19.

Chapter 37

1. Walker, p. 151.
2. *Playboy,* December 1982, p. 97.
3. "Clouseaumania," *Newsweek,* July 21, 1975, pp. 66–67.
4. *The New Yorker,* June 2, 1975, pp. 90–92.
5. "Minkey Business," *Time,* July 7, 1975, p. 47.

Chapter 38

1. Walker, p. 205.
2. Vincent Canby, *The New York Times,* June 24, 1976, p. 26.
3. *Variety,* June 23, 1976, p. 16.
4. "Impressive Array of Talent in Neil Simon's Antic Whodunit," *The Christian Science Monitor,* July 8, 1976, p. 22.
5. Walker, p. 222.

Chapter 39

1. *Playboy,* December 1982, p. 97.
2. "Processing Sludge," *The New Yorker,* January 17, 1977, p. 98.
3. *The New York Times,* December 16, 1976, p. 66.
4. "Purring Along," *Newsweek,* December 27, 1976, p. 57.

Chapter 40

1. Evans, pp. 11–12.
2. Walker, pp. 225–26.
3. *Playboy,* December 1982, p. 97.
4. Ibid., p. 98.
5. *Saturday Review,* October 28, 1978, p. 36.
6. *Maclean's,* August 7, 1978, p. 59.
7. "Inspector Clouseau Strikes Again—And Again and Again," *The New York Times,* July 16, 1978, sec. 2, p. 15.
8. Steven Bach, *Final Cut* (New York: William Morrow, 1985), p. 243.

Chapter 41

1. Walker, p. 230.
2. Walker, pp. 232–233.
3. Sylvester, p. 111.
4. *Variety,* May 23, 1979.
5. "Peter Sellers in Wuwitania," *Newsweek,* June 11, 1979, p. 97.

Chapter 42

1. *Rolling Stone,* April 17, 1980, p. 43.
2. "Peter Sellers' Chance of a Lifetime," *Rolling Stone,* April 19, 1979, p. 63.
3. *Rolling Stone,* April 17, 1980, p. 43.
4. Walker, p. 233.
5. Walker, p. 48.
6. *Rolling Stone,* April 17, 1980, p. 44.
7. Walker, p. 235.
8. "Tube Boob," *New York,* January 14, 1980, p. 69.
9. *The New Statesman,* July 11, 1980, p. 61.
10. "Gravity Defied," *Time,* January 14, 1980, p. 70.
11. Walker, p. 248.
12. *Time,* March 3, 1980, p. 73.

Chapter 43

1. Walker, p. 246.
2. Ibid.
3. Walker, p. 249.
4. Ibid.
5. *Variety,* August 13, 1980, p. 23.
6. "Last Laughs," *Newsweek,* August 18, 1980, p. 85.

Chapter 44

1. Walker, p. 254.
2. *Time,* August, 4, 1980, p. 61.

Index